Evaluating the Cost-Effectiven Counselling in Health Care

When resources in health care are scarce, decisions about the value of counselling must be taken in a highly competitive economic arena. While the principles of economic evaluation are not usually a feature of counsellor training, the authors of *Evaluating the Cost-Effectiveness of Counselling in Health Care* argue that an understanding of the basic theory of economic evaluation is essential for establishing the efficacy of counselling.

Written jointly by a counsellor and an economist, the book is intended to help counsellors and service providers carry out simple cost-effectiveness analysis in their own setting, with a good understanding of the purposes, methods and limitations of the tools they are using. Part One provides a general introduction to the economic evaluation of counselling and related psychological interventions. This includes a definition of terms, an outline of the main types and components of evaluation, chapters on objective setting, costs and outcomes, and other related issues. Part Two concentrates on the practical use of one type of economic evaluation, cost-effectiveness analysis (CEA), providing the reader with examples of how it can be applied in primary and secondary health care settings.

Practical and informative, *Evaluating the Cost-Effectiveness of Counselling in Health Care* will be useful to all those who currently provide or are considering the development of a counselling service.

Keith Tolley is a Lecturer in Health Economics at the University of Nottingham.
Nancy Rowland is a Research Fellow at the Centre for Health Economics, University of York and a counsellor in private practice.

Evaluating the Cost-Effectiveness of Counselling in Health Care

Keith Tolley and Nancy Rowland

London and New York

First published 1995
by Routledge
11 New Fetter Lane, London EC4P 4EE

Simultaneously published in the USA and Canada
by Routledge
29 West 35th Street, New York, NY 10001

Typeset in Times by
Michael Mepham, Frome, Somerset

Printed and bound in Great Britain by
Mackays of Chatham PLC, Chatham, Kent

British Library Cataloguing in Publication Data
A catalogue record for this book is available from the British
Library

Library of Congress Cataloguing in Publication Data
A catalogue record for this book has been requested

ISBN 0–415–07660–9 (hbk)
ISBN 0–415–07661–7 (pbk)

To Michael Greenstone

and

Howard Tolley
(1923 – 1995)

Contents

Illustrations

FIGURES

TABLES

Foreword

This is the first book to address the issues of cost-effectiveness in counselling services. It is a welcome addition to the literature and will be invaluable to consumer and provider alike if its lessons are applied thoroughly and widely.

During the last decade there has been increasing recognition in the National Health Service and the private health care sector that resources are scarce and service practice seems to be almost random, with large variations in the quantity and quality of the care that is delivered to patients of similar age and condition. Such variations beg the question: what is the appropriate method and level of care? There are significant questions in heart and cancer surgery, in the use of drugs and in the use of services such as counselling. Are there data in the knowledge base that can be accessed to determine the appropriate level of care?

Any attempt to 'confuse' decisions about service provision with facts is fraught with difficulty. The quantity and quality of literature in most therapeutic areas is unimpressive. For the majority of interventions, medical and surgical, the effectiveness, let alone the cost-effectiveness is uncertain. Any review of a particular intervention will usually demonstrate too few, often poorly designed and executed trials from which it is impossible to determine whether the treatment 'works' in that it improves the length and quality of the patient's life.

Because of this ignorance and resultant uncertainty about the effects and costs of alternative therapies, the functioning of the NHS internal market is severely impaired. The purchaser's role is to identify local health needs and to meet those needs cost-effectively. As the cost-effectiveness of most services bought by the purchaser are unproven, decision-making is imprecise and inefficient

This book focuses on one service that can be purchased and provided in the NHS market – counselling services. The cost-effectiveness of these services is a matter of dispute and the knowledge base is very limited. Ideally, well-designed trials should have been carried out to determine the effectiveness of counselling interventions. However, knowledge of whether counselling 'works' (that is improves social, psychological and physical functioning) is alone an inadequate basis to determine purchaser choice. Purchasers also need data about cost so that their choices are demonstrably cost-effective. Thus, if counselling therapy A improves a quality of life score by 100, while an alternative counselling therapy B improves the score by 200, the naive might purchase option B. However, if A costs £10 and B costs £50, the cost-effectiveness ratios are 10 per £ and 4 per £ and alternative A may be the 'best buy'.

The purpose of this book is to describe techniques of economic evaluation and demonstrate how these tools of analysis can be used to inform purchasers' choices in the area of counselling service. At present the level of investment in counselling appears to be growing considerably but as with as with so many services in the NHS and all other healthcare systems, this growth is not knowledge based. It is the product of advocacy, often by partisan provider groups, which often seem more related to the provider's self-interest rather than patient welfare and the efficient use of society's scarce resources.

If resources are to be targeted on the provision of services that give most benefit to patients at least cost, health care has to be evaluated carefully. Counselling is no exception to this rule. If practitioners fail to evaluate the cost-effectiveness of counselling inputs, they must expect to be challenged by purchasers and have funding reduced. In the decade to come only knowledge-based services will be provided in healthcare systems and this will benefit patients and taxpayers very much.

Alan Maynard
University of York

Acknowledgements

The authors wish to thank Alan Maynard, David Buck, Pamela Gillies, Jill Irving, Jane Keithley, Robbi Campbell, Stephen Hill and David Miller for their help with this work. Thanks also to Vanessa Waby and the secretarial staff at the Centre for Health Economics, University of York, for their cheerful and efficient typing of the manuscript.

How to use this book

In this book we advocate the importance of the evaluation of counselling and the usefulness of economic evaluation as part of this process. We suggest that there is increasing demand for the provision of counselling services in the state health care sector (Sibbald *et al.*, 1993) within a context of limited funds and resources and that it is important to assess the cost-effectiveness of counselling and other psychological interventions. The new GP contract and the implementation of the NHS reforms in the UK have encouraged health service practitioners to think carefully about the effective and efficient use of resources. Economic analysis does not claim to answer all questions but helps to clarify aims and objectives, inputs and outputs, thus providing information from which decisions can be made.

Written in two parts, the first part addresses the principles of economic evaluation, the second part, the practice of the economic evaluation of counselling. Part I includes a definition of terms and outlines the theory, principles and ethics of economic evaluation and outlines the type of work done by health economists. It also reviews published work on the economic evaluation of counselling in medical settings. Part II focuses on the practical use of cost-effectiveness analysis, as a straightforward and appropriate method to use in counselling contexts. Using examples from counselling settings, it shows how to carry out a cost-effectiveness analysis. Chapter 11 provides detailed case studies of economic evaluation in primary and secondary care. This part addresses the issues of setting objectives and identifying costs and outcomes, as well as demonstrating some of the problems associated with the procedure. Our aim is to equip readers with sufficient knowledge of the purpose, methods and limitations of cost-effectiveness analysis to be able to make good use of the technique in their own setting.

Part I
The principles of economic evaluation

Chapter 1

The economic evaluation of counselling

The relevance of economic evaluation for the NHS
A working definition of counselling
The importance of evaluating counselling
Does counselling work? Research issues
The economic evaluation of counselling
Techniques of economic evaluation

THE RELEVANCE OF ECONOMIC EVALUATION FOR THE NATIONAL HEALTH SERVICE

Economic evaluation is just one part of the overall evaluation of counselling in medical settings, but it is a very important part. In the current climate of change in the NHS and the impact of limited resources, economic analysis plays a powerful role. The present government's commitment to value for money cannot be doubted. The health service is the largest employer in the state sector with public money of £30 billion provided annually to pay for staff, facilities, equipment and patient care. Demographic trends, the continuing stream of new medical and surgical advances and increasing public expectations are placing ever greater demands on the health services, which because of the existence of cash limited funding, has led to lengthening waiting-lists for non-acute health care. Limited funds raise important issues in relation to the development of counselling services in the allocation of NHS resources.

Health service managers will require information on the costs and outcomes of alternative treatment programmes in order to determine priorities for the use of NHS resources. Without that information, decisions will be made according to other more subjective criteria such as historical precedent, managers' personal preference, vague notions of public interest, pressure from government and interest groups and demand from doctors and their patients. GP demand for counselling services is widespread; a recent survey of GPs (Sibbald et al. 1993) showed that 80 per cent of GPs surveyed would like on-site counselling services. Many of these doctors are responding to patient pressure. Without evidence of their effectiveness and data on their cost-effectiveness, counselling services may be viewed as peripheral activity deserving of limited funding, or they may continue to develop in an ad hoc fashion, with no reference to planned policy or population need. Sound evidence is crucial in determining whether or not counsellors are employed. An economic analysis has a key facilitating role to play in ensuring that available resources are used efficiently.

Counsellors have been exhorted (Ross 1989) to deal positively and openly with notions of accountability, cost-effectiveness, cost-benefit analysis, performance indicators and the like. This book aims to develop the reader's knowledge and skills in the economic evaluation of counselling.

A WORKING DEFINITION OF COUNSELLING

While counselling is most commonly perceived as a form of advice giving (a definition irritatingly legitimated by dictionaries (Woolfe *et al.* 1989)), the term may, in fact, cover a whole range of helping methods from psychotherapy to behaviour modification to befriending or advice giving and counsellors may use any or all of these methods. There is, too, a wide range of helpers involved in counselling with workers from many different professions and volunteers in different settings. The range of clients is even greater, encompassing all humanity and its problems (Bolger 1989). It is no wonder that defining counselling presents problems and that those involved with counselling continually refine definition of the term in light of developments in the counselling field, its theory and practice.

A thorough definition of counselling would involve not only describing counselling and differentiating it from associated activities (such as advice giving), but also addressing the issue of who counsels, the methods used by counsellors and a description of the settings in which counselling takes place. Such an investigation is beyond the scope of this book. For a full review of counselling, the reader would do well to refer to Dryden *et al.* (1989), which has a useful introductory chapter describing, in detail, the nature and range of counselling practice.

In outlining a working definition of counselling, it is necessary to touch briefly upon two of the major theoretical issues that currently concern those actively involved in the counselling field, issues which reflect the emergence of counselling as a profession, practised by professionals with a *Code of Ethics and Practice for Counsellors* (British Association for Counselling 1993). Thus the debates on what counselling means to counsellors focus on delineation, definition, inclusion and exclusion. Two such zonal disputes, as Woolfe *et al.* call them (1989), centre on the boundaries (if any) between counselling and psychotherapy, and the differences between the practice of counselling and the use of counselling skills, for example, 'Can a nurse who uses counselling skills in her work caring for patients be said to be "counselling"?' This process of description and definition is an important one and it is to the credit of counsellors and their representative organisation, the British

Association for Counselling (BAC), that time and energy is spent attempting clarification (1989a, 1993).

While the BAC and their colleagues in the voluntary and statutory sector are formally attempting to describe and differentiate skills and processes within counselling and psychotherapy under the auspices of the Department of Employment's Lead Body for Advice, Guidance and Counselling, we will use the terms counselling and psychotherapy interchangeably, believing that in general they overlap more than they diverge. While a broad differentiation might be that psychotherapy tends to deal with deep-seated personal issues and is usually carried out on a longer term basis and in greater depth than counselling, which tends to focus on life problems (Rowland 1992), Einzig points out (1993) that some psychotherapists practise short-term work and some counsellors practise long-term work. If there is a distinction between the two 'talking cures' it lies in practical concerns about the nature of training, the settings in which people work, and the problems and issues with which they are typically confronted (Woolfe *et al.* 1989).

As to the differences between the process of counselling and the use of counselling skills, the BAC maintains that the process of counselling is a complex and highly skilled enterprise which demands training in theory, ethics and practice and an ongoing commitment to personal and professional development on the part of the counsellor, and that this differs from the 'simple' use of counselling skills in a variety of helping situations. While those trained as counsellors represent the 'professional' end of the counselling spectrum, raising issues of training and accreditation, supervision and standards (Woolfe *et al.* 1989), there is also a vast array of individuals of paid and voluntary workers whose primary training is not in counselling but who may have had brief training in, or developed expertise in, the use of counselling skills. Thus doctors, teachers and social workers, to name but a few, use counselling skills in their daily work.

Some counsellors might baulk at hearing these helping activities described as 'counselling', and it is evident that these 'helpers' have varying degrees of experience and expertise. We are not talking about 'good' and 'bad' counselling; such issues must remain the professional concern of counsellors. However, we would agree with Davis and Fallowfield (1991) in taking the broad view and use the term 'counselling' to refer to a range of helping situations, drawing on a base of specialist psychological knowledge and a set of qualities and skills for communicating effectively. This includes those who have developed counselling skills through training or experience but who might have another primary profession such as doctor, teacher, priest and so on; and those who specialise in helping people in emotional distress, such as counsellors, psychotherapists, psychologists and psychiatrists. Therefore, our definition of counselling will include the work done by trained counsellors who help individuals with their 'problems of living', whether psychological, emotional, physical or a complex mixture of each, the work done by psychologists who may use counselling skills along with a variety of specialist interventions (occupational testing, behaviour modification and so on) and those who use counselling skills in their professional lives to do their job effectively, such as doctors or nurse therapists. The content of the book will reflect this diversity.

Given the range of psychological interventions which come under the counselling umbrella, it is useful to refer back to the BAC's *Code of Ethics and Practice for Counsellors* (1993). As there are individuals whose main job it is to counsel, it seems reasonable to take their view of what they do as our baseline, and to include in our definition of counselling other activities that approximate to the definition of counselling, in the spirit if not in the letter. The BAC defines counselling thus:

> The overall aim of counselling is to provide an opportunity for the client to work towards living in a more satisfying and resourceful way. The term 'counselling' includes work with individuals, pairs or groups of people, often, but not always, referred to as 'clients'. The objectives of particular counselling relationships will vary according to the client's needs. Counselling may be concerned with developmental issues, addressing and resolving specific problems, making decisions, coping with crisis, developing personal insight and knowledge, working through feelings of inner conflict or improving relationships with others. The counsellor's role is to facilitate the client's work in ways which respect the client's values, personal resources and capacity for self-determination.
>
> (British Association for Counselling 1993 3:1)

The Association adds that:

> Only when both the user and the recipient explicitly agree to enter into a counselling relationship does it become 'counselling' rather than the use of 'counselling skills'.
>
> (British Association for Counselling 1993 3:2)

Counsellors use a variety of techniques, underpinned by a number of theoretical models with different aims and objectives. Counselling work may be developmental, crisis support, psychotherapeutic, guidance or problem solving. It is a multi-faceted activity which takes place in a variety of settings, for individuals, couples, families and groups. Clients may define themselves in terms of, for example, gender, sexual orientation, ethnic group, age or occupation. Some counsellors have developed special skills (abortion counsellors, bereavement counsellors, cancer counsellors and so on) or work with particular behavioural problems (agoraphobia, drug misuse); other counsellors may utilise a psychodynamic approach to explore and resolve the client's problems. It may be practised on a paid or voluntary basis within a counselling or other occupational setting, or in private practice. Evaluating counselling presents a challenge to most researchers!

THE IMPORTANCE OF EVALUATING COUNSELLING

Given that counselling and related psychological interventions aim to facilitate improved psychological well-being, it is essential to try to evaluate counselling, its processes and outcomes, to identify what makes for effective counselling and effective counsellors. Questions such as 'What is counselling?', 'Does it work?', 'How does it work?', 'Who does it work for?', 'How much does it cost?' have relevance for clients, counsellors, employers, researchers and the NHS.

Individual supervision

The most common form of evaluation in Britain is through supervision of the counsellor's work. Such supervision is considered essential to the ethical practice of counselling. In addressing issues of competence the British Association for Counselling's *Code of Ethics and Practice for Counsellors* exhorts them to monitor their counselling work through regular supervision by professionally competent supervisors and be able to account to clients for what they do and why. Counsellors should monitor the limits of their competence and, along with their employers or agencies, they have a responsibility to themselves and their clients to maintain their own effectiveness, resilience and ability to help clients.

BAC suggests that it is difficult if not impossible to be objective about one's counselling unless there is opportunity to discuss it in confidence with a suitable person. Thus supervision helps the counsellor to evolve practice and in this sense is one aspect of continued training (British Association for Counselling 1987). Counsellor supervision and consultative support refers to a formal arrangement which enables counsellors to discuss their counselling regularly with someone who is experienced and/or qualified in counselling and counselling supervision/consultative support. Its purpose is to ensure the efficacy of the counsellor/client relationship. This involves addressing three main tasks: establishing good standards of practice, developing the counsellor's knowledge and skills and working with the counsellor's response to conducting the counselling. Individual or group supervision may involve a system of peer review or may entail a more experienced counsellor supervising a less experienced counsellor. The agenda will be the counselling work and feelings about that work, together with the supervisor's reactions, comments and confrontations. Exactly what is discussed and how the material is dealt with will vary with different supervisors and counsellors. Supervision is the process by which adequate standards of counselling can be maintained through the continuous assessment of the counsellor's work (British Association for Counselling 1988). Not only does supervision monitor counselling by providing a setting in which individual counsellors are facilitated in their work, it also operates on an organisational level; the cumulative effect of all individual experiences of supervision pervades the culture within BAC. It assists the development of a culture in which there is an openness to new learning and a personal re-evaluation, as well as an expectation that individual experience will be shared and disseminated (Bond 1990a, b).

The drawbacks of the current situation

While the principle of monitoring competence is an admirable one, no guidelines are given as to how counsellors, their employers and agencies should evaluate their work, other than supervision. Bond (1990a, b) argues that this is for the best; that some organisations undertaking similar work have formally relied on research as the means of monitoring the quality of practice but that while counsellors may increasingly welcome research and use its findings to inform their own practice, research does not directly facilitate the process of monitoring the provision of counselling in the way that supervision can. We would argue, however, that while the peer review system of supervision is an essential part of the evaluation process, it leaves many questions unanswered. Because it takes place between individuals or groups of individuals, it is not a documented or researched area and the insights gleaned remain personal to the practitioners taking part. No large scale studies exist to evaluate systematically practitioners' work using core questions, data from which can be amassed and evaluated nationwide, though BAC is piloting a questionnaire to address this aim (Davis 1992).

Moreover, the Association's Research Committee (1989c) notes that evaluation is important both at the micro level (i.e. investigating whether counselling is effective in helping people with their life problems) and at the macro level, namely, the extent to which employers and funding bodies can be persuaded that counselling is cost-effective. They argue that the evaluation of counselling and related psychological interventions can benefit counsellor, client and employer or funding organisation. While counsellor and client evaluation of the counselling process on an ongoing basis is in itself an essential and enabling part of counselling practice, funding bodies will also want to evaluate the way in which an agency provides a counselling service, in terms of numbers of clients counselled, range of services offered, utilisation of resources, outcomes and so on. Until such research is systematically carried out, many questions will remain as to the effectiveness of counselling.

DOES COUNSELLING WORK? RESEARCH ISSUES

Given the different methodologies, subjects, settings and aims, it is not surprising that the evidence for the efficacy of counselling conflicts. While Davis and Fallowfield (1991) note that there is considerable evidence from a number of different areas that counselling can alleviate distress and significantly facilitate psychological adaptation, Bolger (1989) takes the view that conventional outcome research is very hazardous, measures of effectiveness are unreliable, research designs over-simplified and data are over-interpreted. There is no systematic and coherent body of research into counselling in medical settings and much more extensive and better designed research is necessary to answer many questions about what kind of intervention is particularly beneficial to which individuals at what stage and why. In a review of the effectiveness of counselling in general practice,

Corney (1990) notes that subjective accounts of counsellor attachments are positive, with much consumer and GP satisfaction. Studies have indicated that after cessation of counselling, clients make fewer visits to the doctor, fewer psychotropic drugs are prescribed and fewer referrals made to psychiatrists. She suggests, however, that we are at an early stage in refining our evaluation techniques and that most studies of counselling in medical settings are flawed in some way. Ideally, assessments need to be made both before and after treatment, preferably by a researcher unaware of the treatment received. The need for a control group is emphasised as many clients resolve their problems without outside help such as counselling. Corney recommends studies with more than one follow-up assessment so as to get an overview of both short and longer term treatment effects. She stresses the need for measures to be sensitive enough to monitor the subtle changes that may occur after counselling.

Counsellors and researchers attempting to evaluate counselling and related psychological interventions should use a variety of techniques and measures incorporating qualitative and quantitative data. Outcomes include the physical, psychological and social functioning of the individual before and after treatment. Assessment of the patient before counselling should include social and psychological ratings as well as estimates of physical and psychosomatic symptoms. Details of alcohol consumption can also be collected. Measures of outcome may include objective ratings such as criminal offences, health records and measures of illness behaviour such as attendance rates and consumption of psychotropic drugs. Details of health changes in other family members may also be important and may indicate that a preferred treatment might involve family members, rather than focusing on the individual. Further measures such as patients' and professionals' attitudes and satisfaction might be used to address issues about the quality of care. Corney (1992) suggests that evaluative studies should aim to identify those clients who benefit most from counselling so that the most effective use of resources are made. We need to know which therapies benefit which types of problems or patients and which ones are most acceptable to clients. We also need to know more about assessment of suitability for counselling and its effect on outcomes. Finally, we need to know what level of skills in the counsellor are necessary for benefit to occur, and to monitor carefully the qualities of the counsellor/client relationship which facilitate good outcomes.

Such research paradigms seem a far cry from the ongoing monitoring of competence that evolves in counsellor supervision. Bolger (1989) suggests, however, that counselling could and should be evaluated case by case, by counsellors, in addition to large-scale evaluation of numbers of clients grouped according to different types of treatment, different kinds of problems or different types of clients. All counsellors, as they evaluate their own work with their clients, should accumulate results to give some evidence of the outcomes of counselling. Single-case research, when carried out systematically and accurately, is an acceptable form of research, and adds to our body of knowledge.

The BAC Research Committee (British Association for Counselling 1989c) consistently encourages effective research into the development and evaluation of counselling practice, supervision and training, but difficulties remain. Until the problems of evaluating counselling reliably have been overcome, in particular determining what the most appropriate outcome measures should be, it will be difficult to arrive at a valid costing (Fallowfield and Davis 1991). Nonetheless, the body of literature is growing on the evaluation of counselling in clinical settings and a range of qualitative and quantitative outcome measures have been utilised. At the same time, determining the effectiveness of counselling interventions is increasingly preoccupying counsellors who may have no choice but to evaluate their programmes if they hope to receive public funds (Daniels *et al.* 1981). When resources are scarce, the widescale adoption of counselling is unwise without first establishing its effectiveness (Martin 1988).

THE ECONOMIC EVALUATION OF COUNSELLING

Having stressed the importance of the evaluation of counselling, we now return to the importance of the economic evaluation of counselling. Economic evaluation consists of techniques developed by economists to assist decision-making when choices have to be made between several courses of action. In essence, economic evaluation entails drawing up a balance sheet of the advantages (benefits) and disadvantages (costs) associated with each option so that choices can be made. Although the precise forms of economic evaluation may vary the 'cost-benefit' framework is common to all of them and constitutes the distinctive feature of the economic approach (Robinson 1993).

Psychotherapists addressed the issue of the costs and benefits of long-term psychotherapy in the 1980s (Wilkinson 1984; Shepherd 1985; McGrath and Lowson 1986), but the cost-effectiveness of counselling is rarely addressed in studies of counselling. While the literature is discussed in depth in Chapter 5, it is interesting to note that, compared with the studies evaluating counsellor effectiveness, patient outcome and so on, very little exists on economic evaluation. It may be that counsellors are not trained in research and evaluation methods and lack a model of how to carry out economic analysis as part of effectiveness evaluation, or it may be that counsellors perceive their work as more art than science and find it hard to attempt to translate into quantifiable terms the notions of well-being and improved mental health that they hope to foster and facilitate in their work with clients. Yet counselling research is important for the counselling practitioner, especially when there are so many competing systems of counselling and psychotherapy (Bolger 1989). With the growth of interest in counselling and its related activities in occupational and medical settings, the cost-effectiveness of counselling needs to be evaluated.

An earlier review (Rowland and Tolley 1995) of counselling in medical settings shows that scant attention has been paid to the role of economic analysis both in terms of assessing the cost of providing a counselling service or in attempting to quantify the costs and benefits of counselling. Few practitioners or service providers appear to be familiar with the different types of economic analysis i.e. cost-minimisation, cost-effectiveness, cost-benefit and cost-utility analysis, or understand how economic analysis can be of value as part of a wider evaluation. We surmise that practitioners and researchers overlook the role of economic evaluation for a variety of reasons. First, lack of knowledge and understanding of economics dissuades attempts to cost services. Second, economic measures are suspected of being 'crude' and are viewed as only partially useful (e.g. Corney 1990) and third, advocates of counselling in health service settings may predict that counselling will not be shown to be cost-effective so that economic analysis is felt to be better left unexplored. Finally, some practitioners are concerned about the potential misuse of the 'economic argument'; that, given cost constraints, if one treatment is shown to be cheaper than another, the cheaper option will be pursued regardless of other factors, which practitioners may perceive as more important than cost. Thus, for example, if psychotropic medication were shown to be cheaper than counselling, it might be the preferred option regardless of qualitative issues such as possible side effects of long-term medication, including dependency. Some practitioners doubt the ethics of economic analysis as a tool in decision-making with regard to potentially life-saving or life-enhancing treatments. We shall discuss the ethical issues of economic analysis of counselling in health care in Chapter 2. Now, however, we will move on to outline the approaches to economic analysis.

TECHNIQUES OF ECONOMIC EVALUATION

There are several types of economic evaluation, all of which can be applied to counselling in medical settings. The choice of technique depends upon the objectives of the evaluation and the time and money available for collecting data on effectiveness. The main types of economic evaluation are cost-minimisation (CMA), cost-effectiveness (CEA), cost-benefit (CBA) and cost-utility analysis (CUA). Cost-minimisation explores the total cost consequences of using, for example, different medicines given identical outcomes in each case. In each case the outcomes of different interventions are compared using a common unit, such as life years gained. Cost-effectiveness relates the cost of therapies to their differential outcomes and produces measures such as cost per successfully treated patient or cost per life year gained. Cost-benefit analysis uses money as the common unit to compare the benefits of using a given therapy with the associated costs to determine whether the benefits outweigh the costs or vice versa. Cost-utility analysis is a special form of cost-effectiveness analysis that relates the cost of different therapies to improvements in the quantity and quality of life. A measure known as the quality adjusted life year gained (QALY) has been developed by health economists to measure outcomes in cost-utility analysis. In addition, descriptive information can be provided from a cost analysis which assesses the costs of a disease to the NHS, to patients (social burdens) and to the economy as a whole. The techniques of economic evaluation are covered in greater detail in Chapter 3.

The main purpose for undertaking an economic evaluation is to assess how efficiently resources are being used in the pursuit of an objective or set of objectives. This calls into question what economists mean by efficiency. Efficiency is achieved if the resources used on one option have no other use which can be shown to be more worthwhile, that is, if it provides the greatest benefits at least cost. For example, an internal support network for nurses in a hospital might be preferred to the employment of an external counselling service if it is demonstrated to deliver greater value for money. The notion of efficiency raises several questions, such as, how is value for money defined, what are the relevant objectives and options for counselling, what are the relevant costs and benefits and how can they be defined and measured, and ethical questions such as who benefits from counselling services and are the beneficiaries the most deserving cases?

The pursuit of efficiency only arises because of the existence of limited resources. Resources are the staff and other individuals' time (e.g. volunteers), materials, equipment, premises and facilities that are used in providing a counselling service. Economists take as their starting-point the fact that resources are scarce; that there is always greater potential demand for resources than there are the resources to meet demand. If resources were not scarce then there would be no need to choose between different counselling options or between counselling and other treatments that improve well-being. With limitless resources the only criteria for deciding to fund a new counselling programme is in terms of efficacy – that the intervention has been demonstrated to do more good than harm.

Economic factors in health care are becoming more important as demands on healthcare systems increase, often beyond the ability of these systems to satisfy them (Goodwin *et al.* 1990). When demands for resources exceed supply, decisions must be made regarding the allocation of resources. This in turn calls into view questions about treatment effectiveness and treatment cost. Clinicians with limited funds thus need information on which to base decisions about treatment programmes. Economic analysis provides useful information on both costs and effects and is, therefore, an aid to decision-making. In itself, economic analysis is not prescriptive; it does not tell decision-makers which option to pursue. However, it provides essential information to enable decision-makers to formulate rational policies.

SUMMARY

Given that counselling and related psychological interventions aim to facilitate improved psychological well-being, it is essential to try to evaluate counselling, its processes and outcomes, to identify what makes for effective counselling and effective counsellors. Supervision, which is seen as necessary to the process of counselling, does not provide sufficient information, in an easily accessible way, to answer the many questions about the effectiveness of counselling. Counsellors and researchers attempting to evaluate counselling and related psychological interventions should use a variety of techniques and measures using quantitative and qualitative data.

In the current climate of change in the NHS and given limited resources, economic evaluation is an important part of the evaluation of counselling in medical settings. Counselling effectiveness needs to be demonstrated and cost-effectiveness assessed. Scant attention has been paid to the role of economic analysis both in terms of the costs of producing a counselling service or in attempting to quantify the costs and benefits of counselling. There are several types of economic evaluation, all of which can be applied to counselling in medical settings. The main purpose for undertaking an economic evaluation is to assess how efficiently resources are being used in the pursuit of an objective or set of objectives. Efficiency is achieved if the resources used on one option have no other use which can be shown to be more worthwhile, that is, if it provides greatest benefits at least cost. The pursuit of efficiency only arises because of the existence of limited resources.

Economic analysis is not prescriptive, but provides essential information to enable decision-makers to formulate rational policies. The aim of this book is to provide the reader with knowledge of the purpose, methods and limitations of cost-effectiveness analysis so as to be able to make good use of the technique in their own setting. With this understanding, the reader may have some confidence in planning and implementing an evaluation. It is hoped that at a minimum, the book will provide the basic tools for counsellors, service providers and health service managers to develop a proposal for economic evaluation and at best help readers design and conduct their own economic evaluation.

Chapter 2

Economics, ethics and counselling

Introduction
Medical ethics and economics
Resource allocation
Individual and social ethics
The doctor–patient relationship
Cost-effectiveness as policy
The rationale for QALYs
Distributing QALY gains over the life cycle
The continuing debate about QALYs
The problem of discrimination
Economics, ethics and counselling

INTRODUCTION

The economic evaluation of counselling in the health service involves utilising information about the costs and effects of counselling and making decisions about the allocation of resources to finance counselling. The ethical issues associated with the economic evaluation of counselling and resource allocation are often raised by counsellors and doctors aware of potential conflict between the quality and cost of care. Proponents of counselling, who advocate the development of counselling within the NHS, often bemoan the fact that there are scant resources for such development. Some counsellors argue that counselling services should be prioritised in the health service budget, others are concerned about financial restraints affecting the quality of care.

While counsellors are aware of the possibility of conflict between the quality and cost of care, there appears to be no body of counselling literature debating ethics and economics. Economic analysis is usually mentioned only briefly and the ethics of economic analysis are not discussed in depth. Thus, in illustrating some of the arguments about cost and care, we have turned to the medical literature and to the differing viewpoints of philosophers and health economists. The *Journal of Medical Ethics* contains a wealth of discussion about ethics and economics, which counsellors would do well to investigate. Given the importance of this issue, we will begin this book with a discussion of the ethical issues relating to economic evaluation in the NHS. While the authors we cite refer to physicians and patients, to managers and to budget holders, the arguments have relevance for counsellors and for all those who advocate the development of counselling services under the NHS umbrella. As more and more counsellors are taking up a new professional role within multidisciplinary health care, much reflection is needed on the interface between the therapeutic culture and that of the medical world. Moreover, if counselling is to be financed from health service resources, the ethics of efficient resource allocation need to be examined.

There is a fundamental conflict between those counsellors and doctors who are concerned that allowing costs to influence clinical decisions is unethical and those health economists who advocate a systematic deployment of resources. Williams (1992) quotes a letter from a doctor to the *New England Journal of Medicine*:

> Of late an increasing number of papers in . . . journals have been concerned with the 'cost effectiveness' of diagnostic and therapeutic procedures. Inherent in these articles is the view that choices will be predicated not only on the basis of strictly clinical considerations, but also on economic considerations . . . such considerations are not germane to ethical medical practice . . . a physician who changes his or her way of practising medicine because of cost rather than purely medical considerations has indeed embarked on the 'slippery slope' of compromised ethics and waffled priorities.
>
> (Loewy 1980)

In contrast, Williams (1992) argues that a caring, ethical doctor (or counsellor) should take costs into account, indeed that it is unethical not to do so! According to Williams, it cannot be ethical to ignore the adverse consequences upon others of the decisions you make, which is what cost represents. To an economist resources are always scarce; 'what will it cost?' means 'what will have to be sacrificed?' and this may be very different from 'how much money will we have to part with?'. In this chapter we examine arguments for the rational allocation of resources based on cost-effectiveness criteria and the opposing 'slippery slope of compromised ethics' view.

MEDICAL ETHICS AND ECONOMICS

Williams (1992) cites the six basic principles of medical ethics (Ruark *et al.* 1988):

1   preserve life;
2   alleviate suffering;
3   do no harm;
4   tell the truth;
5   respect the patient's autonomy;
6   deal justly with patients.

These principles frequently come into conflict with one another, and resolving such conflicts is central to the art of medicine. In light of a scarcity of resources the principles seem even more difficult to reconcile. How do we make decisions about resources so that we can preserve life, alleviate suffering and deal justly with patients? Decisions need to be made about the fair distribution of resources in general practice, hospital medicine and throughout the NHS.

RESOURCE ALLOCATION

One way to ensure the fair distribution of resources in the NHS is to ensure that there is enough money to go round. Harris (1987) suggests that the value underpinning British society and the health service is that the life and health of each person matters and that each person is entitled to be treated with equal concern and respect both in the way healthcare resources are distributed and in the way they are treated generally by healthcare professionals, however much their personal circumstances may differ from those of others. Life is valuable, and we should give priority to saving lives. If each life counts for one, then the life of each has the same value as that of any. Accepting the value of life generates a principle of equality. Treating individuals as equals when resources are scarce means allocating resources in a way which exhibits no preference. If health professionals (including counsellors) are forced by the scarcity of resources to choose not whether to treat, but who to treat, they must avoid any method of unjust discrimination.

Harris (1987) believes that while it is true that resources will always be limited, it is far from clear that resources for health care are justifiably as limited as they are sometimes made out to be. People within health care are too often forced to consider the question of the best way of allocating the health budget *per se*. Consequently they are forced to compete with each other for resources. Where lives are at stake, however, the issue is a moral one which calls for a fundamental reappraisal of priorities. He argues that the task of health economics is immoral because it tries to find more efficient ways of doing the wrong thing – sacrificing the lives of people who could be saved. The obligation to save as many lives as possible is not the same as the obligation to save as many lives as we can cheaply or economically. Instead of attempting to measure the value of people's lives and select which are worth saving, any rubric for resource allocation should examine the national budget afresh to see whether there is any expenditure that is more important to the community than rescuing citizens in mortal danger. Only if all other claims on funding are more important than that, is it true that resources for life-saving are limited. It is better to overspend a limited healthcare budget than to sacrifice lives. His solution is apparently simple; there is no greater priority than life and health and resources should be allotted to the healthcare budget accordingly.

Levels of funding for the NHS are open to debate; while it may be worth politicking for greater resources to be made available to the health budget from the national budget, the fact remains that resources are limited (and probably always will be) and decisions have to be made about the just distribution of resources. How are these decisions to be made? On what criteria do we decide?

INDIVIDUAL AND SOCIAL ETHICS

Medical ethics are important because the doctor is empowered by the patient to make decisions on the patient's behalf. As Mooney points out (1984), the nature of health and health care requires the doctor to make decisions on behalf of the patient because the asymmetry in information between the two parties results in a serious impairment of the individual's autonomy as a decision-maker. The clinician's job is to protect the patient and to work as best he or she can for that individual. Patients need a medical-ethical code to serve and reassure them that the doctor is acting in their best interests. The relationship between the doctor and the patient is thus paramount. In the present moral climate of the NHS, medical ethics dictates that individual doctors try to maximise the health of individual patients. While medical ethics is currently conceived in terms of the individualistic ethics of duty and virtue, economics embraces a concept of social as well as individual ethics. Each doctor following individualistic ethical objectives will be concerned to maximise the benefit for his or her patients. To this end the doctor will attempt to gain more and more scarce resources to assist in this goal. Such an attempt – which ignores the opportunity cost to other doctors' patients – is legitimised by the ethics of virtue and of duty. Medical ethics in a sense implores the doctor to assume every other doctor's patients out of existence (and also possibly, the potential patients of whom he or she is as yet unaware). Williams (1992) suggests that this is a mistaken view because it cannot be ethical to ignore the adverse consequences upon others of the decisions you make, which is what cost represents.

To have highlighted the fact that individual doctors' values in aggregation are not conducive to the goal of maximising the health of the community at large from the resources available to it may prove rather disturbing for doctors. Thus economic analysis may create discomfort – and the appearance of conflict – within the medical profession. There is frequently an appearance of conflict between medicine and economics, because there is a relative lack of acceptance of the ethics of the common good in medical ethics. As a result, while economics in the field of health has as an objective the maximisation of the health of the community, subject to resource constraints, medical ethics pushes individual doctors to try to maximise the health of each of their patients. Mooney (1984) suggests that certain institutional alterations in the NHS such as new budgeting structures and the acceptance of efficiency as a social goal, would be required to promote the type of behavioural change which will make doctors act in the interests of the common good to a greater extent than has historically been the case.

THE DOCTOR-PATIENT RELATIONSHIP

A further objection is that rational decision-making will interfere with the doctor-patient relationship, in which trust is paramount. The overriding principle governing the actions of a doctor to a patient is that the best should be done for that patient; treatment should not rest on mathematical calculations of cost-benefit. Cubbon (1991), a proponent of economic evaluation, believes that if doctors in the health service were regularly presented with situations in which they have to decide to which of their patients to give time, effort and resources, when this will clearly be to the disadvantage of other patients, they would feel they were playing God and undermining their capacity to relate to them as patients. Judgements in the clinical context have a personal quality and doctors should not be continually consulting principles of economic evaluation. In the formulation of policy, however, the principles should be applied in a thorough way. Cost-effectiveness analysis should be a tool in directing policy decisions about resource allocation rather than in dealing with individual patients. Thus, the impersonal calculating aspect of cost-effectiveness measurement which makes it seem inappropriate as a morality of personal relations is less objectionable in the formulation of policy.

COST-EFFECTIVENESS AS POLICY

Cubbon (1991) submits that planning of services will always need to consider costs and benefits and will always mean that some groups of people will be deliberately deprived of benefits. In a system of competing demands, such as the NHS, the decision-maker, for example a health service manager, might have to choose between the introduction of an acute hospital facility and the expansion of a health promotion programme. Because of the complexity of the alternatives he or she will need to make careful calculations of the costs and benefits. Such a person cannot but play God. The informed formulation of policies affecting the distribution of scarce resources does not go against the grain of our moral intuitions. The people who would benefit from the development under consideration will mostly not be known to policy-makers. Often they will not be known to anybody because they will not yet have become ill. The point is here that decisions will be made as impartially, rationally and fairly as possible.

While one of the objections to the cost-effectiveness approach is that it is unethical to sit in judgement on the value of another person's life and make decisions about treating or not treating accordingly, Williams (1992) believes that judgements about the value of another person's life or more correctly the value of improvements in another person's health are inescapable in a system like the NHS. Such a system is expected to behave in an egalitarian, non-capricious way in discriminating between the well and the ill, between the severely ill and the slightly ill and between those most likely to benefit from a particular treatment and those unlikely to do so, in order that some systematic priority setting can take place in the face of inescapable resource constraints. Every effectiveness decision implies some value judgement.

THE RATIONALE FOR QALYs

Against a background of permanently scarce resources it is crucial that such healthcare resources as are available are used efficiently. To measure efficient standards of treatment, we need a standard of measurement. Traditionally, in life endangering situations, that measurement has been easy to find. Successful treatment removes the danger to life, or at least postpones it, and so survival rates of treatment have been regarded as a good indicator of success. Survival rates loom large in clinical decision-making and clinicians have sometimes been criticised for focusing on survival at all costs – the cost in question being quality of life. It is also important that the help offered not only removes the threat of death to life, but leaves patients able to enjoy the remission granted. In short, it gives them reasonable quality, as well as extended quantity of life. One measure of effectiveness developed by health economists to overcome the objection that survival rates pay no regard to quality of life is by adopting the QALY (quality adjusted life year).

The quality adjusted life year (QALY) is an outcome measure which reflects the fact that most people are prepared to sacrifice some quality of life in order to gain some additional life expectancy and vice versa. If some healthcare activity would give someone an extra year of healthy life expectancy, then that would be counted as 1 QALY. But if the best we can do is provide someone with an additional year in a rather poor state of health, that would count as less than 1 QALY, and would be lower the worse the health state is.

The essence of the QALY concept is that effects on life expectancy and effects on quality of life are brought together in a single measure, and the bulk of empirical work involved in making the concept operational is concerned with eliciting the values that people attach to different health states, and the extent to which they regard them as better or worse than being dead. For the purpose of priority setting in health care, being dead is regarded as of zero life value. A QALY measure can in principle embrace any health related quality of life characteristic that is important to people. Although developed primarily by economists, the QALY is not a measure of people's economic worth, but a measure of whatever aspects of life they themselves value (Williams 1994).

DISTRIBUTING QALY GAINS OVER THE LIFE CYCLE

Williams (1992) investigated the extent to which people are prepared to sacrifice quality of life to increase life expectancy or vice versa. The NHS is underpinned by strongly held but vaguely articulated egalitarian principles; when aggregating benefits across people we have to know what is supposed to be equally valued among people. Even if attention is restricted to outcome measures, the list is quite long: a life year, a QALY, whether the person has already had a 'fair innings', the 'rest of your life', etc. A survey of 400 randomly polled York citizens showed that there was a clear consensus that the time to be healthy was when bringing up children, which is a time in people's lives when they are, in fact, usually healthy but which is obviously a time when people feel extremely vulnerable if they are not healthy. A close second was when you are an infant, the reason here being that a healthy start in life is a good investment for the future. Whether a unit of benefit should have different value depending on who will get it pervades much of the discussion about distributive ethics. The characteristics that are frequently mentioned are age, sex, marital status, whether with or without children, occupation, and whether the person has cared for his or her own health.

A further survey of 700 adults (Williams 1990) gave precedence to the young over the old, non-smokers over smokers, and light over heavy drinkers. Having children of school age made a strong difference in preferential terms, rather than not. Sex and occupation made no difference. Surveys such as this have convinced Williams that there is a strong consensus in Britain concerning discrimination by age, by whether someone has young children, and by smoking and drinking habits. It probably influences treatment almost unconsciously at local levels. We should be clear about the ethical assumptions built into our studies, our practice, and our culture.

THE CONTINUING DEBATE ABOUT QALYs

It is in the area of benefit measurement that the most intense ethical objections to the cost-effectiveness approach arise. They vary from sweeping denials of the right of anyone to sit in judgement on the value of another person's life to more specific accusations of unfair discrimination. QALYs have been accused of being ageist, sexist, racist and of working to the detriment of the least well off (i.e. those least capable of deriving benefits from healthcare resources). Harris (1991) suggests that the worst off members of any society are those with the worst quality of life coupled with the shortest life expectancy. We should not abandon those whose quality is poor to concentrate on the fortunate. He argues that QALYs force us to do precisely this, submitting that QALYs value lifetime over lives and that they value higher over lower quality of life. This means that we should be obliged to maximise lifetime rather than lives and deploy resources accordingly, which is why QALYs are ageist. They direct us to save the lives of those with greater life expectancy rather than less and hence to prioritise medical services which have this effect – paediatrics rather than geriatrics to take just one example. QALYs also dictate that we maximise quality of lifetime rather than simply lifetime. A health service provider faced with rival treatments or treatment centres should prioritise the treatment or treatment centre likely to produce the most QALYs for each patient treated. The maximisation of QALYs encourages healthcare providers to choose, not between treatments, but between the patients who will generate the most QALYs. Harris believes that each person has an equal claim upon the health resources of his or her own society, and that no individual or group or type of individual has a more valuable life or a greater claim to life-saving resources than any other. Thus resources should be used to maximise lives rather than QALYs.

THE PROBLEM OF DISCRIMINATION

Harris (1987) argues that the whole plausibility of the QALY rests on our accepting the possibility that, given a choice, people would prefer a healthier, shorter life than a longer one of severe discomfort. On this view, giving priority to treatments which produce most QALYs for which the cost per QALY is low is both efficient and what the community as a whole, and those at risk in particular, want. But whereas it follows from the fact that given a choice a person may prefer a healthier, shorter life to a longer one of severe discomfort, that the best treatment for that person is the one yielding the most QALYs, it does not follow that treatments yielding the most QALYs are preferable to treatments yielding fewer QALYs for different people who are to receive treatment. With QALY theory that which is given equal weight is not persons and their interests and preferences but quality adjusted life years. If the QALY advocate insists that what he or she wants is to select the therapy that generates the most QALYs for those people who already exist, and not simply create the maximum number of QALYs, then it does matter who gets QALYs – and ageism and other discriminatory factors become important. On the other hand, an evaluation of life or lives without regard to actual or potential QALYs seems very incomplete. QALY maximisation views QALYs as an essential prerequisite for what we regard as important in our lives – health is the *sine qua non* of all that makes our lives valuable to us (Cubbon 1991).

ECONOMICS, ETHICS AND COUNSELLING

Objections to the economic evaluation of health care can be encapsulated in the following three propositions (Williams 1987b):

1   Healthcare priorities should not be influenced by any other consideration than keeping people alive.
2   Everyone has an equal right to be kept alive if that is what they wish, irrespective of how poor their prognosis is and no matter what sacrifices others have to bear as a consequence.
3   When allocating healthcare resources we must not discriminate between people, not even according to their differential capacities to benefit from treatment.

Alternatively:

1   Healthcare priorities should be influenced by our capacity both to increase life expectancy and to improve people's quality of life.
2   A particular improvement in health should be regarded as of equal value, no matter who gets it, and should be provided unless it prevents a greater improvement being offered to someone else.
3   It is the responsibility of everyone to discriminate wherever necessary to ensure that our limited resources go where they will do most good. At the end of the day we simply have to stand up and be counted as to which set of principles we wish to have underpin the way the healthcare system works.

What does this mean for those who advocate the development of counselling in the health service? At present, discussions about counselling automatically raise issues about the quality of care. Counselling is seen, by and large, as an 'extra' service, even a bonus, rather than a mental health care facility that is available in every general practice and hospital. Is counselling to be seen as an 'additional' service, or is it an essential service? Should general practice patients have access to referral to counsellors under the NHS umbrella, as they do to surgeons and physicians? Counsellors need to think about where counselling fits into the health-care system.

Like doctors, counsellors must accurately assess clients for treatment and decide who to accept and who to reject for counselling. The selection criteria need to be reviewed in light of the debate about distributive ethics and resource allocation. Proponents of counselling will need to consider the costs and benefits of counselling to the health service as a whole, bearing in mind that the allocation of resources to counselling will necessarily entail that other treatments are foregone.

SUMMARY

There are many sides to the ethics argument. The major standpoints are that medical ethics are fundamental in the health service and in doctor–patient relationships and that healthcare outcomes involve basic issues of the quality and quantity of life. The QALY provides a tool for investigating explicitly the extent to which people are prepared to sacrifice quality of life expectancy or vice versa. In the presence of scarcity, resources devoted to the health care of the person will be denied some other person who might have benefited from them. Costs represent sacrifices made by other potential patients who did not get treated. Thus, the economist's argument that medical practice should concentrate on those treatments that are cost-effective is designed to ensure that the benefits gained by the treatments which are provided should be greater than the benefits sacrificed by those who were denied treatment. Decisions must be made about resource allocation. If managers and politicians make decisions, will doctors and counsellors be happy to live with the consequences? Counsellors need to think about where counselling fits into the healthcare system and consider the costs and benefits of counselling in relation to other treatments. If counselling is to be financed from health service resources, the ethics of efficient resource allocation need to be examined.

Chapter 3

The main types of economic evaluation

Techniques of economic evaluation
Cost-minimisation analysis
Cost-benefit analysis
Cost-effectiveness analysis
Cost-utility analysis
Financial appraisal
The context of economic evaluation
Which technique: cost-benefit, cost-effectiveness or cost-utility analysis?

TECHNIQUES OF ECONOMIC EVALUATION

A number of techniques of economic evaluation can be used to evaluate counselling services (Figure 3.1). Each technique may help researchers and decision-makers to identify the best allocation of resources between two or more options. In each case the main principle in the measurement of costs is that of opportunity costs – this is an important concept in economic analysis which incorporates the notion of scarcity of resources. The concept of opportunity cost means that a resource (e.g. time) has a value if it has an alternative worthwhile use. For example, the provision of an anti-depressant drug to one group of patients means that the drug may not be available to other patients. As the total supply of drugs is not limitless the drug has an opportunity cost which may be valued using its market price. As a second example, a GP who spends an hour of worktime counselling patient A might alternatively have used that hour to provide medical care to patient B. A GP's professional time is limited and cannot be used for more than one activity at the same time so that the opportunity cost of providing counselling is the value of not using that time for medical care. A simple proxy measure of this cost is the hourly payment rate for a GP. The importance of considering opportunity cost is that even if the GP was unpaid his or her time would still have a value. For example, if it is assumed that the usual payment rate for GPs reflects the value of their service, this rate can also be used to estimate the opportunity cost of any unpaid time used in providing a service. In an extreme case, a resource such as voluntary time, may have zero opportunity cost if the volunteer would not otherwise have a worthwhile use for their time (e.g. if they lay in bed all day). It is clear from this example that most resources, priced or unpriced, will have at least some alternative use value and hence an opportunity cost. Apart from financial appraisals, opportunity cost represents the basic principle adopted in all the techniques listed in Figure 3.1.

The techniques of economic evaluation differ in terms of the measurement of outcomes. Cost-minimisation and cost-effectiveness analysis use a single outcome measure. In a counselling programme a single outcome measure might be a reduction in patients presenting with psychosocial problems. Cost-benefit and cost-utility analysis can incorporate multiple outcomes by valuing them numerically (in monetary terms) or using quality of life indices which include several dimensions of quality of life or well-being. The choice of technique depends on the objectives of the evaluation and the time and money available for collecting data on effectiveness. Before examining the relative merits of each technique, a brief exposition of the purpose of each is provided.

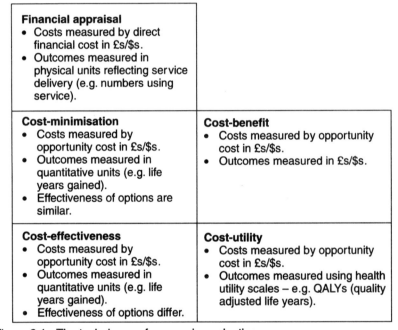

Figure 3.1   The techniques of economic evaluation

COST-MINIMISATION ANALYSIS

This is the simplest form of economic evaluation as it involves only the measurement of the costs of alternative options. The technique can be used when it is known that there is no difference in the effectiveness of each option, but that there may be a difference in cost. Cost-minimisation analysis provides information on which option is found to have the lowest cost. For example, there is evidence to show that the structured use of counselling techniques by GPs has equal benefit compared with the use of anxiolytic drugs (Catalan *et al.* 1984). A cost-minimisation analysis would attempt to assess the cost of GPs using counselling techniques compared with the cost of prescribing anxiolytics and would provide information as to which is the lower cost option, given equal outcomes for both treatments. The least cost option should be chosen, unless additional criteria suggest otherwise.

In order to use a cost-minimisation analysis, there has to be prior evidence that the outcomes of the options are the same. A crucial component of cost-minimisation analysis is that the researcher is properly persuaded that this evidence exists. If this is not the case, it is better to carry out a cost-effectiveness analysis.

In general, difficulties in the measurement of effectiveness of disparate options means that the technique of cost-minimisation analysis will only be used to compare similar options, such as two or more drugs which aim to reduce symptoms or alleviate medical conditions. For example, the British government's 'limited list' of drug prescriptions represents a cost-minimisation exercise. The government's argument is that various drugs are commonly prescribed, some of which are more expensive than others, although they produce the same effects. Assuming this to be the case, the cheapest drug is listed. The reason some doctors challenge the decision, apart from the restriction of clinical freedom, is that they feel some drugs are not as effective as others and so should not be excluded on the basis of cost alone.

COST-BENEFIT ANALYSIS

A cost-benefit analysis involves placing a monetary valuation on all the relevant costs and benefits of the options and assessing which produces the greatest net benefit. For a counselling programme to be deemed worthwhile requires only that the benefits exceed the costs. For example, a health authority might fund several different schemes that would generate positive net benefits, such as the employment of cancer counsellors in general practice or the building of a new hospice for patients with HIV/AIDS. However, if the health authority has a fixed budget and a choice needs to be made between these two options then a cost-benefit analysis will indicate the programme which produces the greatest net benefits, and which should, on this evidence, be purchased.

Unlike cost-minimisation analysis, a comprehensive cost-benefit analysis can be used to make value-for-money comparisons between widely diverging programmes. Hence, in principle, the technique allows comparison between counselling programmes in different health service settings with expenditure on other public and welfare services such as health education, defence and social services. The main difficulty in carrying out a full cost-benefit analysis is that of putting monetary values on many of the inputs and outcomes. For a complete evaluation of counselling and other health programmes, valuations should be put on factors such as stress, anxiety and the time of volunteers, to name but a few 'intangibles'. A cost-benefit analysis is useful for limited evaluations in which the important outcomes can be valued in monetary terms.

COST-EFFECTIVENESS ANALYSIS

Cost-effectiveness analysis is used when both the costs and outcomes of alternative programmes differ, but effectiveness can be compared using a single common measure. For example, the relative effectiveness of employing a counsellor in general practice or training a general practitioner to provide counselling can be assessed using a measure such as patient satisfaction, or reduction in symptoms of depression among patients.

Cost-effectiveness analysis is used for more focused comparisons than cost-benefit analysis. Whereas cost-benefit analysis involves placing a monetary value on all relevant costs and benefits of alternative schemes and assessing which produces the greatest benefit, cost-effectiveness analysis is used when an outcome has already been deemed worthwhile and the main objective of the analysis is to determine how to allocate resources between the different options to achieve the defined outcome. Cost-effectiveness analysis does not provide solutions as to which option to select but clarifies the costs and effects of achieving specific objectives. It can be used alongside other criteria such as acceptability and feasibility. For example, if a group of general practitioners agree that the practice needs to find an alternative to the prescription of anxiolytics for patients with psychological problems, then a cost-effectiveness analysis might be undertaken to help make a choice between the use of a psychologist, a counsellor or a GP with counselling skills for this patient group. Criteria for helping select a particular counselling programme may consist of achieving greatest outcomes for a fixed cost (or budget) or achieving a target outcome at least cost.

One approach to assessing relative cost-effectiveness is to compare the options in terms of the average costs per treated case. Using this criteria the most cost-effective option is that with the lowest average cost. However, a decision-maker may not wish to reject a higher cost option if it is also more effective than the alternatives. Hence cost-effectiveness analysis can also be used to provide information on the additional costs of achieving a greater outcome from a more successful treatment.

COST-UTILITY ANALYSIS

Cost-utility analysis is a technique that has been constructed specifically for evaluating the cost-effectiveness of programmes in which the outcomes are health benefits. It involves the use of a composite numerical scale to represent the multiple health benefits of alternative programmes. When combined with life expectancy data, a measure of the quality adjusted life years (QALYs) gained from an intervention can be calculated. Health economists have designed several such numerical scales, known as health utility scales. Utility scales measure the expressed preferences of individuals for different health states with a higher value or utility being placed on those items which people desire most. The assumption is that a better health state is preferred to a worse health state and so will have a higher 'utility'. There are also a large number of general quality of life scales which are not based on a measure of utility but which can be used to compare the outcome of alternative counselling options, although these vary in terms of their appropriateness and ease of use within an economic evaluation (Bowling 1991).

It might be argued that counselling interventions are unlikely to have a large impact on life expectancy in the same way as, for example, surgical treatment for heart disease. The main benefits accruing from counselling might be expected to be in terms of improvements in well-being or quality of life. Thus, the benefits of a counsellor attachment in general practice might be measured in terms of quality of life gains for the patient and his or her family. The costs per unit gain in patient well-being (or utility) for a patient receiving counselling could be compared with the cost per unit gain in patient well-being gained from the GP providing treatment. As in cost-benefit analysis, however, putting a single numerical value on quality of life is problematic and controversial (Carr-Hill 1989).

FINANCIAL APPRAISAL

Financial appraisal is not a type of economic evaluation as it only measures the financial costs that appear on an accounts sheet. A financial appraisal of a counselling service in a GP surgery will differ from an economic evaluation in several ways. First, the principle of opportunity costing would not be used. This would mean that resources which do not appear on the accounts, such as unpaid overtime, would not be included. In addition, there would be no assessment of whether the financial costs are a reasonable approximation of the true cost of the resources used.

Second, a financial cost would be recorded for the employment of a new counsellor in the GP surgery as this would appear as additional expenditure on the practice accounts. However, costs might not be recorded on the accounts if the counsellor had been re-employed from within the practice – for example, the counsellor might previously have been employed as the practice nurse (a cost is likely to be recorded only for retraining and extra salary to undertake the counselling role). However, this diversion of time from another worthwhile service represents an opportunity cost which would need to be included in an economic evaluation.

Third, financial appraisals use a limited range of output measures usually relating to the effectiveness of service delivery, such as the number of patients seen or patient satisfaction.

Economic evaluations often include financial costs as proxy measures of opportunity cost where these provide the best information readily available. However, economic evaluations use a wider range of costs and outcome measures than are generally used in financial appraisals.

THE CONTEXT OF ECONOMIC EVALUATION

A pragmatic objective currently popular within the Department of Health and other government departments is the goal of cost containment. Alongside this, society has two broader social objectives for the use of human and capital resources:

1   To ensure such resources are used efficiently in order to generate the greatest benefits for society.
2   To ensure those benefits are distributed 'fairly' or 'justly' in society.

The use of public sector resources is often determined in light of the above objectives. In the broadest sense the role of economic evaluation becomes one of examining social efficiency in the allocation of public resources to different sectors such as social services, education, health care, defence, transport and in the distribution of funds within each sector, for example, the provision of counselling services in hospitals or in health centres. Alternatively, the biggest social welfare gains might be achieved by allowing the free market to operate in the provision of goods or services with the product being sold at a commercial price. The product might, for example, be a private counselling service or a more conventional good such as clothes.

While economic evaluation has tended to focus on questions of efficiency (i.e. achievement of the greatest gains at least cost), equity objectives can also be considered. The notion of equity in health care means that the benefits of health services are 'fairly' distributed within society even if the total benefit is reduced. Many commentators argue that issues of equity and efficiency deserve equal consideration in determining the use of public resources for health care (Whitehead and Dahlgren 1991).

Besides the notions of efficiency and equity, the perspective of an economic evaluation can vary, depending on the context. If a counselling service for employees was provided in the private sector, for example in a private hospital, the objective of an economic evaluation might be to assess the costs and benefits of the programme to society (e.g. the benefits accruing from a happier and more productive workforce). From the more limited perspective of the provider agency, the role of the economic evaluation might be to assess the benefits to the private hospital managers of their staff counselling service. This might be assessed in financial terms (i.e. profits) or non-financial terms (i.e. company image). If such a counselling service was provided in the public sector, for example in an NHS hospital, the benefits to society might be measured in terms of the current and future productivity of the medical staff or the specific benefits to the hospital in terms of a reduction in absenteeism.

WHICH TECHNIQUE: COST-BENEFIT, COST-EFFECTIVENESS OR COST-UTILITY ANALYSIS?

The use of financial appraisal will not be considered in depth as it is not strictly a form of economic evaluation. Similarly, cost-minimisation analysis is of limited use as an economic evaluation technique for comparing counselling services due to the requirement of prior evidence of equal effectiveness of the options to be considered. Thus we will focus on the other forms of economic evaluation: cost-benefit, cost-effectiveness and cost-utility analysis. How do these types of economic evaluation compare in their relative theoretical and practical merits for evaluating counselling and counselling services?

Using cost-benefit analysis

Cost-benefit analysis has been the preferred technique for the appraisal of alternative public sector services because it represents the main evaluative arm of a body of economic theory known as welfare economics. As its name suggests, welfare economics is concerned with assessing the efficient use of resources in terms of the benefits for social welfare (Barr 1994). Whether a service is sold in the private market or is paid for by public funds, a cost-benefit analysis should consider all the social costs and social benefits associated with the investment to determine whether society as a whole is benefiting and the extent of this benefit compared to alternative uses of the resources. Several textbooks have elucidated the theory and practice of cost-benefit analysis in assisting the resource allocation problems faced by public agencies (for example, Sugden and Williams 1978; Pearce and Nash 1981).

Economists have tended to use two approaches for valuing the benefits of a service within cost-benefit analysis. One method has been to estimate the value of a service in terms of the greater work and social productivity of individuals resulting as a consequence of their receiving the service. This value is calculated by estimating the extra work an individual is able to perform and multiplying it by the payment rate for that work (or an estimate of the value of the work conducted by non-paid individuals such as volunteers). The second method is to ask potential users of a service what they would be willing to pay for the service for different levels of benefits. For example, a survey could be conducted among patients currently attending a city centre hospital about the perceived benefits of a patient counselling service. The service is free but may be difficult to get to and is only available for a few hours each day. The patients might be asked how much, hypothetically, they would be willing to pay for a counselling clinic more conveniently located with more appropriate opening hours. Different options for the counselling clinic (e.g. different opening times, locations, staffing) could be described to examine how patients' willingness to pay varies with improved service. The responses could then be used to estimate the value of different models of service provision. (It should be noted that while individuals are being asked for their willingness to pay this does not mean they will have to pay a price were such a service to be developed – it is purely a method of valuation.) The value attributed to each level of benefit reflects the overall value of the service to users which could then be compared with the real costs of the service.

However, the outcome measure that might be appropriate to counsellors and decision-makers is not necessarily the monetary value of increased work productivity among those receiving counselling, or service users' willingness to pay valuations. Other more altruistic objectives might be set, especially for counselling services provided within the health service, such as improving the quality of patient care. Alternatively, a profit-motivated manager in a private hospital might see the benefits of a counselling service for hospital employees in terms of the financial returns it can help achieve. If the outcome is positive and staff are satisfied with the counselling service, it might be assumed that the service may contribute to increased productivity of the staff or the image of the hospital. A further benefit is the potential well-being gains for the employees and the secondary effects that might have (for example, for their families). Managers and the providers of a counselling service can then set these outcomes against the costs of the service to help them make decisions as to whether the service in its current form meets their criteria for a worthwhile use of resources.

Converting all costs and benefits to monetary values is likely to be the recommended approach for professionals such as civil servants in the Treasury department at Whitehall, whose objective is to decide how to allocate resources between counselling services, alternative healthcare programmes and all other socially beneficial uses of public funds. In that case, money might be the only feasible common measure of benefit with which to compare the effectiveness of widely diverging services each producing a different set of outcomes. While counsellors need to begin to think about whether counselling is a worthwhile use of resources compared with alternative use of resources (see Chapter 2) our aim here is to demonstrate how an economic analysis can be used to compare alternative counselling options to meet a specified objective.

While a cost-benefit analysis has certain theoretical strengths for measuring efficiency in the use of public resources, there are several reasons why we do not advocate this approach as a practical method of evaluating the relative merits of alternative counselling services in health service settings. Cost-benefit analysis requires monetary values for all relevant costs and benefits of alternative options. There are substantial practical difficulties in undertaking this task in relation to counselling services. For counselling, as with many treatment programmes, the problem of attributing monetary values relates mainly to the measurement of outcomes, or benefits. While it is straightforward to estimate the cost of staff time (e.g. using a counsellor's hourly payment rate) it is less easy to quantify the monetary value of some of the more intangible benefits of counselling services such as a reduction in anxiety or a lower likelihood of suicide. Such measurement appears almost impossible.

Cost-effectiveness or cost-utility analysis?

In our view, the techniques most appropriate for the economic evaluation of counselling are cost-effectiveness or cost-utility analysis. In using these techniques the assumption is made that the provision of counselling in any particular setting has been agreed by the individuals involved (e.g. managers, counsellors) to be a worthwhile use of resources. Cost-utility analysis is best used to help determine whether a counselling service represents the most worthwhile use of resources compared to other health service programmes. Cost-effectiveness analysis is most appropriately used to help decide which type of counselling service represents the best use of resources.

Cost-utility analysis is a specific form of cost-effectiveness analysis in which multiple health outcomes are measured using a common comparable indicator – the QALY. As this is a combined measure of well-being (measured on a 'utility scale') and life years gained from an intervention it should be possible to compare the QALYs gained from a wide range of health programmes, including counselling services and their costs to assess their relative cost-effectiveness. Cost-utility analysis has some grounding in economic theory as the utility measure used in the QALY is derived, albeit loosely, from principles of economic welfare theory. It is also more practical and appropriate for evaluations of the use of health service resources than cost-benefit analysis.

Using cost-effectiveness analysis

While cost-utility analysis could be used to compare alternative counselling service options, we suggest that the technique of cost-effectiveness analysis[1] is probably the most appropriate and practicable for use by counsellors and other service providers. For example, a group of GPs might agree that some form of care and support should be provided in primary care for those patients with 'life problems' or for those who somatise their problems. Cost-effectiveness analysis is concerned with assessing the type of service likely to be the most beneficial and appropriate given the resources available. Cost-effectiveness analysis can also be used to address issues of how much more effective the service might be if it is expanded by using additional resources (such as extra staff or time), or how much reduction in effectiveness is probable from a contraction of the resources available. In this way it supports other criteria for the choice of counselling service such as feasibility, availability of appropriate counselling staff and other resources, political, organisational and cultural acceptability and so on. Cost-effectiveness analysis is a useful tool in decision-making.

While this technique does not have the theoretical rigour of cost-benefit analysis, cost-effectiveness analysis has the advantage of practical simplicity. It can be readily applied by non-economists such as counsellors to help assess whether the resources they have available are being used to best effect and to assess in what way new resources could be used to meet their service objectives and provide the greatest returns. If a counselling service were demonstrated to be cost-effective, this information might be used to back up counsellors' subjective beliefs about the benefits of the service they provide and to help convince managers and budget holders of the value of their service. Even though we suggest that counsellors undertake a cost-effectiveness analysis rather than a cost-benefit analysis, it is still useful for counsellors to list all the possible costs and benefits of the options under consideration to provide supporting evidence to set alongside the results of a cost-effectiveness analysis.

A single measure of effectiveness is needed in a cost-effectiveness analysis in order to compare the relative effectiveness of alternative options. The measure adopted must adequately reflect the objectives of the service. A reduction in psychotropic medication might be the outcome measure to compare counselling in general practice with referral to a clinical psychologist while reflecting the objectives of all parties concerned – the GP principals, the counsellor and patients. A broader outcome measure might be required if a wider set of counselling options are to be compared or if the measure of success is more client orientated. Thus, it may be more appropriate to measure the psychological well-being of users of a GP practice based counselling service in order to compare its relative cost-effectiveness with other counselling services external to the practice, or a different use of resources such as the provision of information leaflets for patients.

It might also be possible to use such outcomes to compare the cost-effectiveness of a counselling service with other mental health services which produce similar types of benefits. However, it would not be possible to compare counselling services with, for example, surgical interventions for heart disease as gains in well-being are unlikely to reflect the full benefits of the latter intervention. In this case, cost-utility analysis (or cost-benefit analysis) is required. We assume that readers will be most interested in how to conduct analyses of alternative methods of providing counselling or addressing a range of psychosocial and stress problems in different healthcare settings and will focus on the use of cost-effectiveness analysis to achieve this aim. However, we deal thoroughly with the merits and issues of using QALYs throughout this book for those readers interested in applying cost-utility analysis or wanting to understand the relevance of its application to evaluating counselling services.

SUMMARY

This chapter outlines various techniques of economic evaluation: cost-minimisation, cost-benefit, cost-effectiveness and cost-utility analysis. Each technique is discussed and cost-effectiveness analysis is advocated for the economic evaluation of counselling. Cost-effectiveness analysis is relatively simple to use and is appropriate for most 'option choice' problems that counsellors are likely to face. While there may be times when cost-benefit or cost-utility analysis might be appropriate, we would argue that given the methodological difficulties (for example, the difficulty of measuring intangible benfits in monetary units) these techniques are best utilised by people trained in economic evaluation. Cost-benefit and cost-utility analyses may be more appropriate when used as part of a large project with specialist support, but can be quite complicated for counsellors conducting a smaller scale evaluation within their own setting.

NOTE

1   We will distinguish cost-effectiveness analysis from cost-utility analysis by defining the former as the technique which uses any appropriate outcome measure other than QALYs. If the evaluation measures QALYs then it is a cost-utility analysis. Hence, appropriate outcomes for cost-effectiveness analysis could be simple measures such as number of clients seen or more 'final' outcomes such as 'psychological well-being' gains. However, in Part II, for simplicity, we use cost-effectiveness analysis as a generic term incorporating cost-utility analysis.

Chapter 4

The components of an economic evaluation

Cost-effectiveness analysis

Introduction
Framework for a cost-effectiveness analysis
The study problem and perspective
The economic objectives
The counselling options
Study design
Cost measurement: identification, measurement and valuation
Outcome measurement
Monetary benefits
Analysing cost-effectiveness results
Example: analysing the cost-effectiveness of counselling in primary care

---

INTRODUCTION

Chapter 3 reviewed the main techniques of economic evaluation and suggested that cost-effectiveness analysis is likely to be the most appropriate technique for assessing efficiency in the use of resources for counselling services. However, we include cost-utility analysis as a special form of cost-effectiveness analysis. Cost-utility analysis differs from a 'conventional cost-effectiveness analysis' in that the outcomes are measured by QALYs reflecting the multiple health benefits of interventions.

This chapter outlines a framework for conducting a cost-effectiveness analysis of counselling interventions. Throughout the chapter we will illustrate the use of this technique in evaluating the cost-effectiveness of counselling for patients suffering from depression in a primary care setting. The evaluation framework can be used to interpret existing studies of the cost-effectiveness of counselling interventions (reviewed in Chapter 5). At the same time the information provided may facilitate the design of evaluations relevant to counselling. In this chapter we outline the basic principles of cost-effectiveness analysis. A detailed exploration of the practical skills and methods required to carry out an analysis will be described in Part II.

FRAMEWORK FOR A COST-EFFECTIVENESS ANALYSIS

There are several inter-related components in an analysis of the cost-effectiveness of a counselling programme. These are outlined in the evaluation framework in Figure 4.1. In this instance, the objective of the evaluation is to produce comparable estimates of the costs and effects of a range of alternative counselling options.

Three stages of evaluation are contained within the evaluation framework.

- *Stage 1* – Prior to the collection and analysis of data, the evaluator needs to consider the purpose and scope of the evaluation. There are three components in this stage: definition of the study problem (Box A), the setting of economic objectives (Box B) and the selection of options for comparison (Box C).
- *Stage 2* – Data collection and analysis consists of the choice of study design for measuring effectiveness (Box D), the assessment of the costs of each option (Box E) and the outcomes from each option (Box F).

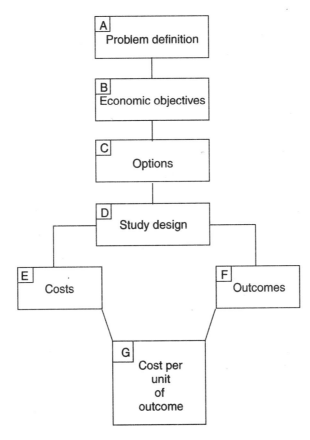

Figure 4.1   The basic cost-effectiveness framework

- *Stage 3* – The production of cost-effectiveness ratios in the form of comparable final cost per unit of outcome measures (Box G). Box G represents the point at which it is possible to determine the relative cost-effectiveness of each of the counselling options considered in the light of the study problem and economic objectives described in Stage 1.

THE STUDY PROBLEM AND PERSPECTIVE

The first step in conducting an economic evaluation is to define the study problem. This might include definition of the problem, its setting and its target group.

For example, in the primary care setting, the study problem might be to identify the most cost-effective strategy for treating the patients suffering from depression visiting the GP. It is important to define the study perspective. Who wants to address this problem? Why are they interested in the problem? What budgets are involved?

The perspective chosen determines the costs to be included in the evaluation. From the perspective of the GP surgery only the costs to the practice would be included. At the other extreme, a societal perspective would include costs to all agencies involved in service provision and personal costs incurred by users of the service. Similarly, the outcome measure chosen to compare effectiveness should reflect the perspective adopted.

The evaluation can be conducted from a number of perspectives. The narrowest perspective would be that of the GP surgery. Alternative perspectives might be the Family Health Services Authority (FHSA) (i.e. all practices within an FHSA boundary) or a National Health Service perspective (which might involve a survey of a cross-section of practices). The choice of perspective depends on who is funding the research and whether any new services that might be recommended as a result of the research. A fundholding general practice might be concerned with how to allocate its budget, resulting in a practice-based perspective. If the FHSA are the main funders and they may be required to allocate additional funds to provide new counselling services, then the evaluation is likely to be conducted from an FHSA perspective. If the Department of Health are the funders then an NHS or societal perspective is likely to be adopted covering all service providers bearing a cost (e.g. the FHSAs, health authorities, local authorities) and the time and money costs incurred by patients themselves.

THE ECONOMIC OBJECTIVES

Once the study problem has been defined, the economic objectives of the evaluation need to be articulated. The objective(s) depend on the study problem and perspective. The economic objective could be defined in terms of improvements in service delivery or in terms of benefits for the service users or society as a whole.

Table 4.1 outlines a range of economic objectives to identify the most cost-effective counselling option for treating patients attending the GP surgery with depression.

Table 4.1 Examples of economic objectives for a counselling service

The economic objectives to identify the counselling option that produces:

1 Lowest cost per patient counselled.
2 Greatest number of patients counselled for a given cost.
3 Lowest cost per unit gain in patient well-being.
4 Minimum extra cost per additional unit gain in patient well-being.

Table 4.1 demonstrates various economic objectives that may help guide the evaluation. For example, one objective might be to identify the counselling option that produces the lowest cost per unit gain in patient well-being or greatest gains for a given cost (objectives 1–3). If the evaluation involves an assessment of the expansion of a counselling service, for example to cover greater numbers of patients, a viable economic objective would be to identify the option that achieves the lowest extra cost for each additional unit gain in patient well-being (objective 4).

THE COUNSELLING OPTIONS

A clear description of the options related to the study problem is required. In our example, a number of options for an economic evaluation of counselling for depressed patients in primary care might be considered.

- Employ a counsellor in the GP surgery;
- train one or more of the existing GPs in counselling skills;
- train the practice nurse in counselling skills.

It is useful, at the outset, to construct a list of possible options, in order to minimise the risk of leaving out a potentially better (i.e. more cost-effective) option in the final evaluation. The range of alternative options selected for the evaluation have to be assessed carefully, as the validity of the findings depend on the most appropriate comparisons being made. For example, the counsellor may prove to be the most cost-effective option for treating patients presenting at the GP surgery with depression. However, if another option which is potentially more cost-effective, such as the referral of such patients to an external counselling agency, was rejected at the initial stage, then the results of the evaluation are likely to be misleading or meaningless. There may, of course, be practical, ethical or political reasons why some potentially viable options are not included in the final option selection which should be made explicit by the evaluator.

To assess the relative cost-effectiveness of the 'active' counselling options with 'current practices', an option known as the 'do-nothing' should be defined. This represents the baseline or control against which the active options are compared. In the example, the 'do-nothing' option is to maintain the current practice of consultations provided by GPs untrained in counselling. In economic evaluations when a do-nothing option is used to represent current practice, there is likely to be a positive cost associated with this option. In some cases the 'do-nothing' option will represent the situation of no alternative service whatsoever. For the purpose of comparison with the 'active options' the 'do-nothing' will in this case have no direct costs associated with it.

STUDY DESIGN

In order to evaluate the relative cost-effectiveness of the treatment options under review the study framework needs to be sufficiently rigorous to be able to measure the association between each option and the outcomes that are desired. Ideally, this means the use of a randomised control trial (RCT), which represents the most scientific and statistically rigorous form of study design (Cochrane 1972). The use of RCTs will be examined in more depth in Chapter 6; in this section we will illustrate the use of an RCT in a simple example. In an economic evaluation of counselling in primary care, the use of an RCT would involve randomly allocating patients to the 'active' options. The counselling options were defined as a counsellor, training GPs in counselling skills and training practice nurses in counselling skills. This would produce three intervention groups (i.e. group 1 receives counselling from the counsellor; group 2 from a GP trained in counselling skills; group 3 from a nurse trained in counselling skills; and a control group – the 'do-nothing' option). The effectiveness of each option would be compared by testing the statistical significance of the difference in patient outcomes. However, for evaluations carried out in work settings by healthcare workers or counsellors the construction of an RCT may be difficult due to limitations on their time, effort, resources, knowledge and data availability. It is probable that counsellors and service providers would require the assistance of researchers in academic institutions skilled in the use of such techniques. Buying in professional help will raise the complexity and cost of carrying out an economic evaluation, but will generate a more reliable analysis of the cost-effectiveness of particular counselling options. In the case studies of Chapter 11 we demonstrate how service providers and academic researchers can work together to plan and conduct an economic evaluation.

A further issue in the use of RCTs is whether it is an ethically acceptable study design for the evaluation of counselling. It may be difficult on ethical grounds for evaluators and counsellors to 'deny' a particular counselling service to a group of individuals who have been randomly allocated to a different and possibly less appropriate option. This danger is inherent in an RCT and may lead the evaluator to use a less rigorous form of randomised controlled trial, whereby some participants are allocated to a counselling option on the grounds that it would be unethical not to do so. Clear evidence that they would benefit less from being allocated to an alternative option, such as usual GP care, might be a case in point. Alternatively, such individuals might be excluded altogether from the RCT, although this could result in small numbers in each group.

For practical and ethical reasons, there is a need to offer a more feasible, albeit less rigorous study design that counsellors and healthcare workers could employ while still having some confidence in the reliability of results produced. A number of designs exist which do not require randomisation, such as semi-controlled trials which can be conducted without randomising users to different groups. For example, in a study of counselling in primary care, GPs would refer patients with depression to the counselling option they decided was most appropriate, rather than randomly allocating them to a treatment option. Another study design is a simple before and after evaluation of the effectiveness of counselling. With this approach the outcome of interest might be measured for the potential service users prior to the implementation of the counselling options, and then measured at defined follow-up times to examine any changes in outcomes. Although there is more likelihood of bias in the results and less certainty that any changes in patient outcomes are attributable to the interventions, such study designs are more flexible and probably more representative of the working practice of doctors and counsellors.

COST MEASUREMENT: IDENTIFICATION, MEASUREMENT AND VALUATION

The measurement of costs depends on the perspective of the evaluation and its economic objectives. Three interrelated steps of cost identification, measurement and valuation need to be considered in determining the costs of each option in an evaluation:

1 Identification: the range of resource inputs to include in the costing.
2 Measurement: the approach to collecting resource use data for cost estimation.
3 Valuation: the method for estimating the unit cost of resource inputs.

Identification

Resources are time and material inputs that can be used in alternative ways. In our example of counselling in primary care the inputs would certainly include the time of GPs, nurses and counsellors spent counselling and time involved in administration but might also include the use of surgery facilities (e.g. premises, heating, lighting, stationery), the production and provision of self-help leaflets.

Whichever perspective is adopted in an economic evaluation it is important to estimate opportunity costs. The time a GP spends counselling a patient cannot be reused to treat another patient for hypertension. Hence the cost of a GP providing counselling in the surgery would include the value of the doctor's time diverted from other activities (this value could be estimated by taking the current gross salary of a GP). This would be a positive cost unless the doctor concerned had sufficient worktime flexibility to provide additional counselling without foregoing time spent with other patients, other activities and without working longer hours, as home life and leisure time also has a value.

Patients may incur a money cost in travelling to the surgery for counselling. Similarly, they may also give up time, which has an alternative use value – either earnings lost from taking time off work or the value of foregone leisure time. In addition, intangible costs would be incurred if the counselling resulted in greater distress and anxiety rather than less.

Measurement

There are two approaches to collecting data on resource use. The direct and more comprehensive approach is to conduct a data collection exercise in which information on resource use is collected either prospectively (so that resource use is monitored as it occurs) or retrospectively (whereby resource use is estimated after the service has been provided using such methods as medical records or staff recall of their time involved in counselling). However, the direct methods, (particularly prospective data collection) are costly in terms of research time, resources and effort. Short cuts can be taken to produce crude estimates of resource use and cost. This might involve the use of a combination of financial accounts, best guestimates and informed assumptions of resource use and cost.

Valuation

The valuation of opportunity cost requires a unit price to be attached to each resource input identified. If a counsellor spends one hour with a client the value of that time can be measured using the equivalent payment rate for a counsellor (e.g. gross weekly salary divided by hours worked). This reflects society's valuation of using the counsellor's time to provide counselling rather than providing some other service. In this case the financial cost (the salary paid) is the same as the opportunity cost. However, if the counsellor would otherwise be unemployed (i.e. their time could not be used in any other way) then strictly the opportunity cost would be zero. Conversely, a volunteer's time providing counselling would not represent a financial cost, but could represent an opportunity cost of value to society, in that some other beneficial activity might have been given up (e.g. alternative voluntary work or leisure time).

In general, economists use market prices (e.g. salary, price of materials, health service prices or tariffs) to reflect opportunity cost. If this does not adequately represent their true value or opportunity cost, or a market price does not exist, then a proxy measure of unit costs should be estimated (known by economists as 'shadow prices'). The extent to which shadow prices are estimated depends on the inaccuracy of market prices, the amount of unpriced resource inputs and the time available to estimate unit costs.

An economic evaluation of counselling in primary care for patients with depression would include the measurement of costs to the practice if this was the perspective adopted. If the perspective was that of the NHS, the costs to all agencies (e.g. the practice, FHSA) would be included and if a societal perspective was adopted personal time and money costs to service users and their companions would be included. Within these cost components the evaluator would need to define the specific resource inputs to be included and methods of data collection.

OUTCOME MEASUREMENT

To compare the cost-effectiveness of alternative options, a common outcome measure is necessary. It would not be possible to compare the cost-effectiveness of a counselling programme with a non-counselling option if different outcome measures were used for each option. For example, data might be collected on the reduction in depressed patients consulting their GP as a result of patients having received counselling from a practice counsellor, but this could not be compared with an alternative option, such as GPs providing advice to patients about smoking cessation with the number of patients quitting smoking as the outcome measure. In this case a more general outcome measure, such as improvements in patient quality of life would be required to compare relative cost-effectiveness. In comparing alternative counselling options, for example the work of a practice counsellor with a nurse trained in counselling skills, a specific outcome measure is required. One such measure might be the reduction in patients' depression using a numerical scale such as the Beck Depression Inventory (Bowling 1991).

There are three types of outcome measure for assessing the effectiveness of counselling interventions within an economic evaluation:

1 Process indicators.
2 Intermediate outcomes.
3 Final outcomes.

Process indicators

These are used to measure effectiveness in the delivery of counselling. Process indicators (PIs) can be divided into two sets:

1 PIs measuring the effectiveness of the 'supply' of each counselling option (supply process indicators) such as the proportion of general practices in an area that have decided to provide a specialist counselling service.
2 PIs measuring the 'demand' for each counselling option (demand process indicators) such as the proportion of eligible patients aware of, or who use a counselling service at the surgery. These indicators provide a measure of the target group coverage, awareness and uptake of each counselling option.

Process indicators are measures that can only be used for very narrow economic evaluations of the cost-effectiveness of alternative methods of service delivery (for example, using a demand process indicator such as the number of patients who use a counselling service).

Intermediate outcomes

These represent the influence of counselling on the attitudes, intentions and behaviour of service users. This represents the middle stage between the provision and uptake of counselling and the impact on quality of life, well-being or final health state. To have an impact on quality of life some change in attitude or behaviour needs to occur subsequent to receiving counselling. This change can then be used to provide a measure of intermediate outcome. For instance, the short-term impact of different counselling options for patients with depression within a primary care setting could be assessed by comparing the attitudinal statements of patients in each group (e.g. 'I feel much happier now', 'I can cope with my life to a greater extent now').

Final outcomes

These are measures of well-being, quality of life and other health benefits of counselling. For example, the effects of counselling patients with depression in a primary care setting could be measured using the Beck Depression Inventory or the General Health Questionnaire. Numerous psychological well-being and general quality-of-life or health instruments exist that could be used in an economic evaluation of counselling (Bowling 1991). Examples of general quality-of-life measures are the Sickness Impact Profile, which assesses the impact of ill health on behavioural functioning (Bergner *et al.* 1981); the Nottingham Health Profile (Hunt *et al.* 1980); the SF-36 health profile (Ware and Sherbourne 1992). However, each of these measures contains a numerical scale for each of several dimensions of well-being including mobility, physical pain and psychological state, which can make their use in cost-effectiveness analysis difficult as this requires a single scale to be able to compare the effectiveness of various options.

Final outcome measures can enable comparison of the cost-effectiveness of counselling with other types of programme that affect the well-being, quality of life and general health state of individuals. A final outcome measure frequently used for comparing the cost-effectiveness of different health programmes is life years gained. For instance, in an assessment of the cost-effectiveness of nicotine gum prescription for smokers and the effects of surgery for heart disease, an estimate of life years gained could be used to compare the health benefits from each option. However, this is unlikely to be an appropriate outcome measure for counselling options which tend to have a relatively low impact on life expectancy, but may have a high relative impact on quality of life.

Cost-utility analysis (which in Chapter 3 was defined as a specific form of cost-effectiveness analysis) allows comparisons between counselling and other treatments that have different effects on patient survival probabilities and quality of life (e. g. treatment for heart disease). The outcome measure used in cost-utility analysis is the quality adjusted life year (QALY) (Williams 1985). Estimates of life expectancy are adjusted for the quality of life expected, with quality of life measured on a scale from zero (quality of life equivalent to that if dead), to one (quality of life if in perfect health). There are several such quality of life scales (defined by health economists as utility scales). These include the Rosser disability-distress matrix and the EuroQoL index (Williams 1985; Bryan *et al.* 1991). Work is currently underway at the University of Sheffield to devise a new single index scale using a general health profile measure – the SF-36 (Brazier 1993). Within an economic evaluation QALYs provide a comprehensive measure of health outcomes that can be combined with cost data to determine priorities for allocating resources between programmes that affect health status (Drummond 1989). However, cost per QALY gained estimates can also be used to compare different counselling options, such as the use of counsellors, GPs or nurses trained in counselling skills for patients with depression attending the GP surgery.

MONETARY BENEFITS

If a cost benefit analysis is used to evaluate a counselling service, then the outcomes (or benefits) would need to be measured in monetary units. The main benefit measure for a counselling service for patients with depression in primary care could, for example, be savings in prescribed drugs expenditure. While most economic evaluations of counselling have used cost-benefit analysis (reviewed in Chapter 5), we are not focusing on its use due to the complexities in using this technique. Moreover, the limited range of outcomes that can be measured in monetary units (such as drug savings) can be incorporated into a cost-effectiveness analysis by including such items in a measure of net costs (i.e. costs minus savings). This method is described in Chapter 10.

ANALYSING COST-EFFECTIVENESS RESULTS

The final part of a cost-effectiveness analysis is to produce and interpret the results in order to determine which intervention represents the most cost-effective option. The data can be analysed, using average, incremental or marginal costs.

Average costs

The end stage of an economic evaluation is to bring together the cost and outcomes data to analyse the relative cost-effectiveness of each of the options considered in relation to the original economic objectives. In almost all economic evaluations one of the economic objectives will be to compare the estimate of costs per unit of outcome for each option. In the example we have used in this chapter, this would involve comparison of the costs per unit increase in patient quality of life for the patients receiving counselling from the counsellor, GP or nurse options. The decision-maker could then select the option which has the lowest average cost per unit increase in quality of life, although this might be conditional on the total resource cost not exceeding the budget available, or the total gain in quality of life meeting a minimum target level.

Incremental costs

An economic objective might be to provide information to enable decision-makers to judge whether the additional costs of a more expensive but also more effective counselling option might be worthwhile. This is known as an assessment of incremental cost-effectiveness and it might lead to a different conclusion from that formed from comparison of average costs. For instance, employing a counsellor in general practice may be more costly than training practice nurses in counselling skills but could result in a greater effectiveness in terms of improved well-being of depressed patients. The decision is then whether the extra effectiveness of the counsellor is thought to be worth the additional cost. Information of incremental cost-effectiveness can assist decision-makers in the selection of the most effective option for the resources available.

Marginal costs

Alternatively, an assessment might be made of the costs of expanding (or contracting) an existing service. This is known as an analysis of marginal cost-effectiveness. For example, a counsellor might initially provide a service two days per week. If the service was expanded so that the counsellor was employed full time (five days per week) the marginal cost would be the value of an additional three days of counsellor time. The extra benefits of employing a counsellor full time could be measured to examine the marginal cost-effectiveness of extending the service. An assessment of marginal costs is important if, for example, a small expansion of a service results in a large increase in effectiveness. For instance, a counselling session of thirty minutes per patient may produce poor outcomes compared to providing longer sessions of between forty-five minutes to one hour.

Discounting

A general behavioural principle used in economic analysis is that people or agencies prefer to delay costs but wish to obtain immediate monetary benefits. Thus future benefits and costs should have a lower valuation than current benefits and costs. This is known as discounting. It is based on individuals' time preference for current consumption and explains why, for example, consumers may prefer to pay for a fridge-freezer using interest-free credit rather than spending a lump sum, or will only deposit their money in a restricted access savings account if a high rate of interest is paid. Hence, if the costs and money benefits (e.g. health service savings) of counselling extend beyond one year then the principle of discounting should apply. Let us assume that there are two sets of options with the same nominal total costs and benefits but different time-scales for these costs and benefits. In general, individuals prefer to delay a cost of £100 by one or more years if possible, but would rather receive £100 now rather than delay its receipt for one or more years. If discounting is applied the options for which the costs are immediate and the benefits only accrue in the longer term will appear less cost-effective than the options with delayed costs and immediate benefits. However, economists are currently in disagreement as to whether non-monetary benefits such as QALYs should be discounted at all, so discounting of final outcomes is not a hard rule to which economic evaluations need to adhere (Parsonage and Neuberger 1992).

Sensitivity analysis

In most economic evaluations it is necessary to analyse data further so as not to rely solely on a comparison of a single cost-effectiveness ratio for each option. A range of estimates (i.e. low, medium or high) for costs, outcomes and discount rates should be utilised to allow for uncertainty in these variables. The impact of different estimates on the relative cost-effectiveness of the options should then be examined. If relative cost-effectiveness changes, the issue of uncertainty may need to be remedied by the collection of better data on the costs and outcomes of the options.

Equity objectives

Finally, it might be necessary to assess whether the counselling options meet specified equity objectives. The pursuit of economic objectives (which represent efficiency objectives) may conflict with equity objectives (Culyer 1980). This has resulted in an emphasis in the use of cost-effectiveness analysis on assessing whether or not an intervention produces the greatest total benefits for a given cost. The issue of whether this benefit is equitably distributed in society has been only a secondary concern.

However, it is possible and perhaps appropriate for an evaluation of a counselling programme to have a predefined equity objective, such as ensuring equal access for all patients to counselling. Alternative methods of providing counselling that meet this equity objective could then be compared to assess their relative cost-effectiveness.

EXAMPLE: ANALYSING THE COST-EFFECTIVENESS OF COUNSELLING IN PRIMARY CARE

The principles of cost-effectiveness analysis can be illustrated by adding some figures to the example we have used throughout this chapter – the provision of counselling in a primary care setting for patients with depression. More detailed case studies will be introduced in Part II.

The study problem facing an FHSA might be to compare the relative cost-effectiveness of four options for providing counselling in a primary care setting (i.e. GP as counsellor, nurse as counsellor, and counsellor, plus a 'do nothing' option). Let us assume in this instance that successful treatment is measured by a reduction in the number of consultations with patients for depression. The objective is then to identify which option produces the lowest cost per one per cent reduction in patients consulting with depression. The FHSA have defined a target reduction of 50 per cent in numbers of patients attending with depression, to be achieved at the least possible cost (i.e. this is a specific economic objective). In order to simplify the calculations we will assume that a randomised control trial is acceptable on practical and ethical grounds. A study is thus set up whereby 100 patients identified as potentially benefiting from counselling are randomly assigned to each of the intervention groups – A, counselling GP; B, counselling practice nurse; C, practice counsellor. A further group of 100 patients receive routine GP care (representing the control or do-nothing option). After a one-year trial, results show that the control group has experienced no reduction in patients attending with depression, but the reduction in groups A, B and C is 40 per cent (n=40); 45 per cent (n=45) and 55 per cent (n=55) respectively. The GP routine care group represents the baseline against which the active options can be compared.

The total cost to the FHSA of each option relative to the routine care option is £40 per counselling session for the GP, £10 for the nurse and £20 for the counsellor. With this data the cost per one per cent reduction (compared to the routine care group) for the three options are:

£100 for the GP as counsellor option
£22 for the nurse as counsellor option
£36 for the practice counsellor option.

On the basis of these calculations the cost-effective option appears to be the nurse as counsellor option. However, for managers with cash-limited budgets this evidence may not provide sufficient guidance for decision-making. The reduction in patients with depression of 45 per cent does not meet the FHSA target of a 50 per cent reduction; the counsellor option meets this target but at a higher total cost. The question is then whether an option which produces a greater total gain is worth the extra costs incurred. The total cost of the counsellor option is £2,000 for the 100 patients (£20 x 100) and £1,000 for the nurse for a relative effectiveness of 55 per cent and 45 per cent respectively. Hence, with a difference in total costs of £1,000 the incremental cost-effectiveness to achieve an additional 10 per cent reduction in patients with depression by employing the counsellor is £100 for each additional one per cent reduction.

In this hypothetical illustration of the use of cost-effectiveness analysis, it can be seen that while the technique aids decision-making, it can only help make informed decisions about resource use along with consideration of other criteria. The example provided is simplistic – it has not included sensitivity analysis, discounting or consideration of equity objectives. These issues are dealt with in the case studies of the North Brownstead Practice and the Smithland Trust Hospital in Chapter 11.

Summary

This chapter outlines a framework for the economic evaluation of counselling focusing on the use of cost-effectiveness analysis. The basic components in the evaluation have been demonstrated using a hypothetical example of three 'counselling options' for treating patients attending GP surgeries suffering from depression. No attempt has been made to provide a detailed account of the methods for carrying out an economic evaluation – Part II covers each component of the framework in depth.

There are two main uses for the framework outlined in this chapter: first, as a tool for reviewing literature. With some minor modifications the framework can be used to interpret the content, coverage and quality of previous cost-effectiveness and cost-benefit studies of counselling, psychotherapy or mental health interventions. The framework illustrates the techniques needed to interpret and assess the quality of the methods and results of economic evaluations. In Chapter 5 evaluations of primary and secondary healthcare settings are reviewed, using a modified version of the framework.

Second, the framework can be used to plan and conduct an economic evaluation. It provides guidelines for counsellors and others involved with counselling on how to conduct a cost-effectiveness analysis of alternative counselling or psychotherapy options in healthcare settings. Part II provides details of the specific steps and potential problems likely to be faced by researchers in planning and conducting a cost-effectiveness analysis.

Chapter 5

The cost-effectiveness of counselling
Reviewing the evidence

Introduction
Is counselling beneficial?
The value of cost-effectiveness and cost-benefit analysis
Counselling in primary care: costs and outcomes
Counselling in secondary care: costs and outcomes
The review studies
Summarising the evidence: scope, generalisability and comparability
    criteria

INTRODUCTION

Psychosocial problems are a significant cause of morbidity in the UK. It has been estimated that approximately 30 per cent of the adult population have experienced symptoms of anxiety or depression, and that up to 40 per cent of those consulting their GP have a probable psychiatric disorder (Dowrick 1992).

In health settings patients with problems as diverse as bereavement, sexual dysfunction, chronic illness and disability, HIV/AIDS, alcohol and drug problems, marital difficulties, occupational stress, unemployment and redundancy, racial discrimination, difficulties with sexual orientation or a combination of psychosocial or 'life problems' might be presented to health professionals and counsellors. Moreover, counselling or support might be required for health professionals and other staff experiencing occupational stress.

This chapter examines the literature on the effectiveness and cost-effectiveness of counselling. First, we undertake a general review of the evidence for the cost-effectiveness of counselling and psychotherapy interventions in healthcare settings. Second, we conduct a more detailed review of a selection of published studies of the cost-effectiveness of counselling interventions. Chapter 4 outlined the cost-effectiveness evaluation framework. In this chapter we apply this framework to review and assess five studies. The framework is slightly modified here so as to review studies using different types of economic evaluation techniques (i.e. cost-benefit analysis or cost-effectiveness analysis).

There are few cost-effectiveness or cost-benefit evaluations of counselling and those selected represent some of the more rigorous evaluations published in the last ten years. The first three studies (Dryden *et al*. 1989; Maguire *et al*. 1982; Ginsberg *et al*. 1984) use cost-benefit analysis to evaluate counselling interventions in a primary care setting, the fourth (Scott and Freeman 1992) does not clearly define a setting or technique (although it can be defined as a cost-effectiveness analysis) and the fifth (Robson *et al*. 1984) is a cost-effectiveness analysis of counselling in a secondary care setting.

Our aim is not to cover every economic study conducted in this field, but to take a selection of studies published since 1980, deemed of sufficient quality to be published in peer-reviewed medical journals, in order to demonstrate the application of the framework for reviewing economic evaluations. This may help counsellors and other non-economists to review and criticise economic studies of counselling and psychotherapy interventions.

Finally, we summarise the existing evidence on the cost-effectiveness of counselling using three criteria: scope of the studies, generalisability of findings and comparability of findings. These criteria help assess the quality and policy relevance of existing studies. Scope relates to the range of objectives, types of cost-effectiveness analysis methods used and range of interventions analysed. Generalisability relates to the overall relevance of the study results beyond their specific contexts or settings. Comparability represents the extent to which results from different studies can be compared to identify cost-effective counselling interventions. This depends not only on scope and generalisability considerations but also on the variations in the methods used for measuring costs and outcomes.

IS COUNSELLING BENEFICIAL?

Counselling and psychotherapy outcome research has tended to focus on two main questions. First, does counselling offer any greater benefits than a placebo therapy,[1] that is, does it work? Second, can counselling reduce the utilisation of health services and hence offset health service costs?

Is counselling more effective than placebo?

There has been little agreement as to whether counselling and psychotherapy has any effect or is more effective than offering individuals a suitable placebo therapy. An early study (Eysenck 1952) found no difference in patient benefits between a group receiving psychotherapy and a control group with similar symptoms but who did not receive psychotherapy. A meta-analysis of several hundred studies in which psychotherapy and placebo options were compared confirmed this finding (Prioleau *et al*. 1983).[2] Thus it has been argued that psychotherapy is an expensive placebo and requires more evidence to justify use of limited health service resources (Lancet Editorial 1984; Wilkinson 1984, Shepherd 1985; Pringle and Laverty 1993). In contrast, proponents of psychotherapy argue that brief, short-term intervention is more effective than placebo and is cost-effective in that it reduces healthcare costs (Lesser 1979). In a meta-analysis of nearly 500 controlled studies, Smith *et al.* (1980) concluded that on average psychotherapy interventions produced an increase in well-being that was 80 per cent greater than that achieved by the controls. This finding, coupled with some evidence of a reduction in healthcare utilisation, means that some commentators in the UK believe that the cost of psychotherapy in the NHS is low relative to other procedures such as renal dialysis and the care of the chronically ill, and can provide significant benefits for human well-being (Aveline 1984; Bloch and Lambert 1985).

Debate has focused on the relative methodological merits and weaknesses of the meta-analysis conducted by Smith *et al.* (1980) and Prioleau *et al.* (1983). One problem with both these studies is that in many of the articles reviewed the placebo was another therapeutic intervention, such as relaxation training, so that different therapeutic options were being compared rather than psychotherapy versus no therapy. The difference in effectiveness of these options should be considered in relation to their differences in costs to determine appropriate cost-effective strategies for improving the psychosocial well-being of clients. This is an entirely appropriate focus for evaluation as in many cases there may be no alternative to counselling or psychotherapy that will achieve the same type of outcome.

Utilisation and costs

In the USA Mumford *et al.* (1984) reviewed 58 studies of the effectiveness of outpatient psychotherapy and conducted an analysis of health insurance claims over the period 1974–8. They presented evidence of a mean reduction in the utilisation of inpatient and outpatient medical care of 10 per cent to 33 per cent, using a variety of outcome indicators (e.g. hospital days, admissions and assessment of cost savings). Psychotherapy had the greatest impact on utilisation of hospital inpatient care and associated costs. A large relative decline in utilisation was also found for older subsets of patients. A similar pattern emerged from the analysis of health insurance claims.

An early US study (Goldberg *et al.* 1970) of 256 patients attending an outpatient mental health therapy programme found, 12 months after referral, a 13.6 per cent reduction in the number of patients seen for non-psychiatric services and a 15.7 per cent reduction for laboratory or X-ray procedures. The study patients were all prepaid members of a community practice health plan (Group Health Association of Washington). The study consisted of a simple before/after design whereby service utilisation 12 months after referral was compared with the 12-month period prior to referral.

Over a four-year period 1974–8 Schlesinger *et al.* (1983) examined the health insurance claims of people with a first diagnosis during 1975 of one of four chronic diseases (diabetes, hypertension, obstructive airway disease and ischaemic heart disease). Based on charges for inpatient treatment they found by year 3 a marginally lower average cost for patients who had been receiving outpatient mental health treatment (n=723, mean cost \$820) compared to the no-mental health treatment group (n=1188, mean cost \$870). However, for patients who attended three or more outpatient visits for mental health treatment the cost difference was larger (e.g. \$545 for the group with 7–20 visits). Over the four-year period the mean cost for medical care was greater for the mental health treatment group. If the costs of providing the mental health treatment were included the study found statistically significant lower mean costs only for the group with 2–6 visits for mental health treatment in year 3. Mental health treatment was found to have no significant impact on outpatient costs – the authors argued that outpatient care was necessary for maintaining and improving the quality of medical practice for people with chronic illness and so no cost savings should be expected. Schlesinger *et al.* (1983) claimed their study represented an examination of the 'cost-offset' effect of psychotherapy, although this represents a form of cost-benefit analysis, with benefits measured as medical care savings.

The 'cost-offset' hypothesis was also tested in the primary care setting in the USA in a study of the costs of ambulatory medical care (i.e. number of non-psychiatry visits) of 400 patients with mental health problems such as schizophrenia, organic brain syndrome and personality disorder (Borus *et al.* 1985). These patients were attending a health centre in Massachusetts and had received a mental disorder diagnosis in 1978, which represented the reference year. The study compared the ambulatory care utilisation and charges of a sub-group of these patients who received specialist mental health treatment during the reference year (n=198) with an 'untreated' sub-group (n=202). Comparisons were made 24 months prior to and 24 months post the reference year. The 'treatment offset effect' was defined as a decrease in post-reference month visits or charges for the treated sub-group relative to the untreated sub-group. Similar to the findings of Mumford *et al.* (1984) for inpatient costs, Borus *et al.* (1985) found 24 months after the reference month a lower ambulatory care utilisation and mean cost for the treated group versus the untreated group. Utilisation and costs associated with more severe mental health disorders such as schizophrenia were also examined. The mean cost difference was between \$110–\$113 for both severe and less severe cases. However, including the visits and charges for these cases, specialist treatment resulted in an opposite outcome of higher utilisation and costs for the treated sub-grouping for non-psychiatric and psychiatric visits combined, the mean cost difference at 24 months after the reference month being \$446 for severe cases and \$91 for less severe cases.

One problem with the US 'cost-offset' studies is that none have employed a rigorous study design. In addition, instead of measuring direct costs, charges for medical care have been used, a reduction of which are a poor indicator of cost savings. All the studies are US based and their findings have a low transferability to other contexts and settings such as the UK. Despite these reservations, the evidence might be sufficient to hypothesise that while costs of inpatient care might be offset by psychotherapy and mental health treatment, overall healthcare costs might be higher. If attention is paid only to cost savings the effectiveness of psychotherapy might well be questioned. Mumford and Schlesinger (1987) have argued that any cost-offsets should be seen as incidental effects and not the goal of psychotherapy which should focus on improvements in emotional status and other 'human' benefits.

THE VALUE OF COST-EFFECTIVENESS AND COST-BENEFIT ANALYSIS

In the early 1980s there was a surge of interest in the application of the techniques of cost-effectiveness and cost-benefit analysis to the evaluation of psychotherapy. While several commentators have argued strongly for the use of cost-effectiveness analysis to evaluate psychotherapy interventions (Goldberg and Jones 1980; Yates and Newman 1980a, 1980b; Demuth and Yates 1981), there has been resistance to the introduction of economic evaluation. Demuth and Yates (1981) identified four statements which have been used to argue against therapists using cost-effectiveness analysis for the purposes of self-evaluation.

1   Therapeutic outcomes, such as human and emotional benefits, are not readily quantifiable.
2   The feeling that of higher priority is the need to undertake more strictly controlled evaluations of the efficacy of various counselling interventions (i.e. the evaluation of efficacy represents an assessment of whether a counselling intervention does more good than harm).
3   The fear that evaluation will demonstrate that counselling is an expensive luxury, and that any benefits can only be achieved at high cost.
4   The measurement of costs is something that economists are qualified to do, not psychotherapists.

Demuth and Yates (1981) refute each of these points. They argue that it is possible to identify proxy measures of effectiveness such as client satisfaction ratings. They state that a balanced development of psychotherapy provision requires both a programme of efficacy evaluations and more pragmatic evaluations of cost-effectiveness in healthcare settings. Citing evidence that psychotherapy for schizophrenia is of lower cost and more effective when carried out in outpatient departments rather than as part of inpatient care, they argue that changing service practice can result in reduced costs and greater effectiveness. Finally, Demuth and Yates indicate that counsellors are in a better position than economists to collect and analyse cost and outcome data for their services.

While there is a recognition of the role of cost-effectiveness analysis in evaluating counselling some commentators accept this only begrudgingly or try to promote its use in a 'softer' more subjective manner. Wolberg (1981) argued that in the USA empirical work has demonstrated that psychotherapy produces a benefit for two-thirds of people who receive it, but that it is very difficult to specify the factors that lead to these gains. He accepts that 'to finance psychotherapy without limits would probably be unwise', but concludes that the main issue is the need to understand psychotherapy better.

In a review of the literature in the UK Corney (1990) suggested that the evidence pointed to two-thirds of patients who receive counselling in the primary care setting obtaining a benefit. The danger with evaluation is that it might lead to counselling being dismissed as ineffective if it fails to produce benefits, while the real problem may lie with the study design so that, for example, a good therapeutic method might be carried out by poor practitioners. Cost-effectiveness analysis has become a popular 'buzz' phrase. There is a risk that it will be applied to the evaluation of counselling and psychotherapy services without proper consideration of its use and without an adequately robust evaluation framework (McGrath and Lowson 1986).

One argument against applying the full rigours of cost-effectiveness to psychotherapy has been that it tends to adopt the perspective of the healthcare purchaser or provider, but rarely that of the patient (Canter 1991). Three patient case studies were presented by Canter whereby the use of psychotherapy produced important benefits for the individual and so appeared cost-effective. However, he focuses only on subjective benefits to three subjects and does not attempt to quantify the costs or accurately measure the benefits. It is important to quantify the total benefits to all patients receiving psychotherapy so that the cost-effectiveness of psychotherapy from a societal perspective can be examined.

Although it is true that many of the costs and benefits of counselling and psychotherapy are intangible, it is still possible to conduct cost-effectiveness analyses of such interventions. Goldberg and Jones (1980) compared the use of a large psychiatric hospital with a small psychiatric unit in a district general hospital for treating a cohort of first admission schizophrenic patients. They divided the costs and benefits of each option into those that were 'hard' (i.e. quantifiable) and those that were 'soft' (i.e. intangible). The 'hard' costs and benefits were examined from two perspectives – the community (provider agencies such as the hospital, local authority, social security) and the patient and his or her family. In both options the benefits exceeded the costs, but there were net monetary benefits estimated for the small DGH psychiatric unit compared to the large psychiatric hospital. 'Soft' costs and benefits were defined as 'those effects of a service which cannot readily be expressed in financial terms, such as relief of symptoms and distress and improvements in psychological adjustment'. In the Goldberg and Jones study the soft costs and benefits were listed and compared for the two options and non-quantitative judgements made about which service was superior on each intangible dimension.

As Table 5.1 shows, the district general hospital is judged to offer a superior service in terms of all but one of the costs and benefits listed. The authors have used this approach to include intangibles within the framework of a cost-benefit analysis. An alternative approach might be to include 'soft' costs and benefits within a cost-effectiveness analysis framework, although the nature of this technique (a single outcome measure) will necessarily reduce the scope of the evaluation. Although the items in Table 5.1 are not quantifiable in monetary terms a numerical outcome can be recorded for most – for example, patient weeks employed or ratings of leisure can be measured numerically. Indicators such as these can be used as the measure of effectiveness in a cost-effectiveness analysis.

Table 5.1   Intangible costs and benefits of a district general hospital (DGH) versus a psychiatric hospital in the treatment of chronic schizophrenia

	Superior services
Costs	
Inpatient days	DGH
Patients needing changes in drugs or dosage	DGH
Sociability – number of impairments	DGH
Employability – relatives' views	Psychiatric hospital
Patient adopts strange postures	DGH
Benefits	
Sociability – no. of assets	DGH
Heterosexual performance	DGH
Patient weeks employed	DGH
Work ratings	
drive	DGH
constructiveness	DGH
realism	DGH
Leisure rating	DGH
Marital adjustment rating	DGH

Source: Goldberg and Jones (1980)

COUNSELLING IN PRIMARY CARE: COSTS AND OUTCOMES

Attention in the 1990s has focused on mental health services, as a reduction in mental health problems is one of the principal areas in the government's *Health of the Nation* strategy (Department of Health 1992). As with most health promotion initiatives, primary care is seen as a central setting for the provision of mental health services, in particular for counselling and psychotherapy services (Dowrick 1992). While counselling in general practice is growing, this has been piecemeal and without sufficient attention given to ensuring that counsellors have adequate qualifications and training opportunities or clarification of the costs and outcomes desired.

As Waydenfeld and Waydenfeld acknowledge (1980), counselling is notoriously difficult to assess. Most studies address the issue of validity by using multiple outcome measures. Thus, the impact of counselling services in primary care is measured using a variety of qualitative outcome data (e.g. patient satisfaction, patient well-being) and quantitative data (e.g. consultation and prescription rates) before and after counselling. As Ives points out (1979), subjective assessments of global improvement are notoriously subject to bias and other sources of error.

However, it might be assumed that an improvement in the patient's condition would be expected to be reflected by his or her behaviour with the general practitioner so that the number of doctor/patient contacts and the number of prescriptions for psychotropic drugs for each patient in the months immediately preceding referral and after discharge might provide more objective measures. Given that time and medication are probably the most costly elements of primary care, they deserve attention. Attendance rates and prescriptions provide quantifiable 'hard' data, for which costs can be easily calculated. However, of the studies which utilise such quantitative measures, few attempt to assess costs.

Three types of evaluation of counselling in primary care have been undertaken:

1 Studies using multiple outcome measures but without cost analysis.
2 Studies including cost analysis.
3 Studies that attempt a more complete economic evaluation using cost-benefit or cost-effectiveness analysis.

Studies involving multiple outcome measures

In a multi-centre, two-year study, Waydenfeld and Waydenfeld (1980) used 'as many criteria as they could' in assessing the outcome of 38 counselled clients in a study involving 35 general practitioners and nine counsellors. Measures included surgery attendance figures, prescriptions and assessments by the doctors, patients and counsellors involved. On before and after counselling comparisons, taken over six months on either side, attendance at surgery fell by 31 per cent with a similar reduction in the number of prescriptions issued. Patients, doctors and counsellors registered high levels of satisfaction with the provision of on-site counselling. However, of the doctors interviewed five thought their workload was unchanged, two admitted some relief and two felt their workload had increased through their greater personal involvement and through discussions with the counsellor. The authors conclude that surgery counselling fills a definite need and could be considered for extension nationally.

Earll and Kincey (1982) carried out a controlled trial in which 50 consecutive potential referrals for psychological treatment from one general practice were randomly allocated either to behavioural treatment or routine general practitioner care. The patients' use of NHS resources was assessed during the treatment period and at a follow up comparison point, when the patients' subjective ratings of their progress were also obtained. The treated group received significantly less psychotropic medication than the control group, though this difference was not maintained at the longer term follow-up. There were no differences in general practice consultation rates, or in subjective ratings of patient improvement, though the level of patient satisfaction was high. The authors conclude that further studies should be set up to discover what GPs and clinical psychologists should do to maintain short-term effects of behavioural treatment in primary care.

In Ashurst and Ward's study (1983) of the Leverhulme counselling project, the hypotheses tested were:

1 that counselling will reduce the prescription of psychotropic drugs;
2 that counselling will reduce the number of consultations with general practitioners;
3 that a counselling service based in the primary medical care setting will be found acceptable to patients and their general practitioners.

In a detailed report (1983), there were no outcome differences on the reported data from 406 patients presenting with minor neurotic disorders who were randomly assigned to counselling or to routine general practitioner treatment. Patients who received counselling (treatment) were no less likely to reduce their dependency on or use of anti-depressant drugs than those who did not receive counselling (the control). While treatment group patients were likely to reduce their use of tranquillisers while they were being counselled, counselling was associated with an increased likelihood of tranquillisers being prescribed subsequently. The control patients were slightly more likely to end their use of psychotropic drugs. Counselled patients used more general practitioner time, seeing their doctor slightly more frequently and for slightly longer than the controls. Patients who rejected counselling, however, were less likely to feel better and twice as likely to continue using psychotropic medication, than those who accepted counselling or the controls. While high proportions of clients valued the help they received there was no striking difference in outcomes between the groups.

In a study focusing on quantitative data, Koch (1979) describes 30 general practitioner consultations with patients with psychological problems referred to a clinical psychologist for behaviour therapy. Consultations for advice and psychotropic drugs were compared during one year before and after treatment and were found to be reduced by over 50 per cent following treatment. Contact with clinical psychology services, therefore, considerably reduced the demand made by these patients for general practitioner time. The mean number of consultations per patient in the year after completion of psychotherapy was 5.46, which represented a significant reduction when compared with pre-treatment rates. Consultation rates for advice and psychotropic medication were significantly lower than before treatment with little change in physical drug consultation rates. At follow-up it was noted that all three types of consultation rate increased slightly compared with rates during treatment. Repeat prescription rates were reduced significantly as a whole and specifically for psychotropic medication.

The interaction with clinical improvement was significant ($P=0.001$).[3] In both consultation rates and repeat prescription variables, the percentage of physical drug therapy rates was increased. Koch therefore advocates close liaison between clinical psychologists and general practitioners. He notes that in further studies entry criteria should be more rigorously defined and a control group monitored, so as to enable clarification of which reductions were more than part of the natural history of change. Such studies should also assess general practitioner referrals to expensive hospital-based psychiatric services.

However, it may be that rates of consultations and prescriptions are unrepresentative of longer term rates or may be atypical for one particular time under study. Freeman and Button (1984) showed that three quarters of the patients in a group practice referred to a clinical psychologist during a three-year period showed marked reductions in the consulting and psychotropic drug prescription rates in the six months after treatment compared with the six months leading up to treatment. However, the rates for the whole practice revealed a general decline over the period of study. Furthermore, examination of the records of all patients with at least one psychosocial problem over a six-year period has shown that encounters for psychosocial problems tended to be concentrated in a relatively short period, 'the worst year', rather than being evenly distributed over the whole six years. It is concluded that the natural history of most psychological disorders is one of crisis and remission and that it may be difficult to interpret reductions in consulting and prescribing rates after referral to a psychologist or counsellor unless trends for the whole practice are known.

In light of this, Blakey (1986) attempted to assess rates of consultation and prescription for patients referred to clinical psychologists and their immediate families, for three-year periods both before and after referral. Patients and their children consulted more and had more medication prescribed before referral than control groups, this tendency being particularly prevalent in the year before referral. After the contact with the psychologist there was a decrease in all these indices in the short term. There were long-term decreases in psychotropic drug prescriptions for patients and in both consultations and prescriptions for their children. The results show that the effect of the intervention was more than a short-term one.

Studies with basic cost data

Ives (1979) describes the service provided by a part-time clinical psychologist attachment to two group practices. A total of 238 patients were seen over a period of 26 months. Of those completing therapy, 72 per cent made satisfactory progress. In the three months after stopping treatment patients made significantly fewer (36 per cent) visits to the surgeries and received significantly fewer (50 per cent) prescriptions for psychotropic drugs than in the three months before referral. These changes were maintained one year later in the three-month period twelve to fifteen months after discharge. On this evidence, Ives argued that the provision of such largely successful therapy for a population of patients for whom adequate treatment was previously unavailable should be expanded. He noted that the rate of referral to psychiatrists did not alter, at least at the smaller practice for which figures were available. The study includes brief mention of financial data, noting that a reduction in medication has cost reduction benefits, although Ives did not directly quantify these. However, brief mention was made of potential drug cost savings. Based on a random sample of 30 prescriptions issued to patients this was estimated at an average of £1.19 per item (price year not defined but is likely to be 1976 or 1977, the period over which the study was conducted). Unfortunately, it is difficult to use this estimate to assess the likely benefits to practices or to the NHS.

In a study which undertook a simple cost analysis, Anderson and Hasler (1979) surveyed the subjective and objective effects of counselling on the first 80 patients who used a newly established part-time counselling service in a health centre. There was an improvement as measured by the feelings of the patients and doctors and through some reduction in the use of psychotropic drugs and medical consultations. The cost analysis focused on the change in use of psychotropic drugs. The total cost of drugs issued to all 80 patients for a three-month period before counselling was compared with a similar period after counselling sessions had ceased. It was estimated that the reduction in drug costs for the total group was £76.92. This figure was based on the unit cost of 100 tablets of the prescribed strength calculated from the December 1977 issue of MIMS. The net cost reduction would have been much greater owing to the additional costs of dispensing fees, container allowances and cost allowances. The cost of consultations was not calculated, although most patients reduced their use of doctor consultation time after counselling. The authors conclude that in the short term counselling offered an alternative to the use of psychotropic drugs and enabled some people to reduce or discontinue medication. It may also be linked with a reduction in the demand for medical time, although it is not possible to say whether this would have happened in the practice without the counselling service. Anderson and Hasler felt that, in general, a readily available and accessible counselling service had been an important development in the provision of primary care in the practice. However, they acknowledged that the results of this study should be treated with caution. No attempt was made to estimate costs for the counselling service or to compare outcomes (there was no control group). Statistical techniques were not used and the study took place over a short period of time.

Economic evaluations

A number of studies have been conducted to examine specifically the costs and benefits associated with the provision of counselling in primary care. The use of cost-benefit analysis (CBA) has been dominant in the economic evaluation of counselling interventions conducted to date. However, the application of CBA in these studies has invariably been flawed in some way.

Three of the studies reviewed here are CBAs (although only one explicitly claims to be a CBA, the other two represent forms of CBA). A basic CBA was conducted by Robson et al. (1984) in evaluating the role and effectiveness of the employment of clinical psychologists in the primary care team. Ginsberg et al. (1984) conducted a more complete CBA using a randomised controlled trial to collect data on the effectiveness of behavioural psychotherapy using a nurse therapist compared to routine care from a GP. The third study by Maguire et al. (1982) also represents an economic evaluation of nurse counselling compared to the 'do-nothing' alternative of providing routine health care in primary and secondary sector settings. The patient group analysed in this study were women who had undergone mastectomy for breast cancer. Finally, a study by Scott and Freeman (1992) aimed to compare the clinical efficacy, patient satisfaction and cost of three specialist treatments for depressive illness with routine care by general practitioners.

COUNSELLING IN SECONDARY CARE: COSTS AND OUTCOMES

There has been virtually no assessment of the cost-effectiveness of counselling services provided in the hospital setting. As we demonstrated earlier most research has focused on the potential cost savings and other specific health service benefits (reductions in treatment) associated with mental health and psychotherapy services. In the main this research has been USA based and carried out more than ten years ago, with consequent difficulties in the generalisability of the results to the present UK context. A Dutch evaluation of the cost-effectiveness of psychiatric consultations with depressed medical inpatients is reviewed in detail in the next section, (Hengeveld *et al.* 1988).

We have been unable to find UK studies evaluating the provision of counselling services for hospital staff who might be at risk of stress and burnout. In recent years some interest has been shown in the development of stress support systems for health professionals working in the hospital setting. It is hoped that the alternative options for addressing this problem are properly evaluated using cost-effectiveness analysis and other evaluation techniques. We include a case study evaluation of options for reducing stress among nurses working in a hospital setting in Chapter 11, which may encourage more and varied economic evaluations of different aspects of counselling in secondary care.

THE REVIEW STUDIES

As noted earlier, we have modified the cost-effectiveness evaluation framework introduced in Chapter 3. The categories used to assess existing evaluations of counselling using different economic techniques are:

- Study problems, objectives and options
- Study design
- Cost and outcome measurement
- Results

Study 1 – Robson, M.H., France, R. and Bland, M. (1984) 'Clinical psychologist in primary care: controlled clinical and economic evaluation', *British Medical Journal* **288: 1805–8.**

Study problem, objectives and options

The study problem was to assess GPs' referral patterns to psychological services and to evaluate the effectiveness and cost-effectiveness of 'psychological treatments'. Effectiveness was measured by the monetary savings in drugs and other services (therefore the study was a CBA). The perspective adopted was that of the National Health Service. The general objective was to assess the effectiveness and cost-benefits associated with the use of clinical psychologists in primary care for counselling patients with psychosocial problems. An economic objective was to assess the potential drug savings associated with the use of a clinical psychologist for counselling these patients. The estimated financial savings were then to be compared with the costs of the clinical psychologist (CP) intervention.

There was one 'active' option in the evaluation consisting of four clinical psychologists (three working at any one time) employed on a sessional basis (one or two sessions per week) for up to ten weeks in one health centre (consisting of six GPs). A 'do-nothing' option was selected which was routine GP care, including possible referral of patients with psychosocial problems. The trial appears to have been carried out in the early 1980s.

Study design

A randomised controlled clinical trial was designed whereby patients identified by a participating GP as potentially benefiting from psychotherapy (n=429)[4] were randomly allocated to an intervention group (n=229) receiving up to 10 weeks counselling from a clinical psychologist or a control group (n=200) receiving routine GP care. No details were given of the patient selection criteria. A high percentage were male (72 per cent); as it is more usual for women to be referred with psychosocial problems some discussion of this pattern would have been useful. The trial lasted 52 weeks during which there were several follow-up assessments of outcome (at 14, 22, 34 and 52 weeks).

Cost and outcome measurement

The direct costs to the health service of the time of the clinical psychologists was based on their net payment per session in 1981. The figure stated in the paper was £17.71 per session for a senior clinical psychologist, although it is not clear if this is the gross or net cost (the latter excludes national insurance and superannuation payments). The cost estimate should be based on the former for a proper assessment. No attempt was made to include other health service costs such as overheads through the use of primary care facilities (e.g. office space for the clinical psychologists) or the clinical psychologists' travel costs. The costing of the CP service is inadequate for use in a cost-benefit analysis, if the purpose of this analysis is to determine whether the programme is a worthwhile use of resources (i.e. benefits exceed costs).

However, the authors' main aim was to assess the cost of clinical psychologists so as to illustrate the extent of the potential drug savings from the service. The main focus was on estimating the difference in drug prescribing costs between the intervention group and the control group up to one year after patients entered the trial. The cost of prescribed drugs was calculated from prescriptions returned by the Prescription Pricing Authority and were divided into three categories:

Category A = those drugs acting on the central nervous system including all psychotropic drugs.
Category B = drugs for gastrointestinal, nutritional and skin conditions.
Category C = all other drugs that were used, to control for overall changes in prescribing patterns during the study.

The costs of drugs prescribed to each patient were assessed on a monthly basis over the year trial. Drug savings represented the measure of monetary benefits of the clinical psychology service. Data for three further outcome indicators were collected in order to assess the effectiveness of the service:

1   Psychosocial ratings measuring the severity of the problem, the effect on the patient and the effect on patient's household.
2   The number of visits to hospital outpatient departments were recorded using data from the local district health authority. Unit costs of these visits were estimated although not used in the analysis.
3   Visits to the GP were calculated for 34 weeks prior to the trial, 10 and 24 weeks after the intervention started.

Results

The difference in outcomes between the intervention and control group using the four sets of measures was conducted. The authors found statistically significant gains for the intervention group in the short term (up to 24 weeks) in terms of improved psychosocial ratings, less frequent GP visits and less category A drug expenditure. The authors commented that insufficient referrals to hospital were made to provide reliable data for this outcome measure. However, the gap between the two groups was found to decrease up to the end of the full 52-week study period. Using this evidence Robson *et al.* (1984) argued that most of the psychosocial problems presented by patients were short-term 'life transition' events which could be dealt with by the use of brief, low-cost psychotherapy in the primary care setting.

There was only a limited attempt to assess the costs and benefits of the clinical psychologist service focusing on the drug cost savings as the measure of benefit. Robson *et al.* (1984) estimated a cost reduction of £4.05 per patient year in expenditure on category A drugs with a total of 114 patients seen in any one year. They argued that the total estimated saving of £462 per year this produced was significant as this alone represented 28 per cent of the sessional costs of the four clinical psychologists employed in the study (based on an annual cost for the CPs of £1,629). For the reasons stated above this cost-benefit comparison is purely illustrative and cannot be used to derive any conclusions about the cost-effectiveness or otherwise of the CP service. There was no requirement for the costs to be discounted because of the short time profile of the trial (one year). In addition, no sensitivity analysis was conducted to test the reliability of the cost and outcome measures and results. The equity implications of the results were not discussed. However, as the authors point out, 'we know that this calculation is approximate but there are, moreover, considerable social and economic benefits, shown by the other measures' (ibid. 1808).

Based on the outcome results the main conclusion of the authors was that CPs in the primary care setting provided an effective service for patients with psychosocial problems, both for the patients well-being and for more effective use of health service resources. Robson *et al.* (1984) did not attempt to assess the value of these benefits, merely suggesting that with the use of the right techniques it would be possible to undertake a more complete CBA of the CP service.

Study 2 – Ginsberg, G., Marks, I. and Waters, H. (1984) 'Cost-benefit analysis of a controlled trial of nurse therapy for neuroses in primary care', *Psychological Medicine* 14: 683–90.

Study problem, objectives and options

The study aimed to examine whether nurse therapy for neurotic patients (mainly phobics and obsessive-compulsives) in the primary care setting was a worthwhile use of resources. The perspective adopted was that of society, which meant that health service costs, personal costs and indirect costs were identified. This study was a follow-up to earlier studies which had compared the cost-effectiveness of nurse therapists with psychiatrists and psychologists providing behavioural psychotherapy (Marks *et al.* 1983). On the basis of the findings from these studies, Ginsberg *et al.* wanted to identify whether the benefits of the most cost-effective option, the nurse therapist, exceeded the costs. The CBA framework applied in this way can be used for addressing issues of whether an intervention represents a worthwhile use of resources, in this case from the perspective of society.

However, care must be exercised in the interpretation of the results from studies which claim to be CBAs even if conducted from a perspective of society. Relevant costs and benefits might still have been omitted (e.g. costs and benefits to the family of the patient receiving counselling) which if included would have altered the cost-benefit ratio to produce an opposite conclusion from that originally obtained.

Study design

The 'active' option in the evaluation was defined as behavioural psychotherapy given by a nurse therapist in a health centre setting. The 'do-nothing' option was the provision of routine care from the GP. The study design was a randomised controlled trial with patients receiving the active option representing the intervention group, and those obtaining routine care the control group. Sixty-six patients attending four health centres (twenty GPs) in London over the period 1978–81 who met specific diagnostic selection criteria (neurotic conditions and with a high professional expectation of responding positively to behavioural treatment) and who consented to participate, were included in the trial (n=29 in the intervention group; n=37 in the control group). The intervention and control groups were well matched in terms of their clinical and demographic characteristics. A two-year study period was chosen for each patient with assessments carried out at entry to the study, and at 6 months, 1 year and 2 year follow-up. Two sources of data were used for the CBA. First, GP notes provided information on the number of visits by the patient to the GP and drug prescriptions. Second, an economic questionnaire enabled data to be collected on patient socio-economic circumstances and education record, the impact of their disorder on work and income and the time and money costs incurred in visiting the GP/nurse therapist and the use of other services (e.g. social workers, counsellors).

Cost and outcome measurement

The value of psychotherapy was assessed by calculating the additional costs and benefits of the nurse therapy service compared to usual GP care. The costs of the psychotherapy service covered the time and expenses of the nurse therapists, practice overheads, extra treatment costs (all NHS costs) and the time and money costs incurred by patients in receiving the service. The average annual cost of treating each patient was calculated using different scenarios of the numbers of patients completing treatment each year (in the range of 40 to 60 patients per year). Certain costs varied with the level of activity. Nurse therapist costs and practice overheads decreased progressively with higher patient throughput,[5] while the costs per patient of nurse therapist travel, extra treatment expenses and patients'/relatives' costs were fixed.

The additional benefits of nurse therapy were measured in monetary terms through an examination of the change in average net costs associated with neurosis at one-year follow-up among patients in the intervention and control groups. At entry to the study the social cost of neurosis was calculated covering estimates of productivity losses from patients' absences from work (representing at least 75 per cent of the total costs for each group, NHS treatment and care costs and patients' and relatives' time and money costs incurred due to the problem). These costs for the nurse therapy group were compared with those with the control group to identify savings (benefits) associated with the former. Intangible costs of stress and anxiety (benefits related to the nurse therapy option) were not quantified.

Data from the economic questionnaire was used to identify resource use for several items included in the costing (e.g. personal expenses, number of home visits from the GP, days absent from work). A full list of unit costs for health service items was provided in an appendix. There is no information as to whether the unit cost estimates, which come from health service sources, are net or gross (i.e. the latter includes national insurance and superannuation). If they are not gross costs, they could be poor estimates of the opportunity cost of resources.

Results

At one-year follow-up average cost savings of 4 per cent were found for the intervention group (from £598 at entry to £574 at one year, 1981 prices). The net benefit after one year of the psychotherapy service was estimated at £152 per patient. This was calculated as the reduction in costs found for the intervention group (£24 per patient) plus the extra costs for the control group (£128 per patient (i.e. £24 + £128 = £152)). However, the only variables demonstrating a statistically significant difference (at $p<0.05$) between the intervention group and control group were the average costs of non-NHS resources, GP visits and hospital services. In total the difference in net costs for the two groups was only statistically significant at $p<0.15$.

The patient throughput figure was estimated to be 46 per year, based on findings from a national follow-up of the average number of treatments completed by nurse therapists in routine conditions. Under this scenario the costs were estimated as £255 per patient year (1981 price year). The ratio of benefits (i.e. savings from a reduced level of neurosis) to the costs of the psychotherapy service is only 0.6. In none of the other patient throughput scenarios was the ratio greater than 1. The authors argued that if the benefits of treatment lasted only one year the psychotherapy service did not appear to be a worthwhile use of resources. This finding has to be treated with caution if, as we argued earlier, important costs and benefits that could significantly alter the C-B ratio have not been included in the evaluation.

The authors calculated the benefit to cost ratios for scenarios in which the benefits lasted up to five years (with costs and benefits discounted at 5 per cent per annum). Under the baseline estimate of patient throughput the benefit:cost ratio becomes favourable with benefits lasting for two years or more, reaching 2.73 at year 5. The greater the patient throughput the better the ratio (e.g. 3.43 for 60 patients per year and 5 years' duration for benefits). However, this finding is based on the assumption that the benefits remain constant over this time period and that the costs remain the same whether benefits are achieved over one or five years.

The experimentation with different scenarios of duration of benefit and patient throughput for nurse therapy represents a form of sensitivity analysis. However, a full sensitivity analysis would probably involve closer examination of other uncertain variables such as the discount rate chosen and the use of different assumptions regarding the costings.

The authors recognised that there were flaws in the study design but concluded from the results that 'the tangible benefits to society from employing a nurse therapist for this clinical population usually exceed the costs, even when all the intangible benefits are omitted'. However, this conclusion appears too optimistic as the numbers in the evaluation were small, few economic differences were statistically significant and many patients either did not complete the trial or failed to return economic data.

Study 3 – Scott, A.I.F. and Freeman, C.P.L. (1992) Edinburgh primary care depression study: treatment outcome, patient satisfaction, and cost after 16 weeks', *British Medical Journal* 304: 883–8.

Study problem, objectives and options

The study problem was to identify a cost-effective method for the treatment and care of patients visiting the GP with depression related to social and relationship problems. The perspective adopted was that of the NHS, as only health service costs were assessed. The economic objective was to compare the costs of a number of specialist treatments in the primary care setting with the provision of routine GP care for depressed patients and assess their relative effectiveness in terms of reduced depression, recovery rate and patient satisfaction with treatment. The authors claimed that the study was an (incomplete) cost-benefit analysis. However, as they did not measure the benefits in monetary units, the study was a form of cost-effectiveness analysis.

Four specific options were defined. The three specialist treatments were:

1 the prescription of a psychotropic drug, amitriptyline, by a psychiatrist with brief counselling provided;
2 cognitive behaviour therapy from a clinical psychologist;
3 counselling and case work by a social worker.

The fourth option, routine care by the GP was the 'do-nothing' option. This involved GPs in following their normal procedure including referral to other agencies.

Study design

The study design consisted of a prospective RCT. A total of 63 GPs in 14 primary care practices asked all patients who were about to undergo treatment for depressive illness to participate in the study. The study covered a two-year period between 1987–9. In total 121 patients who consented to participate were randomly allocated to the four treatment groups, with routine GP care representing the control group. All treatments were given over a 16–week period, with an independent assessor collecting data on patient clinical and demographic characteristics at week 0, and then assessing change in depression ratings and recovery rates (defined as achieving a level of depression below a specified target) at weeks 4 and 16.

Cost and outcome measurement

The main cost component included in the evaluation was the time incurred by the therapists within each option. This was costed at 1986–7 prices although there was no detail regarding the source of cost data. For example, it is not clear whether the cost represented gross payment rates or the salary of the therapists. The costs of hospital services due to referral of depressed patients by the GP were included, again without details of the costing methods used. A third cost component was the cost of drug therapy which was based on 1987 NHS prescription prices. These data are easily available but because of subsidies the prescription price is not a particularly reliable reflection of the opportunity cost of the therapy. The authors deal only very briefly with the costing methodology, but refer to Personal Social Services Research Unit Discussion Paper 647 (1989) on the methods of costing hospital and community care. This suggests that some thought has gone into undertaking a proper costing, which is not immediately obvious from the information provided in the paper.

Three sets of outcome measure were used in the study. The main measure was the changes in depression ratings for each of the option groups at weeks 4 and 16. The level of depression was measured using the Hamilton rating scale for depression. The recovery rate was defined as the proportion of patients who managed to reduce their rating on the Hamilton scale to below 7 (the mean for each group varied between 15.7 for the social work counselling group to 19.7 for the GP care group). The third measure was patient satisfaction with the service received, for which a four-point scale was used.

Results

The authors undertook separate analysis of the relative effectiveness and costs of the options. The main conclusion arising from their analysis of changes in depression ratings was that there was very little difference in the effectiveness of each option. After 16 weeks only the social work counselling group had significantly better reductions in depression rating and recovery rates compared to the GP care group, but this group also contained less severe cases in terms of the initial depression rating (from a mean for the social work group of 15.7 to 4.9 on the depression rating and 72 per cent recovery rate compared to 19.7 to 8.4 for the GP group and 48 per cent recovery rate). There was a marked improvement in depressive symptoms in all treatment groups over 16 weeks. The results showed that psychological treatments, even though lengthy, were most positively evaluated by patients, with social work counselling being assessed most favourably in terms of meeting needs and helping with problems.

While the evidence of the outcomes pointed towards the social work counselling being the most effective option, initial analysis of the costs demonstrated that this was four times more costly to the health service than the GP care option in terms of therapist time alone (£121 compared to £26 per treatment). There was only a small cost differential between the three specialist options. Although both cognitive behaviour therapy and social work counselling involved more face-to-face contact than the amitriptyline treatment from the psychiatrist, the costs per treatment for the specialist groups were similar because clinical psychologists and social workers are less expensive to employ by the hour.

The GP took only a handful of appointments, but practice doctors referred some patients to other NHS specialists and facilities such as health visitors and psychiatric day hospital (which were costed). In addition, GPs prescribed more drugs than the specialists which reduced the cost differential. The total average cost per treatment for GP care was £55, which was still less than half the cost of the specialist treatments.

The main conclusion derived from this evidence was that the additional costs associated with specialist treatments of new episodes of mild to moderate depressive illness presenting in primary care were not commensurate with their clinical superiority over routine GP care. However, the authors stated that this finding might alter if it was discovered that specialist treatment produced a significantly lower relapse rate among patients, arguing that a proper cost-benefit analysis was required in order to address this issue.

Study 4 – Maguire, P., Pentol, A., Allen, D., Tait, A., Brooke, M. and Sellwood, R. (1982) 'Cost of counselling women who undergo mastectomy', *British Medical Journal* 284: 1933–5.

Study problem, objectives and options

An earlier study had demonstrated the effectiveness of counselling in reducing psychiatric morbidity (mainly trauma and depression) associated with mastectomy (i.e. the surgical removal of a cancerous breast) for women with breast cancer (Maguire *et al.* 1980). The study problem in this paper was therefore to focus on an assessment of the costs and benefits (savings) of employing a specialist nurse to offer counselling to women prior to and after surgery. The perspective adopted was that of society – the costing was comprehensive covering the NHS, local authority costs and those incurred by the patients, their family and friends. Although it was not clearly stated by the authors, the evaluation was a form of CBA as the costs of the nurse counselling scheme were set against the net savings to society from a reduction in psychiatric problems associated with breast cancer.

The active option considered was counselling pre and post operation provided by a specialist nurse. No details were given regarding the type of counselling offered except that the nurse had received three months training prior to the start of the scheme. The setting for the counselling service was not clearly identified –

presumably it could be provided in the primary care setting, in hospitals or at the patients' homes. Each would have different cost implications. The 'do-nothing' was the provision of usual treatment and care only for patients undergoing mastectomy.

Study design

Women receiving counselling represented the intervention group and those receiving usual care represented the control group. In the original evaluation of outcomes a case-control trial design was used whereby women in the intervention and control groups were matched as closely as possible for such characteristics as marital status, age, social class and stage of disease. A total of 152 women took part in the original effectiveness study. Of these, 110 consented to take part in the costs assessment (*n*=62 for the intervention group and *n*=48 for the control). One problem was that the controls participating in the costs study had relatively less severe psychiatric and social problems compared to those controls who did not consent. This might have resulted in an overestimate of the potential net cost savings associated with the counselling service. These problems of reduced response and selection bias might have been overcome if the economic evaluation had been conducted at the same time as the effectiveness study. Follow-up of patients was conducted over a period of 12–18 months after surgery.

Cost and outcome measurement

The costing was comprehensive in its scope, including both direct and indirect cost estimates. However, no attempt was made to include intangible costs. For both the intervention group and control group the following cost components were estimated and compared:

1 NHS costs included the costs of the specialist nurse (consultation time, travel time and expenses, time and expense of contact by phone/post, provision of extra aids), inpatient psychiatric care and drug therapy, other hospital-based services and time of primary care specialists (GP, district nurse) and drugs provided by the GP.
2 Local authority and social services department costs included social worker, health visitor and home help time and the provision of a service bringing meals to the patients' homes ('meals on wheels').
3 Costs to the community. This consisted mainly of the indirect costs of lost productivity from relatives taking time off work to care for the patient after surgery and accompanying them to hospital. Only paid time off work was included under this heading.
4 Patient personal costs included loss of earnings (this could alternatively be viewed as the value of lost productivity to society, but should not be included as both as this would result in 'double-counting' of costs). Other personal costs

were the cost of travel, child minding, home help, self-medication, alcohol, additional household bills, clothing, increased spending on social services, additional spending on holidays (less savings on holidays and leisure activities).

5   Direct costs to family and friends included loss of wages from taking time off work to care for the patient and accompanying them to the hospital. This cost was not included as an indirect cost because the time off work was unpaid (a proxy value was used but no further details were available). However, this represents a loss of productivity and could have been included under costs to the community.

Data on resource use, health service contacts and personal costs were derived from questionnaire surveys with the women in the study, a questionnaire and diary of contacts completed by the specialist nurse, a psychiatrist involved in post-mastectomy care and a research nurse assessment of the type of support received by the patient 12–18 months after surgery. The paper provided no details of the method used for estimating unit costs, stating that this was available in an (unpublished) working paper. It would have been helpful had the authors presented some basic information on the costing methods used.

Results

The total cost for the intervention group receiving nurse therapy at £1,499 per patient was marginally greater than that for the control group at £1,478 per patient (price year not given, mean period of follow-up of 16 months per group). Excluding the direct costs of the specialist nurse consultation time, travel time and expenses and contact by telephone/letter (estimated at just under £28 per patient) and nurse training (costs of £25 per patient), the net benefit of the counselling service was estimated at £32: £1,478–[£1,499–53]. These costs and savings (benefits) were not discounted. This can be justified by the short time span of the follow-up, but if analysis had been conducted over a time period of two or more years then the issue of whether to discount would have had to be addressed by the authors. One major shortfall was that no attempt was made to allow for error or uncertainty in the cost estimates or the data they were derived from. The use of sensitivity analysis with a range of high and low estimates and scenarios for different possible time spans for the impact of the counselling programme would have incorporated some necessary caution into the interpretation of the results.

The direct cost of the specialist nurse only contributed £27.66 per patient to the total cost estimate. A large proportion of the total costs were incurred in the other categories, in particular indirect costs (i.e. loss of work productivity). In total this was £696.28 for the intervention group and £789.25 for the control. Hence this represented a large estimated net benefit for the programme (£92.97). Because of difficulties in accurate estimation there is much controversy over whether lost productivity costs should be included in evaluations, especially as they often dominate the costs (Drummond *et al.* 1987). The authors have largely avoided this problem by measuring patient time off work as a personal cost (i.e. loss of wages). However, uncertainty remains concerning the valuation of the costs of family and friends who took either paid or unpaid time off work to look after the patient or accompany them to the hospital. These have been included as indirect costs. At a minimum a sensitivity analysis should have been conducted on these estimates. If the indirect costs were excluded a net benefit would have been a net cost of £61 (authors' calculations).

The difference in indirect and personal costs offset virtually all other estimated savings from the counselling intervention. However, if the aim of the study was to convince health service managers (the scheme had been funded by North-West Regional Health Authority) of the value of the counselling service a primary requirement is likely to be to demonstrate benefits to the NHS. Fortunately, the authors estimated a small net benefit to the NHS (NHS costs for the counselled group were £87.38 per patient compared to £98.90 for the control). They argued that additional net savings were probable over time as the fixed costs of the initial nurse training declined in importance.

The conclusion reached was that a substantial reduction in the psychiatric morbidity associated with treatment for breast cancer and improvements in quality of life (examined in an earlier paper) could be obtained at a negligible net cost to society. Maguire *et al.* supported its wider introduction within the NHS, although the methods and results from this one study do not provide sufficient evidence of the cost-benefit of counselling in this context.

Study 5 – Hengeveld, M.W., Ancion, F.A.J.M. and Rooijmans, H.G.N. (1988) 'Psychiatric consultations with depressed medical inpatients: a randomized controlled cost-effectiveness study'. *International Journal of Psychiatry in Medicine* 18(1): 33–43.

Study problem, objectives and options

The authors stated that the most frequent psychiatric disorder among general medical inpatients is depression. The study problem was to assess the effectiveness and cost-effectiveness of consultation-liaison (C-L) counselling among depressed patients. The perspective was that of the hospital in which the study was conducted. The economic objective was to identify whether counselling could produce medical cost savings in addition to improvements in patient mental health (i.e. reduce depression).

The active option was the provision of a series of C-L counselling sessions to patients identified as mildly depressed. A standard package was not offered, but counselling was tailored to the individual needs of the patient. In general this consisted of illness counselling and discussion of the impact on the family. Hence the duration, number and content of the sessions varied. There is a potential bias problem if the accuracy of the psychiatrist assessment of patient need varies. Some patients might be getting a better service than others. However, this approach is more likely to mirror practice and directly aid practical decision-making than an evaluation of the cost-effectiveness of a standard package of counselling.

In order to compare the effectiveness of the counselling programme a 'do-nothing' option was included, consisting of routine medical care only (no psychiatric consultation) for patients identified as mildly depressed.

Study design

The design was a randomised controlled trial. All patients admitted to three general medical wards of a Dutch hospital between September 1984 and March 1985 were asked to participate. Of those consenting who were identified as at least mildly depressed (i.e. had obtained a score of 13 or more on the Beck Depression Inventory (BDI)) each alternate patient was allocated to the C-L group to receive both counselling and routine care (the consult group), with all other patients allocated to the 'do-nothing' to receive routine care only. The patients in the two groups were well matched on sex, marital status, previous hospital use and severity of illness, although the consult group, had a lower mean age and higher mean BDI score (not statistically significant). However, there were only 33 patients in the consult group and 35 in the control group, which is a very small number for making outcome comparisons. In addition, the main outcome measure, the BDI, was only administered with 17 and 23 patients in the consult and control group respectively. Follow-up covered the time over which patients were in hospital, an average of 19 days for both groups.

Cost and outcome measurement

Cost measurement was limited. The direct costs to the hospital of the time of the psychiatrist in the provision of counselling was estimated. The costs of drug therapy for the consult and control groups were estimated to assess whether counselling resulted in reduced prescribing and hence cost savings. The costs of screening and identification of depressed patients by a medical student were not included, although if this cost is the same for both groups the relative cost-effectiveness will not be altered. No details were provided of the source of cost data or the method used to calculate the cost estimates, which appear to be crude approximations.

Two sets of outcomes were measured for the consult and control groups. First, a number of components of medical resource use were measured. This covered hospital length of stay, number of laboratory and other diagnostic tests, number of consultation requests to other specialists and prescribing of psychotropic and analgesic medication. Second, the BDI at discharge was measured for patients in the two groups to identify whether the counselled patients had achieved a greater reduction in depression.

Results

Although the study claimed to be a cost-effectiveness analysis, the main emphasis in the results and discussion was on the comparison of the outcomes for the consult and control groups. Comparison of medical resource use had found no statistically significant difference between the groups at discharge in each component examined except drug therapy. For this reason only the savings in medication was costed. The total financial saving was estimated at $341. There was a statistically significant reduction in mean BDI for the consult group at discharge compared to BDI at admission (from 20 to 13.2), but not for the control group (from 18.8 to 15.9). This reflected a benefit in terms of psychological well-being related to the counselling. The authors argued that the drug savings were a low estimate because they did not include intangible benefits from a reduction in associated side-effects of drug therapy and the higher psychological well-being from reduced reliance on drug therapy.

The total costs of C-L time were roughly approximated to be $1,000 (based on 59 hours of psychiatrist time input over the trial period). The authors pointed out that this extra cost was not offset by the financial savings in drug prescribing. Implicit in the discussion is that the authors had expected to find benefits from a reduced length of stay and hence cost savings for the consult group, as had been found in other studies of psychiatric intervention. Net costs were positive but the main finding of a reduction in depression (increase in psychological well-being) pointed towards the intervention being cost-effective. However, the authors noted a number of problems in making any firm conclusions from this study regarding cost-effectiveness.

SUMMARISING THE EVIDENCE: SCOPE, GENERALISABILITY AND COMPARABILITY CRITERIA

We can use the evaluation criteria of scope, generalisability and comparability to provide an overall summary of the economic data from the five studies reviewed. The interpretation of these criteria is provided in Table 5.2.

Table 5.2 Evaluation criteria: scope, generalisability and comparability

Scope	What are the range of objectives, perspectives and counselling options included in the studies?
Generalisability	What is the relevance of the study results beyond their specific contexts and settings?
Comparability	Can the study results be compared to identify cost-effective counselling interventions? This depends on the methods used to measure costs and outcomes.

Scope

Three of the five studies reviewed were evaluations of counselling and psychotherapy interventions in the primary care setting, and a fourth (the study by Maguire *et al.* on the costs of counselling women undergoing mastectomy) did not specify the setting but presumably could be primary care, home or hospital based. The other study reviewed involved the provision of counselling for medical inpatients suffering from depression. This balance generally reflects the scope of work on the economic evaluation of counselling, which in the UK at least has focused on primary care as the 'natural setting' for the location of counselling services. In the USA there has been more interest in the provision of counselling, psychotherapy and other mental health services as ways of reducing hospital inpatient utilisation and costs.

In each of the review studies bar one the counselling option was compared with a 'do-nothing' option (routine care). Only the Scott and Freeman study compared more than one active option (three specialist interventions). This approach enabled a comparison both of the cost-effectiveness of the different specialist interventions and an assessment of the marginal costs and benefits of the specialist interventions compared with routine GP care. In the other studies reviewed only the latter issue could be addressed. A health service perspective was adopted in three studies, while two studies also included the perspective of patients and their families (Ginsberg *et al.* 1984 and Maguire *et al.* 1982).

Ginsberg *et al.* claimed explicitly in the title of the paper to be undertaking a cost-benefit analysis. The cost analysis of Maguire *et al.* can also be viewed as a cost-benefit analysis. The other studies can be defined as cost-effectiveness analyses. However, they were really only partial economic evaluations with more focus on effectiveness than costs (with both sets of data presented separately).

Generalisability

Four of the review studies used a randomised controlled trial study design. Each of the counselling studies adopted a pragmatic design which generates data appropriate for policy orientated economic evaluations useful for assisting resource allocation decisions. The Maguire *et al.* study used a less controlled, but still rigorous study design – a case control evaluation. The study designs used appear to be fairly robust and pragmatic and therefore potentially useful as a basis for making generalisable policy statements. The limitation in most of the studies is the small sample sizes in the intervention and control groups. Only the Robson *et al.* study has a sizeable study population with 429 patients allocated to a counselling group and usual GP care group. In the other studies the total patient population included in the final analysis does not exceed 110.

The generalisability of the evaluations and results within an NHS context or other countries depends on the study design used – the use of a controlled trial improves generalisability as there is more control of confounding factors such as

Table 5.3 Main results from the review studies

Study and options		Costs (£s)	Monetary Benefits (£s)
1 Robson et al. (1984) Patients allocated to:			
• Clinical Psychologist at GP surgery (active option, n=229)	Total per year	1,629	462
vs			
• Routine GP care (do-nothing, n=200)	Per patient	17.71	4.05
2 Ginsberg et al. (1984) Patients allocated to:	Per patient year (1981 prices)		
• Nurse therapist providing 'behavioural psychology' at GP surgery (active options, n=29)	1 year benefit	255	152
vs	2 year benefit	130	152
• Routine GP care (do-nothing, n=37)	5 year benefit	56	152

	Outcomes			
3 Scott and Freeman (1992)	Costs per treatment (1986-7 prices) £s	Mean depression rating at week 0	Change in depression rating at week 16	Recovery rate %
Patients allocated to:				
• Amitriptyline (drug therapy) prescribed by psychiatrist (active option, n=26)	120	18.2	-10.2	58
vs				
• Cognitive behaviour therapy from clinical psychologist (active option, n=29)	115	18.3	-11.6	41
vs				
• Counselling/case work from social worker (active option, n=29)	121	15.7	-10.8	72
• Routine GP care (do-nothing, n=29)	55	19.7	-11.3	48

Table 5.3 (continued)

	Costs of interventions £s	£s	Net benefit £s (intervention – control)	Outcomes	
				Depression rating at	
				Admission	Discharge
4 Maguire et al. (1982) Patients allocated to: • Nurse therapy (n=62) vs • Usual care for mastectomy (do-nothing, n=48)	53 – *Per patient costs/benefits (16-month period)*	1,446 1,478	32 –		13.2 15.9

	Costs/benefits		**Outcomes**	
	Total costs of intervention $s	Drug cost savings $s	Admission	Depression rating at Discharge
5 Hengeveld et al. (1988) Patients allocated to: • C-L Psychiatrist (n=33) vs • Routine hospital care (do-nothing, n=35)	1,000 – *Total costs/drug savings at follow-up*	341 – *Outcomes per patient*	20 18.8	13.2 15.9

Notes:
See text for details of costs/benefits included.

1 Robson et al.
Primary care setting.
Price year not given.

2 Ginsberg et al.
Primary care setting.
C-B estimates based on best estimate of 46 patients treated per year, 5 per cent discount rate for costs incurred in years 2 to 5.

3 Scott and Freeman
Primary care setting.
Costs per treatment cover time of therapists, and drug costs for amitriptyline and GP care.
Depression ratings measured using Hamilton Depression Index.
Recovery rate is proportion of patients recording a score of less than 7 on the Hamilton Index after 16 weeks.

4 Maguire et al.
Setting undefined.
Price year not given.
Patient costs follow-up for 16 months.

5 Hengeveld et al.
General hospital medical ward setting.
No price year given.
Patients followed up from admission to discharge. Average length of stay for 2 groups some at 19 days.
Depression ratings measured using Beck Depression Inventory (BDI), only patients with rating of 13 or more (moderate depression) were included in the evaluation. Patient numbers refer to those whose BDI was recorded at admission and discharge.
The change in the do-nothing option BDI was not statistically significant at P≤0.05.[6]

the specific circumstances in which the evaluation was carried out. The studies reviewed are limited in the extent to which they have conducted rigorous controlled trials which therefore constrain the generalisability of the results. However, in many cases a less rigorous study design (with less generalisability) is the best that can be achieved given the cost and complexity of randomised controlled trials.

Comparability

The cost and outcome results have been presented in different ways in each of the five studies, which means it is very difficult to make direct comparisons. Table 5.3 summarises the main cost and benefit/outcome results for each study. The cost estimates produced in the studies by Maguire *et al.*, Ginsberg *et al.* and Scott and Freeman are detailed and appear to be based on sound costing principles (although little information on methods is provided in the papers). In contrast, the Robson *et al.* and the Hengeveld *et al.* studies include only very basic cost data. In the Dutch study the cost estimates appear to be crude approximations.

Comparisons could still be made if a common measure was used within a cost-effectiveness evaluation framework (e.g. comparisons of costs per unit of outcome). To make comparisons across studies and settings usually requires the use of general final outcome measures, such as quality adjusted life years or specific measures of psychological well-being. Three studies included a final outcome measure – Hengeveld *et al.* and Scott and Freeman measured the relative effectiveness of the options using changes in psychiatric morbidity among counselled patients and those receiving routine GP care. However, the instruments used had different rating systems which makes direct comparisons across studies impossible. In addition, comparisons were made even more difficult as none of the studies attempted to combine cost and outcome data to derive cost-effectiveness ratios (i.e. cost per unit of outcome) for the active options.

The 'cost-effectiveness' studies incorporated other intermediate outcome measures such as patient satisfaction, recovery rates and reduced health services utilisation indicators. Once again these were not combined with cost data to examine costs per unit of outcome.

Although direct comparisons cannot be made because of different follow-up periods and different applications of cost-benefit analysis, there is more scope for comparing the results from the studies of Ginsberg *et al.* and Maguire *et al.* as similar sets of costs and benefits were included. For different counselling interventions (nurse therapist in GP surgery v counselling women undergoing mastectomy) both studies found net benefits for counselling under certain conditions. Hence both could represent a worthwhile use of resources, but more detailed comparative analysis is required to identify which achieves the greatest net benefits in different circumstances. The studies were comprehensive in that patient costs and benefits were included in addition to direct health service costs and benefits.

All of the studies missed out a relevant aspect of the economic evaluation process. None conducted a sensitivity analysis – indeed only Ginsberg *et al.*

attempted to adjust the results to allow for uncertainty in key variables (e.g. cost and outcome measures). Also, this was the only study to consider the issue of discounting future costs and benefits to a present value. None of the studies mentioned equity in the distribution of costs and outcomes related to each option in the evaluation.

It is only possible to draw some tentative conclusions from the findings of these studies. Apart from Scott and Freeman, the studies were favourable (with conditions) towards counselling and psychotherapy being a more cost-effective use of resources compared to depressed patients receiving usual care in primary and secondary settings.

SUMMARY

The evidence for the cost-effectiveness of counselling is limited. Empirical work in the 1970s and early 1980s was mainly conducted in the USA and focused on issues of the efficacy of psychotherapy and the testing of a 'cost-offset' hypothesis – that psychotherapy was beneficial for reducing in-patient costs due to mental health problems. There is conflicting evidence for efficacy. However, most of the studies found limited support for a cost-offset effect due to psychotherapy.

In the USA there has been much debate in the psychotherapy literature concerning the usefulness of cost-effectiveness analysis for evaluating different programmes. In many cases its value has been promoted although there seems to be little understanding of the application of the empirical research technique which has been undertaken.

In the UK most studies of the costs and outcomes of counselling interventions have been conducted within a primary care setting. Most fall short of a full economic evaluation. Several studies that attempt a cost-benefit or cost-effectiveness analysis have been reviewed in depth in this chapter, using the economic evaluation framework outlined in Chapter 4.

There are few evaluations of counselling in the secondary care setting – we have reviewed one study from The Netherlands. Three criteria have been used to summarise the evidence from the review studies: scope, generalisability and comparability. It should be possible for counsellors, and others wanting to carry out a literature review in a particular area of counselling evaluation to use these criteria to summarise evidence.

NOTES

1   Placebo therapy is any intervention that patients perceive to be of benefit.
2   Meta-analysis is a technique in which the outcomes data from a range of studies employing similar methods are pooled in order to increase the statistical reliability of the results (Ingelfinger *et al.* 1994).
3   Statistical significance has been defined here as P value being less than 0.01. Different P values can be set to increase or decrease the precision of the results. A P value of less

than 0.01 means that the probability is that in 99 out of 100 cases the result is not a chance event. (For more detail see Chapter 7 of Ingelfinger *et al.* 1994).

4   The character n is typically used in evaluations to represent the number of participants in a group.

5   Economists call this economies of scale.

6   Statistical significance has been defined as being P value is less than 0.05. This represents the probability that in 95 out of 100 cases (i.e. 95 per cent confidence) the change in outcomes is not a chance or random event.

Part II

The practice of economic evaluation

Chapter 6

Pre-analysis stage
Problem definition, objectives and options

Introduction
Defining the counselling study problem
Setting economic objectives for counselling
Defining counselling options
Options in the case studies

INTRODUCTION

The framework for conducting a cost-effectiveness analysis of counselling was introduced in Chapter 4, and was utilised in our critique of published studies in Chapter 5. The next three chapters examine in detail the methods for an economic evaluation of counselling interventions, using two case studies from primary and secondary care settings.

In Chapter 3 we discussed the difference between a cost-effectiveness and cost-utility analysis, the latter being a form of cost-effectiveness analysis which uses quality adjusted life years (QALYs) as the outcome measure to compare the effectiveness of different health service programmes. For simplicity, in the following chapters the term 'cost-effectiveness' will be applied in a generic sense to cover both cost-effectiveness analyses (CEAs) and cost-utility analyses (CUAs).

The two case studies cover a general practice team (the North Brownstead Practice) and a hospital management team (in the Smithland Trust Hospital). Both service providers have planned to set up and evaluate a counselling intervention. The case studies will demonstrate the stages of an economic evaluation, beginning with the definition of the study problem, the general and economic objectives of the evaluation and the selection of counselling options to be evaluated. The steps included in this process help to clarify the scope and purpose of the evaluation, the desired outcomes and the potential methodological problems which may arise.

DEFINING THE COUNSELLING STUDY PROBLEM

Definition of the study problem involves three steps:

1 Identification of the issue for evaluation.
2 Identification of the appropriate method of analysis.
3 Identification of the perspective for evaluation.

Step 1: The issue for evaluation

Identification of the issue for evaluation involves consideration of the rationale for implementing a counselling intervention. For example, staff in the North Brownstead Practice might have noticed an apparent increase in patients consulting with psychosocial problems. They may have felt they lacked the time and skill to treat these patients, tending to prescribe drugs as the standard response. Some of the doctors may have felt that this was not necessarily the best course of action for the patient and an unnecessary strain on their drug budget. Alternative treatments, such as counselling interventions may have been considered. However, there may not have been sufficient information to support or reject these deliberations.

The Smithland Trust Hospital might have noticed high levels of absenteeism among its nursing staff which might be attributed to occupational stress. The management may want to examine methods of improving staff morale, perhaps including the provision of a counselling service. In both cases an evaluation of one or more counselling interventions to address the identified problem would be an appropriate course of action.

Step 2: Choosing a method of cost-effectiveness analysis

It is important to select the appropriate method of analysis for a cost-effectiveness evaluation. There are four methods of carrying out a cost-effectiveness analysis of counselling and related interventions within the healthcare setting:

Method 1: CEA within a healthcare setting

This would involve analysis of the cost-effectiveness of alternative strategies and methods of providing a counselling service within a healthcare setting. An example of this type of evaluation for the North Brownstead Practice would be a comparison between employing a practice counsellor or the use of a clinical psychologist.

Method 2: CEA between healthcare settings

This would involve analysis of the cost-effectiveness of alternative counselling services in different primary and/or secondary service settings. For example, the development of an on-site counselling service in the North Brownstead Practice could be compared with GPs referring patients with psychosocial problems to the Community Mental Health Team.

Method 3: CEA between health service programmes

This would involve analysis of the cost-effectiveness of counselling services compared to alternative health service interventions such as drug treatment for diabetes or health education for HIV prevention. The method could also be used to compare a counselling service with alternative interventions within the same health care setting or service context. This might involve comparison of instituting a counselling service in the North Brownstead Practice with the option of continuing to use psychotropic drug therapy and doctors' advice for patients presenting with psychosocial problems. Alternatively, the method could involve comparison of a counselling service with other health programmes in other service contexts such as surgery for heart disease, immunisation as part of a preventive healthcare programme and so on.

The cost-effectiveness of such healthcare programmes have been assessed using QALYs as the measure of outcome (Williams 1985, 1987a). Using the QALY as a common outcome measure allows the results to be incorporated into a summary table of relative cost-effectiveness known as 'cost per QALY league tables'. League tables are discussed further in Chapter 10.

Method 4: CEA of the allocation of public sector resources

This would involve analysis of the cost-effectiveness of allocating public sector resources to counselling services (i.e. allocated by the Department of Health (DoH) through the NHS) compared to allocating resources to other welfare or public services such as education (allocated through the Department of Education), social security (allocated through the Department of Social Security) or defence (allocated through the Ministry of Defence).

Our focus is on providing counsellors, service providers in primary and secondary care, health service purchasers and other health service managers with the tools to conduct one of the first three methods of cost-effectiveness analysis listed above. The fourth method, CEA for the allocation of public sector resources, is beyond the scope of most service providers and policy-makers at the local level and will not be considered in detail.

Selecting a method   In order to select the appropriate method of evaluation, a general idea of the alternative service options is required. The Smithland Trust Hospital might already be running a staff support group but might want to examine the impact of introducing a new counselling service for nurses (Method 1: CEA within a healthcare setting). The Family Health Services Authority (FHSA) might be interested in the use of a counselling programme in the North Brownstead Practice and other general practices within their boundary compared to using the

Community Mental Health Team (Method 2: CEA between healthcare settings). The North Brownstead evaluation might focus on the impact of an on-site counselling service on the prescription of psychotropic drugs (Method 3: CEA between healthcare interventions).

Step 3: Choosing a perspective

Defining the perspective of the evaluation is important because it determines the range of costs to be calculated. There are two broad perspectives: the agency and the societal perspectives. The latter includes personal costs.

A single agency perspective represents the narrowest form of evaluation. A study might be conducted with the interests of one agency uppermost in the design of the study and the desired results. This agency might be the service provider such as the general practice or the funder of the evaluation, such as the FHSA. Table 6.1 outlines the range of single agency perspectives that could be adopted for primary and secondary care. For primary care based counselling an appropriate single agency perspective at the local level would be the GP practice (either one or several in a locality) and at the regional level the FHSA or Health Commission. For counselling in secondary care, an appropriate single agency perspective at the local level would be the hospital (i.e. general or specialist) whilst at the regional level this could be a District or Regional Health Authority. The Department of Health would represent a single agency perspective at the national level.

Table 6.1 Single agency perspectives*

Setting	Geographical Organisation		
	Local	Regional	National
Primary care	GP practice	FHSA	Dept of Health
Secondary care	Self-governing trust hospital, health authority hospital, private hospital	Health Commission* District Health Authority Regional Health Authority Health Commission	Dept of Health

Note: * New institutions and mechanisms developed in the 1990s in response to the NHS reforms include Health Commissions (responsible for purchasing health services on behalf of a consortium of District Health Authorities and FHSAs), GP fundholders and Self-Governing Trust hospitals. One or more of these could be chosen to represent the perspective of the evaluation.

A broad agency perspective would examine the cost impact on some or all of the key agencies involved in the provision of a counselling service. The study would then be conducted with the interests of several agencies more or less equally represented in the design of the study and the results.

At the most general level (in which individual agencies would not necessarily have to be identified) the perspective adopted could consist of the health service. Thus, the evaluation of a counselling programme might be undertaken at the national level from the perspective of the NHS whereby the costs incurred by all health service providers are included. Private sector service providers could also be included in the evaluation.

Compared to the agency perspective, the societal perspective also involves consideration of the personal costs incurred by the users (i.e. patients, clients, family, friends and other 'non-professionals') of the counselling service. An evaluation of counselling in general practice from a societal perspective would include the direct costs to the practice and associated agencies such as the FHSA and personal costs incurred by patients attending the surgery for counselling sessions. Such costs include foregone leisure or work time and out-of-pocket expenses.

Which perspective?

The perspective selected depends on the decision-making context of the evaluation. A general practice may want to conduct a financial appraisal (see Chapter 3) to examine the costs of introducing a counselling service in terms of the overall impact on their budget. Evaluation would thus be from the practice perspective and only the financial cost incurred within the practice would be relevant. Utilising the principle of opportunity costing (see Chapter 8), an economic evaluation from this perspective would require all the practice resource inputs in the service to be identified and included (i.e. both newly employed resources such as a counsellor and practice resources which have been diverted from another use).

In contrast, were the Department of Health to examine the possibilities of increasing the number of counsellors employed in primary care as part of a public health strategy they would probably adopt a societal perspective. The rationale would be that as society's resources would be used to provide counselling the evaluation should recognise this in the costing. However, this does not preclude the Department of Health from adopting an agency perspective, such as that of the Government (i.e. the DoH or NHS), nor does it preclude the GP practice adopting a societal perspective. As a general principle it is advisable for all evaluations to adopt the societal perspective. Appropriate cost elements identified from such an evaluation could be used to provide data for evaluations adopting narrower perspectives.

However, there may be practical reasons for not adopting a societal perspective. To a large extent the choice of perspective depends on the source of funding for the evaluation. For example, a fundholding practice may want to implement a counselling programme, but require external funding if it is to evaluate the service. This may result in the selection of a different perspective (for example, a multi-agency or societal perspective) than if the practice alone had funded the trial.

Which perspectives might be adopted by the North Brownstead Practice and the Smithland Trust Hospital for their proposed evaluations? Each might decide that a single agency perspective is most appropriate. The North Brownstead Practice evaluation could be carried out from the perspective of the practice (as the service provider) or the FHSA (as the administrative body). The emphasis would then be on the assessment of the costs of resources employed by the practice or funded and administered by the FHSA (e.g. staff time, equipment). The Smithland Trust evaluation might be carried out from the perspective of the hospital to examine the costs of providing a counselling service. Alternatively, both the North Brownstead and the Smithland Trust evaluation could be conducted from the NHS perspective in which all health service resources used in the counselling programmes would be identified and included.

SETTING ECONOMIC OBJECTIVES FOR COUNSELLING

General objectives

Having identified the issue for evaluation the next stage is to specify its objectives. This will assist in the identification of appropriate outcome measures against which to evaluate the effectiveness of, for example, a counselling service.

Setting objectives for a cost-effectiveness analysis is a two-stage process. The first stage is to define a set of general objectives appropriate for the healthcare setting in which the evaluation is to take place. The second stage is to identify those objectives that can be evaluated using a quantitative outcome measure. These are used to produce economic objectives for cost-effectiveness analysis (i.e. specified in terms of costs per unit of outcome).

General objectives are illustrated in Table 6.2. Alongside each qualitative objective a quantitative outcome measure is defined. This enables the evaluator to identify the type of effectiveness data that would be required for addressing each objective. The North Brownstead Practice might define a number of objectives for a counselling programme. One objective might be to reduce the number of patients presenting with psychosocial problems and a second might be to increase the quality of life of these patients. Another objective might be to reduce the costs of drug therapy. General objectives of the Smithland Trust could be defined as the reduction of staff stress in order to control absenteeism, reduce staff turnover and to raise staff morale. Other general objectives might reflect the recent shift in the UK to a competitive healthcare market and medical labour market. For example, the management of a newly formed Self-Governing Trust Hospital may have as an objective the presentation of a good image among potential healthcare purchasers and staff.

These examples provide the basis for the detailed case study evaluations in Chapter 11. Other examples might have been developed, such as using the practice counsellor to support members of the primary care team, or an evaluation of specialist counselling for patients (e.g. cancer counselling) in the hospital setting. However, the two examples chosen are currently topical issues in health service research and policy in the UK.

Table 6.2 Setting objectives and associated quantitative outcomes

Setting	Qualitative objective	Quantitative outcome
Primary care e.g. North Brownstead Practice evaluation	Reduce the number of patients returning to the GP with psychosocial problems.	Percentage reduction in numbers over a six-month period.
	Increase quality of life of patients presenting at the GP surgery with psychosocial problems.	Gain in quality adjusted life years (QALYs).
	Reduce prescription of psychotropic drug treatments.	Reduction in psychotropic drug expenditure.
Secondary care (e.g. Smithland Trust Hospital evaluation)	Reduce the level of absenteeism and turnoveramong nurses.	Percentage reduction in staff turnover.
	Increase morale among nurses.	Reduction in absenteeism day/ per year.
	Improve image of hospital in labour market.	Improvement in staff stress ratings. Improvement in staff morale. Staff satisfaction ratings.

Economic objectives

Having identified the general objectives of counselling interventions, the next step is to define economic objectives. These are related to the final cost-effectiveness indicators that will help decision-making. At this stage the notion of target outcomes and cost constraints are discussed. In the context of setting economic objectives targets are not supposed to be a prescriptive marker designed to audit performance, but are to be used by the evaluator to help to determine objectively initial expectations of outcome, and to monitor actual outcome against this. Hence it is to be used as a guide to identifying economic objectives.

Both costs and outcomes are incorporated in an economic objective. Objectives such as the achievement of the greatest outcome (without consideration of cost) or the achievement of minimum cost (without consideration of outcomes) do not represent economic objectives. It is not possible to determine cost-effectiveness without combining the two. There are two types of economic objectives for which targets can be set:

A The achievement of the lowest cost per unit of outcome. The economic objective is to reach a target outcome for the minimum cost outlay.

B The achievement of the greatest outcome per unit of cost. The economic objective is to obtain the greatest outcome for a given cost outlay.

Table 6.3 Alternative economic objectives: examples for the primary care setting

Setting	Economic objectives	Target outcome	Time	Cost limit £
Primary care e.g. North Brownstead Practice)	A Achieve target reduction in patients presenting with psycho-social problems at minimum cost.	10 %	6 mths	Minimise average cost
	B Achieve maximum reduction in patients presenting with psycho-social problems for given cost outlay.	Maximise reduction in numbers	6 mths	20,000
	C Achieve target reduction in patients presenting with psycho-social problems for given cost outlay.	5 % reduction	6 mths	15,000
	D Achieve additional reduction (above 10 per cent) in patients present-ing with psychosocial problems for a given extra cost.	Additional 3 % reduction	6 mths	+1,000
	E Achieve reduction in patients presenting with psychosocial problems from expanding a counselling programme.	Additional 3 % reduction	6 mths	10,000

Economic objectives are illustrated using the North Brownstead Practice evaluation (Table 6.3). In economic objective A, the North Brownstead Practice might set a provisional operational target to reduce the number of patients presenting with psychosocial problems by 10 per cent over a 6-month trial period by adopting a counselling intervention that achieves this target at least cost. In economic objective B the Practice may attempt to achieve the largest possible reduction in patients presenting with psychosocial problems given a maximum cost outlay on a counselling intervention of, for example, £20,000 over a 6-month trial period. The objectives are not mutually exclusive – the two types may be combined. Thus, the North Brownstead Practice may wish to achieve a target reduction in patients presenting with psychosocial problems of 5 per cent with a cost constraint to the practice of £15,000 over a 6-month period (economic objective C).

Incremental and marginal cost-effectiveness objectives

Instead of deciding between interventions solely on the basis of lowest average cost per unit of outcome (for example, increased morale, improved quality of life, reduction in numbers of patients presenting with psychosocial problems), the evaluator might set an additional objective in terms of incremental or marginal cost-effectiveness. This involves two types of economic objective. First, objectives can be set for the costs and outcomes of a more costly but also more effective intervention (incremental analysis). Thus, the North Brownstead Practice might decide that a more costly counselling intervention is worth additional resources if it achieves an objective of an additional outcome of 3 per cent reduction in numbers of patients presenting with psychosocial problems (above the target of 10 per cent) per extra £1,000, even if this exceeds the predetermined cost limit (Table 6.3, objective D).

Second, the evaluator might need to decide not whether to implement a counselling programme, but whether to expand or contract a current counselling programme (marginal analysis). In assessing marginal cost-effectiveness, the North Brownstead Practice might wish to examine the consequences of employing a second (part-time) counsellor in the surgery if demand for the first counsellor appears high. The Practice might set an economic objective for the second counsellor of an additional or marginal reduction in patients presenting with psychosocial problems of 3 per cent over 6 months for the extra cost (of £10,000), in addition to a 5 per cent reduction found from an earlier evaluation of the employment of the original counsellor (objective E).

More than one economic objective can be set for counselling interventions, particularly if the evaluation is being conducted from more than one perspective. Economic objectives set by managers at the Smithland Trust Hospital for the counselling service may well differ from those set by the Department of Health. The former could include the objective of achieving a 5 per cent increase in the uptake by staff of the counselling service for a given cost, or raising staff morale (measured using a simple rating scale of staff satisfaction) while the main objective of the Department of Health might be to obtain an improvement in staff productivity measured by a reduction in absenteeism.

It is not necessary to give strict targets for outcomes or cost limits if this is not feasible. As a minimum, the general form of desired economic objective should be specified (e.g. to maximise outcomes or minimise costs or to achieve an increase in outcome from an intervention at a 'reasonable' marginal cost). Setting targets simply assists the evaluator in specifying initial objectives for counselling services. These should not be viewed as unalterable objectives, especially if it becomes obvious at a later stage in the evaluation that they were too ambitious or appear to be too easy to attain.

DEFINING COUNSELLING OPTIONS

Selecting options

The final part of planning a cost-effectiveness analysis is to define and select the alternative options to be included. First, the range of options to be included depends on the CEA method used. An evaluation conducted within or between health service settings might compare different counselling interventions. In comparing counselling with other healthcare interventions one or more of the options should represent a counselling intervention but at least one of the alternative options should be a non-counselling option.

Second, a list of all potential options should be drawn up and ranked to help final selection. The criteria for ranking and selection of options is a matter of discussion between those involved in the evaluation. Any number of options can be selected although too many will result in a costly and complicated evaluation. It is rare to find more than four options included in evaluations of healthcare programmes (see Drummond *et al.* 1987). The final option choice has to be undertaken carefully as the validity of the cost-effectiveness results depends on the most appropriate comparisons being made. For example, the informal use of a staff support group may prove to be more cost-effective than the employment of a counsellor in the Smithland Trust Hospital. However, if a third appropriate option, which is also potentially more cost-effective (such as the use of a 'time-out' facility whereby staff can take a limited number of days off work for stress-related reasons) is not considered, the end results could be misleading.

The option ranking determines which options to include in the final evaluation. The ranking and selection depends on several criteria such as feasibility, ethical and political acceptability, evaluation and set-up costs. If the final list of options remains too long (for example, if insufficient funds exist to include all selected options in the evaluation) a further assessment of each option is needed. This will involve detailed assessment of the acceptability and feasibility for inclusion of each option.

Third, each option included in the final evaluation should be defined and described so as not to exclude the possibility of better options being overlooked. For example, the use of a counsellor might be an appropriate option, but to define the option in terms of client work, (e.g. eight sessions of the counsellor's time working with individuals and two sessions on marital and group work) would probably be too specific. Instead it would be better to define the general option as the employment of a counsellor and examine variants within this option such as allocating some of the counsellor's time for marital and group work compared to working only with individuals in the GPs surgery.

The 'do-nothing' option

In all cost-effectiveness evaluations it is important to define a 'do-nothing' or baseline option. This option represents the current provision of care in health service settings. In each case the do-nothing option can take the form of no formal provision of counselling (with zero costs and outcomes assumed) or the use of approaches that are currently in existence (which will have a positive cost and outcome). For example, an 'active' option might be the introduction of a counselling clinic for patients with problems of sexual dysfunction. If the new clinic is compared with the use of an existing part-time counsellor who is currently undertaking this work, the latter would represent the baseline or 'do-nothing' (i.e. current practice) option.

OPTIONS IN THE CASE STUDIES

Table 6.4 provides an example of the final options that might be selected for inclusion in an evaluation by the two case study service providers with consideration given to the method of cost-effectiveness analysis and perspective adopted.

We will assume that the evaluation in the North Brownstead Practice has arisen because of the doctors' concern that they are seeing an increasing number of patients with psychosocial problems. Their general response has been to offer patients medication and extended repeat consultations, which has put severe pressures on the drug budget and on doctors' time. They might decide to conduct an evaluation of alternative counselling options within the surgery (Method 1 CEA) from the practice perspective. The general objective could be to reduce the number of patients presenting with psychosocial problems within a cost limit of £20,000. Two 'active' options to be included in this evaluation are:

1 Employment of a full-time counsellor located in the surgery.
2 The purchase of the services of an NHS employed clinical psychologist (CP) to provide counselling for patients with psychosocial problems. The CP is based in a Community Mental Health Team (CMHT) unit five miles from the surgery and is available to the surgery for two sessions per week.

The do-nothing option which reflects existing practice is the usual care and support provided by the GP to patients with psychosocial problems. This could vary according to the clinical practice of the doctor involving advice giving and reassurance, drug therapy or a combination of both.

Again, the North Brownstead doctors might carry out further analysis to address another objective – that of reducing the psychotropic drug bill. This involves a cost-effectiveness analysis conducted from the perspective of the practice (the third type of CEA method). This could contain the same options (including the do-nothing option) as in the evaluation described above, but include GP prescription of psychotropic drugs to patients with psychosocial problems as another option.

Table 6.4   Option selection for the case studies

Type of CEA and option	North Brownstead Practice	Smithland Trust Hospital
Method 1		
Perspective	GP Surgery	Hospital
Active options	Counsellor	Counsellor
	Clinical psychologist	Staff support group
Do-nothing option	GP usual care and support	No counselling
Method 2		
Perspective	FHSA	
Active options	Counsellor	Not considered
	Referral to Community Psychiatric Nurse in by the hospital Community Mental Health Team	
Do-nothing option	GP usual care and support	
Method 3		
Perspective		
Active options	Not considered	Society
		Counsellor
Do-nothing option		Other health service options

The FHSA might decide to undertake an evaluation of local practices including the North Brownstead Practice comparing the cost-effectiveness of a counsellor employed in the surgery with the referral of patients with psychosocial problems to the Community Mental Health Team (Method 2 CEA). The Community Mental Health Team has recently employed a new Community Psychiatric Nurse (CPN) whose duties include the provision of counselling to these patients. The 'do-nothing' option is once again the use of the GP to provide routine care.

Smithland Trust Hospital

The Smithland Trust Hospital may want to compare alternative counselling services within the hospital. The hospital managers have set a number of objectives (reducing staff absenteeism, staff turnover, and improving staff morale). The evaluator might chose two 'active' options for the provision of a staff support facility – the use of a counsellor employed full time in the hospital to provide counselling for nurses and a staff support group provided by a counsellor on a weekly basis. The do-nothing option would reflect the current situation of no counselling provision.

The DoH might be interested in comparing the cost-effectiveness of counselling options in a hospital setting such as the Smithland Trust with other types of healthcare interventions. A society perspective could be adopted for this evaluation (which represents the third method of CEA outlined above – Table 6.4). The health service alternatives could be as diverse as cervical cancer screening, coronary artery bypass grafting or surgery to remove varicose veins. This evaluation may be too difficult for the service providers to undertake – the option list could become very large and arbitrary decisions about which to exclude may have to be taken. The alternative approach is to use evidence from published studies of the cost-effectiveness of various health programmes. 'Cost-effectiveness' league tables are readily available (see Maynard 1991). However, unless a representative cross-section of interventions are included in a league table the interpretation of relative cost-effectiveness results could be misleading (see Chapter 10).

SUMMARY

This chapter outlines the steps involved in planning a cost-effectiveness analysis of different counselling services. We have emphasised the importance of careful planning and consideration of study objectives and options. There are three main stages: defining the study problem, setting general and economic objectives and selecting options for inclusion in the analysis. In defining the study problem, the main issue of the evaluation should be addressed. This includes selecting the main CEA method, which varies according to whether comparisons of counselling options are made within a setting, between settings or with alternative healthcare services. The perspective for analysis can be that of a single agency (e.g. GP practice), of multiple agencies (in the NHS) or of society. The economic objective is to achieve the greatest outcome for least cost. Specific cost limits or target outcomes may be devised. Final options for the evaluation have to be selected carefully as the validity of the cost-effectiveness results depends on the most appropriate comparisons being made.

Chapter 7

Data collection I
Study design

Introduction
Randomised controlled trials
Before/after study design
Study design and short cuts to cost and outcome measurement

INTRODUCTION

This chapter describes the selection of an appropriate and feasible study design. Once the study problem and its objectives have been defined and options have been selected, the next stage is to set up a trial period for the cost-effectiveness analysis involving costs and outcomes data collection. Within a cost-effectiveness analysis the study design influences the extent to which the counselling outcomes can be attributed to each intervention (i.e. its statistical robustness). The study design also provides the framework for the collection of resource use data as part of the cost analysis. There are two types of study design:

1 Controlled trial – these are evaluations carried out under controlled conditions, usually within a specific service setting. If well designed, controlled trials provide statistically robust outcomes data for cost-effectiveness analysis. However, they are difficult and costly to construct.
2 Before/after study design – these are evaluations carried out in service settings where existing conditions are incorporated into the study. Before/after studies provide a practical study design for simple cost-effectiveness analyses and are more appropriate if time is limited, but they are less likely to provide statistically robust outcome data.

RANDOMISED CONTROLLED TRIALS

The most robust study design is the randomised controlled trial (RCT). The RCT is most frequently used in clinical research to establish the efficacy of healthcare interventions, in particular new drug therapies, under controlled 'laboratory' conditions (Cochrane 1972). Chapter 5 described randomised controlled trials initiated to assess the efficacy of counselling interventions. The efficacy results could be combined with costs data to compare the cost-effectiveness of the interventions.

An important feature of the RCT is that patients (or service users) who have provided informed consent to participate in a trial are randomly allocated to either one or more 'active' intervention groups or to a control group (the baseline or do-nothing option). The purpose of randomisation is to reduce systematic bias in outcomes related to differences in the characteristics of individuals included in each group.

Options in an RCT need to be specified carefully. It might be specified, for example, that a counsellor employed as part of an intervention must have BAC Accreditation and use a particular therapeutic approach, such as non-directive counselling. The other 'active' options and do-nothing option should also be defined. The study should be approved by the local Ethics Committee.

An RCT could be used in an evaluation such as that of the North Brownstead Practice. Those patients presenting with psychosocial problems and who consent to participate in the evaluation would be allocated randomly between the three option groups described in Chapter 6: the practice counsellor, the clinical psychologist and GP consultation (the 'do-nothing' or control option).

The Smithland Trust Hospital case study might also take the form of an RCT, whereby nurses who consent to take part in the study are randomly allocated to the two 'active' option groups: the counsellor and counsellor-led weekly staff support group. The counsellors working within each option could use an agreed therapeutic approach. A third group of nurses might be reminded that they can discuss problems with senior nursing staff. This group is the control, representing routine conditions.

If possible, the participants in an RCT should be unaware that there is an alternative intervention they could be receiving. The patients are thus 'blind' to the study design. Full knowledge of the study design might affect their attitudes and behaviour. For example, patients with psychosocial problems attending the North Brownstead Practice who are randomly allocated to the control group may derive additional distress from the knowledge that other patients are receiving the services of a counsellor or clinical psychologist. In practice, it is difficult to ensure the complete segregation of patients in each of the option groups.

The outcomes of interest from each option are measured over the trial period and the differences between them tested for statistical significance using a standard test such as students-t or chi-square (Altman 1991). The principle is that if the difference in outcomes is 'statistically significant' then a null (or baseline) hypothesis, that there is no difference in the effectiveness of the options, can be rejected. For instance, the practice counsellor and clinical psychologist options in the North Brownstead evaluation might result in a reduction of numbers of patients returning with psychosocial problems of 10 per cent and 5 per cent respectively over a 6-month period. The null hypothesis is that, statistically, the counsellor option is no more effective than the clinical psychologist, the apparent difference being caused by chance. If this is accepted it means that if the trial was repeated again the counsellor option would demonstrate a reduction in number of patients with psychosocial problems of 5 per cent. The difference in the outcomes of both these options could be compared with that for the GP consultation option to examine whether the active interventions are any more effective, statistically, than the do-nothing option. The likelihood of rejecting the null hypothesis depends on a number of factors:

1 The level of precision required in the test. This is determined by the power of the test chosen – the weaker the power the more likely it is that a difference in outcome will be statistically significant and the null hypothesis will be rejected.
2 The sample size. The greater the number of patients in each group the more reliable is the test of significance and the higher the probability that a given difference in outcomes will be statistically significant.
3 The difference in outcomes. The greater the difference in outcomes the more likely that, other things being equal, this will be statistically significant.

There are a number of texts on medical statistics where detailed discussion of tests of statistical significance within RCTs can be found. A useful text is Altman (1991). In an RCT of efficacy, intervention compliance is 100 per cent (or assumed to be so). However, in practice it is important to examine all the factors that influence the effectiveness of a counselling intervention, including non-compliance of patients. This could be incorporated within a pragmatic RCT designed to measure levels of effectiveness in practice settings after efficacy has been established. If cost data are collected at the same time as testing efficacy, cost-effectiveness can be examined prior to a counselling intervention being introduced as part of a service. In primary and secondary care settings it is more difficult to withdraw an intervention that is not cost-effective than to introduce a new policy that is cost-effective.

However, there are practical problems in setting up an RCT in primary and secondary care settings. Clinical conditions may not be sufficiently controlled for examining the independent impact of counselling interventions. Moreover, the service provider may not be sufficiently confident that he or she has the technical and statistical skills required to construct the study design or analyse results. Service providers may also object to the use of an RCT to evaluate the cost-effectiveness of counselling interventions due to the practical or ethical difficulties in randomly allocating patients to different intervention groups. One possibility would be to allow those patients with a strong preference to select the group they want to be allocated to. These patients could be excluded from the main evaluation, although they may still generate useful data for separate analysis.

An alternative to random allocation within a controlled trial would be to match people in the counselling and control groups according to similarities in key characteristics such as age, sex and medical history. This is known as a case-control study design. For instance, nurses participating in the Smithland Trust Hospital evaluation might be allocated to the counselling and staff support options so that the two groups are matched as closely as possible in terms of age and experience criteria (or whatever criteria is judged to be the most important). With this method more care needs to be taken to avoid bias in the allocation of individuals to option groups, which would reduce the reliability of an association between the counselling intervention and the outcomes recorded. For example, even if nurses allocated to intervention groups in the Smithland Hospital were well matched on age and experience, the allocation process may result, for instance, in a significantly higher proportion of individuals in the counselling group who have positive attitudes towards counselling. In an RCT random allocation reduces the possibility of such selection bias occurring systematically.

BEFORE/AFTER STUDY DESIGN

A before and after study design is appropriate if a counselling service is already being provided in the healthcare setting or if there is a need to assess the cost-effectiveness of the counselling options within usual service provision conditions and it is felt that an RCT is not feasible. The main feature of this approach is that the key outcome measures are recorded after participants have received counselling and compared with an assessment of the situation prior to their receiving counselling.

A before/after study design in the Smithland Trust evaluation might take one of two main forms. First, if the counselling service and the staff support group were being introduced for the first time the evaluation would consist of measuring, for example, the stress levels of staff receiving each intervention at a post-counselling follow-up. At this time they would also be asked whether there had been any change in stress levels compared to before the counselling intervention. Alternatively, the stress levels of staff could be measured prior to the introduction of the interventions.

Second, if one of the options, for example the staff support service, existed prior to the evaluation this could represent the 'do-nothing' option in a before/after study. The costs and outcomes of the staff support service in the 'before' phase could be compared with the counsellor option in the 'after' phase. If the staff support service continued after the introduction of the counselling option, staff using either service would simply be asked to compare stress levels with a time prior to when they started using this service. The change in outcomes from each intervention could then be compared to assess relative effectiveness and be combined with costs data to compare cost-effectiveness.

The main advantage of the before/after study design is that it is the simplest and often most practical approach to use. It can be performed at low cost compared to a controlled trial and causes less disruption to normal service practice. The design represents the most pragmatic basis for the analysis of the cost-effectiveness of counselling interventions in service settings.

The main problem with this approach is that it has a relatively low reliability in establishing the effectiveness of counselling interventions. It does not adequately enable the control of bias due to confounding factors such as the impact of domestic/home conditions on stress levels which leads to problems in attributing measured outcomes to the interventions. A further problem is a lack of control over the numbers and characteristics of people in each group, which can lead to problems of bias and low reliability due to small sample size. For example, 90 per cent of nurses may be using the staff support group with only 10 per cent receiving specialist counselling. Those in the latter category may consist only of female nurses while the staff support group is mixed. This is likely to lead to further problems interpreting the relevance of outcomes relating to the counselling option unless the sample size is very large (which entails more costly evaluation).

STUDY DESIGN AND SHORT CUTS TO COST AND OUTCOME MEASUREMENT

Within both types of study design it is possible to take short cuts to cost and outcome measurement. However, it seems unwise to go to the time and expense of setting up an RCT for the outcome evaluation only to use rough and ready methods of costings. If only limited time and resources are available for cost estimation the evaluator is advised to use a form of before/after study design. Short cuts for cost and outcome measurement are provided in Chapters 8 and 9.

SUMMARY

A summary of the complete data collection phase of an economic evaluation presented in Chapters 7, 8 and 9 is provided at the end of Chapter 9.

Chapter 8

Data collection II
Cost measurement

INTRODUCTION

The detailed measurement of the costs of the options in an economic evaluation involves three steps: the identification of the main cost components (i.e. labour, non-labour and overheads) and resource inputs (e.g. staff time, materials and equipment, premises); the measurement of the physical quantities of each resource used; and the estimation of unit cost (e.g. hourly cost of counsellor time). The cost components included depend on the perspective and objectives of the evaluation.

For the second and third steps there is a range of techniques that can be applied, depending on the time and resources available for the evaluation. For the measurement of the physical quantities of resource inputs the evaluation could use monitoring forms, questionnaires, time use diaries (for staff time inputs), evaluator observation or by including options which have clearly defined levels of resources inputs. For the estimation of unit costs, 'prices' and resources could be used (e.g. salary rates for staff) or 'proxy' unit costs could be estimated (e.g. production cost of a leaflet or estimated value of 'unpriced' volunteer time).

Although the three-step approach is the most complete method for estimating costs, we provide a number of 'short-cut' approaches to costing. If the time for evaluation is limited or detailed data cannot be collected evaluator estimates and financial accounts can be used.

A decision needs to be made as to whether to undertake bottom-up costing, which involves the estimation of the amount of resources used by each patient in the trial, or direct total cost estimation. The latter involves adding up the total resources used in an option and is most appropriate when specific service users cannot be identified (due to the difficulty or expense of doing so, or because there are no readily identifiable service users – for example, an evaluation of the cost-effectiveness of material produced to provide information about a counselling service). An average cost per patient can be calculated by dividing the total cost by the number of patients using the counselling service. It is also important for the evaluator to include an assessment of the costs of all relevant resource inputs of an option in order to assess the total cost of implementing the counselling service.

The production of an average cost per patient for any defined time period and therefore is essentially a static process. Analysis of marginal costs (i.e. the extra costs of an expansion of a counselling service or greater number of service users) adds a dynamic element to the evaluation. Consideration of marginal costs and fixed and variable cost components can produce very different results.

Another costing issue is the analysis of indirect costs, a measure of lost economic and social productivity while receiving counselling (e.g. from time taken off work or diverted from another socially beneficial activity in order to receive counselling). Finally, a cost of illness evaluation would be conducted to assess the direct health service costs and indirect costs (e.g. lost work and social productivity) associated with a disease or condition. For instance, a cost of illness assessment of psychosocial problems could be undertaken to examine the burden this places on society and therefore the potential benefits of providing counselling services to reduce this burden.

CALCULATING TOTAL COSTS – AN OVERVIEW

In cost-effectiveness analysis the total cost of each option needs to be calculated. In a complete costing three steps are involved in directly estimating the total cost of each option:

1 Identify the cost components and resource inputs included in the cost assessment. The main cost components are labour, non-labour and overheads. For a single agency perspective such as the GP surgery a resource input for the labour cost component would be the time input of a counsellor.
2 For each cost component, identify the quantity of resources used in providing an option (e.g. 10 hours of counselling time per week for the counsellor option).
3 Estimate a unit cost for each resource input (e.g. £23 per hour for counsellor time, covering direct patient/client contact time, supervision, administration and planning time).

Table 8.1 outlines the costing process. The resource inputs for each option are identified, including labour, non-labour and overheads cost components. Examples of resource inputs for a counselling option are presented in Column 1, Table 8.1. The cost of each resource input identified in Column 1 is calculated by multiplying the physical quantity of each resource input (Step 2, Column 2) by its estimated unit cost (Step 3, Column 3). Adding together the cost of each resource input produces a total cost estimate for the option. For example, a counsellor (labour component) might provide a total input of 10 hours per week over a 6-month period at a unit cost of £23.00 per hour. This produces a total cost of £5,980. In addition, 500 leaflets might be distributed to patients receiving counselling over this period at a unit cost of £0.50 per leaflet, and therefore a total cost of £250. Summing these two resource costs produces a total cost to the health service provider for the option of £6,230 (Table 8.1).

Table 8.1   Direct agency costs over a six-month trial for a counselling option

Cost components R	Resource quantities Q	Unit costs £s C	Total cost (TC) £s Q x C
Labour			
Counsellor time (Rl)	260 hours (Q1)	23 (C1)	5,980
Practice nurse time	–		
Non-labour			
Self-help leaflet (R2)	500 leaflets (Q2)	0.50 (C2)	250
Postage	–		
Telephone			
Overheads			
Office space	–		
Electricity	–		
General administration			
			6,230

The principles of cost estimation can be summarised by a simple equation. If R represents the resource inputs for each option (Column 1, Table 8.1), Q represents the quantity of each resource used in the intervention (Column 2, Table 8.1) and C is the unit cost of each resource input (Column 3, Table 8.1), then the total cost (TC) of the option is:

$$TC = RQ_1 \times RC_1$$

where:
TC = Total costs
RQ_1 = Quantity of resource R1 . . . . . . r
RC_1 = unit cost of resource R1 . . . . . . r

Applying this notation to the data in Table 8.1, R1 could be counselling time and R2 could be the self-help leaflet. Q1 represents the hours of counsellor time

(10 hours per week) and Q2 the number of leaflets produced (500). C1 is the unit cost of counsellor time (£23 per hour) and C2 the unit cost of the leaflet (£0.50 per leaflet). Table 8.2 summarises the total cost of the option using this notation.

Table 8.2 Notation for option costing (see Table 8.1)

R1 = Q1 [£260] × C1 [£23] = TC1 [£5980]

R2 = Q2 [£500] × C2 [£0.50] = TC2 [£250]

R1 + R2 = [Q1.C1] + [Q2.C2] =TC1 + TC2 = £6230

Table 8.3 outlines a more detailed list of possible cost components and resources, appropriate physical units with which to measure resource quantities and sources of unit cost.The next three sections explain in more detail the costing process outlined above and in Table 8.3.

Table 8.3 Costing a counselling service

Cost components	Measurement of physical quantities	Unit/total cost measure
Direct service costs		
Labour		
Health professionals, time (service provision, travel)	Time units (e.g. hours, days, weeks, months, year)	Market price – gross salary
Other staff time	Time units	Market price – gross salary
Volunteer time	Time units	Market price of equivalent paid staff or non-worktime values
Non-labour		
Materials	Physical amounts	Market price or estimate of production cost
Postage	Volume of mail	
Telephone	No. of calls/units used	Market price
Travel	Miles	Market price Public transport fare; NHS travel allowances for car travel; petrol price paid

Table 8.3   (continued)

Cost Components	Measurement of physical quantities	Unit/total cost measure
Capital		
Equipment	Type of equipment/	To produce EAC:*
Buildings	type of building	(i) Estimate Market Value (MV) or replacement cost (RC) of capital
		(ii) Estimate capital lifespan (n) and discount rate (r) and apply formula: $EAC = MV$ or $RC \times [1-(1/1 + r)^n]$†
Overheads		
Office space + furnishing	Proportion of total space	Estimated rental cost to produce an EAC or % add on to total costs (labour + non-labour)
Utilities (electricity, gas, water)	As a proportion of total units according to space occupied	Market price of utilities or % add on to total costs (labour + non-labour)
Central administration + management	Percentage of total used in service setting	Market price of admin/management or % add-ons
Personal costs (service user, companions)		
Travel time	Time units	Value of work time
Time in service use	Time units	foregone (net earnings lost) or non-worktime foregone
Travel expenses	Car wear and tear Petrol used, fare for public transport/taxi	AA/RAC schedules, market price, fare paid
Other out-of-pocket expenses	No. of hours receiving a counselling service, books purchased, OTC†† drugs	Charges for services, prices paid per hour, market prices
Intangible costs (due to service use)		
Anxiety	Level of anxiety	Proxy value for
Stress	Period of time involved	anxiety/stress caused

Notes: * EAC= Equivalent Annual Cost.
† This formula is presented here for illustration only – a table of annuity factors for calculating EACs is provided as Annex 8.1. The use of Table 8.3 is discussed in the section on capital resources, p.113–14.
†† OTC = over the counter drugs purchased at a pharmacy.

IDENTIFYING THE COST COMPONENTS

Labour, non-labour and overheads are cost components appropriate for an evaluation of the provision of a counselling option conducted from an agency perspective (e.g. the health authority, the FHSA, the GP practice). The costs to be included in the analysis depend on the perspective adopted. For an evaluation conducted from an agency perspective, the evaluator needs to consider how to measure the physical quantities of resource inputs related to the cost components. Examples of resource inputs are presented in Table 8.3. What cost components and resource inputs might an evaluation from an agency perspective include? The evaluator in the North Brownstead Practice might decide only to examine the direct labour and non-labour inputs for each option (which then need to be listed), but decide not to consider overheads due to difficulties anticipated in measurement. In contrast, in the Smithland Trust Hospital evaluation it might be decided to include an estimated cost for the premises used by each option. For example, the counsellor might be provided with an office in which to provide counselling, which was previously used for another purpose.

If a societal perspective is adopted, two further sets of cost components need to be considered – direct personal costs and intangible costs. The main types of direct personal cost are listed in Table 8.3:

- Travel and attendance time – the time used in travelling to and attending a counselling service.
- Out-of-pocket expenses – expenditure incurred from using counselling services (e.g. travel expenses, service fees, expenses for materials purchased as a direct result of receiving counselling).

In addition, the service user might incur intangible costs from anxiety, stress or other psychosocial problems which may occur as a consequence of participation in a counselling programme (for example the 'stigma' of referral to a counselling service). Anxiety might occur as a result of non-participation if the individual is aware of but cannot gain access to the counselling service (e.g. due to transport problems).

The evaluator conducting a cost-effectiveness analysis from a societal perspective should decide which components of personal costs are to be included. If a societal perspective was adopted for the North Brownstead Practice evaluation, the evaluator might decide only to include an assessment of the additional out-of-pocket expenses incurred by patients and their families due to attending the surgery for counselling. Using a societal perspective the Smithland Trust Hospital might decide to attempt a complete evaluation of personal costs including the time and money expenses incurred by nurses in using the counselling service and to measure any intangible costs they might incur from receiving counselling.

Adding together the direct agency, personal and intangible costs produces an estimate of the total costs to society of each intervention. Few evaluations are likely to include all cost components and resources. In particular, intangible costs are difficult to measure and are often excluded from cost-effectiveness evaluations. However, it is useful at the start of the costing process to list all the potential costs relevant to the perspective adopted, even if measurement difficulties mean that some cost items will not be quantified in the final analysis. This approach was adopted by Goldberg and Jones (1980) in their analysis of the relative intangible costs and benefits of a district general hospital and psychiatric hospital setting for the treatment of chronic schizophrenia. This study was reviewed in Chapter 5.

MEASURING THE QUANTITY OF RESOURCE INPUTS

Table 8.3 (column 2) illustrates a range of measures of the physical quantities of resource inputs. Labour resources are measured in units such as minutes, hours, days, weeks and months. Non-labour resources (materials and equipment) can be measured in terms of amounts used (e.g. number of self-help leaflets, number of (and/or time of) telephone calls). A variety of measures is needed for overheads, for example time input of central management and administration, heating and lighting, office equipment and space. Overheads can be difficult to measure, usually requiring identification of that part of the total amount used that is due to the operation of a specific service. The calculation of overhead inputs is dealt with in a later section. The following section focuses on the collection of data on direct labour and non-labour resources used in a counselling intervention and on personal costs.

COLLECTING RESOURCE USE DATA

There are two broad approaches to collecting data on the quantities of resources used in the provision of counselling and other options. Prospective data collection involves resource use identified at the time of the activity. Retrospective data collection involves resource use identified after the activity has occurred. Specific methods for collecting resource use data considered in this section are:

1   Monitoring forms.
2   Questionnaires.
3   Time use diaries.
4   Evaluator observation.
5   Secondary data sources.
6   Using strictly defined options.

Methods 1–3, if well designed, provide a relatively rigorous approach to collecting resource use data. The evaluator with limited time and resources might adopt a less detailed method, such as 4–6 above.

Monitoring forms

A well-designed monitoring form can be used for the prospective collection of resource use data. It can be used to record the time input of counsellors, other health professionals and volunteers within each option. A monitoring form is a useful method for recording small or irregular time inputs. For example, the number of hours the clinical psychologist spends in the North Brownstead Practice providing counselling and the number of visits over a defined time period can be recorded to identify the average weekly and total time involvement over the evaluation period. Moreover, the use of equipment, facilities, drug therapy, the provision of information sheets and other resources associated with a counselling option can be recorded at the time of use. Thus, information sheets handed out at the staff support group sessions as well as the use of facilities and hospital administration overheads could be recorded on a monitoring form. If a societal perspective was adopted the monitoring form could be used to record the time patients spent seeing the counsellor, clinical psychologist or GP in the North Brownstead evaluation.

For the Smithland Trust Hospital the time of nurses in attending at the staff support group or in consultation with the counsellor would be recorded. However, a monitoring form is not convenient for the routine collection of information on other personal costs such as time in travel, out-of-pocket expenses and intangible costs. Additional questions would be required to obtain this information which means other methods of data collection are likely to be more suitable.

Table 8.4 provides an example of a simple monitoring form that might be used in the North Brownstead Practice evaluation for recording details of the counsellor time spent with patients, leaflets distributed, facilities used and other related activities. It may be possible for the evaluator to abstract some of this information from patient case notes.

Table 8.4 Monitoring form: counselling service in GP surgery

Patient no.*	Time in counselling/ consultation	Materials used	Facilities used	Other inputs
1	25 mins with counsellor	Leaflet provided	Counsellor's office	Telephone call to CPN Admin for 20 mins
2	30 mins with counsellor	Leaflet provided	Counsellor's office	Admin for 10 mins
3	20 mins with clinical psychologist	–	–	–
4	–	–	–	–

Note: * Alternatively, this column could be defined in terms of a time period, for example day/week number, and resource use recorded on a per day/week basis.

Questionnaires

Questionnaires can be used for the collection of retrospective data on resource use. Two alternative approaches can be adopted. First, the health professionals involved in the provision of a counselling service could complete a questionnaire which requests information on their time commitment to the service (e.g. hours and whether daily, weekly or less frequent input), and the use of other materials and resources. In the North Brownstead evaluation, questionnaires would be given to the counsellor, clinical psychologist, GPs and other health professionals involved. In the Smithland Trust evaluation this would include the counsellor, the staff support group facilitator and managers. It should be possible to produce a standard questionnaire suitable for completion by all health professionals involved. Because some of the questions may not be relevant for all health professionals, the questionnaire should be designed so that respondents need answer only selected questions.

An alternative less costly but also less detailed approach is to provide key respondents with a questionnaire requesting information on the time input of the counsellor and other health professionals in the counselling intervention. Thus, the questionnaire might be given to the counsellor employed by the North Brownstead Practice or Smithland Trust or a doctor/manager in each healthcare setting who has a good knowledge of the counselling programme and evaluation. Information on the use of non-labour resources and overhead facilities could also be provided.

A number of issues need to be considered in the development, design and administration of a questionnaire survey. To start, the researcher must decide whether to administer the questionnaire through personal interviews with each health professional/volunteer involved in the counselling programme or by respondent self-completion. The former approach involves an interviewer and hence is the more costly method of data collection. The timing of the questionnaire is also important. It is best to collect information as soon after the intervention as possible so that respondents are not being asked about events too far in the past when there are likely to be errors in recall. For example, the clinical psychologist in the North Brownstead evaluation might be asked to estimate the time spent over the previous three weeks of the trial in counselling patients referred, and the facilities and materials used.

If a societal perspective is adopted, the data relating to personal costs and intangible costs are best collected using questionnaires. In addition, the time input of counsellors and the use of materials and medications could be estimated from patient questionaires. For example, patients in the North Brownstead practice and nurses in the Smithland Trust could be asked to complete service use questionnaires. Questions could cover the mode of travel, time and distance involved in travel, travel expenses, time using the counselling service, the payment of any fees for using the service, other out-of-pocket expenses and drugs prescribed by the GP. This information could be requested from the service user and the informal carers or volunteers who accompanied them. Intangible costs can be identified by asking service users about anxiety or worries regarding the use of the counselling service.

Once again, the evaluator needs to decide on the relative merits of administering the questionnaire by interview, by self-completion, as part of the counselling session or to be taken away and returned by post. How and when to administer the questionnaire will affect the response rate. The researcher also needs to decide whether or not to offer incentives to encourage completion (e.g. financial payments, entry to prize draw).

Time use diaries

This method is used to collect data on labour resource inputs. Time use diaries involve individuals in regularly recording their time input into a service. The diary might be completed on a daily or hourly basis. In addition, it could be used to identify time spent on key activities, such as time the North Brownstead Practice counsellor spends seeing clients, and the time spent in associated planning meetings and administration. The accuracy of time input estimates can be increased if time use is recorded at frequent intervals (e.g. every hour), although this involves a high degree of participant commitment. It is more feasible to encourage diary completion on a daily basis, although this might involve less precision due to inaccurate recall. If the time use diary is completed less than daily there are likely to be major problems of recall. Table 8.5 shows a time use diary that was used to evaluate the costs of the time inputs of speech therapists employed at specialist Communication Aids Centres for the speech impaired in England and Wales (Chamberlain *et al.* 1991).

The duration and time of year over which a diary is to be completed can affect the reliability of this method. Ideally, a minimum period of one year is required in order to reduce the impact of weekly variations in time use. However, counselling trials may not be conducted over this length of time and if they were, the use of such an instrument is likely to be difficult to administer, costly to implement and require much goodwill from the participants. Long time periods pose problems of 'participant fatigue' resulting in errors in the recording of time use and low completion compliance, especially for more detailed diaries.

Shorter time periods have lower administrative costs and place less demands on participants, resulting in more incentives to complete a time use diary satisfactorily. The minimum acceptable period is one week (any less than this is unlikely to produce meaningful data). Preferably the period should cover at least two weeks (and more for individuals with a lower time input). The main drawback is the possibility of choosing an atypical time period resulting in bias and errors in the time use records. It is best for each health professional to complete the time use diary in two or three spells over the course of a trial in order to reduce seasonal bias.

A time use diary would be an efficient method of time use data collection if completed by those health professionals who spend more than 50 per cent but less than 100 per cent of their working time involved in one or more of the interventions included in the evaluation and by all those who have a regular involvement which

Table 8.5 Example of time use diary (partially completed)*

Name:

Job Title: Speech Therapist

Grade: Senior I

Use functions:

Key Letter	Function in Communications Aids Provision
A	Direct patient contact
B	Indirect patient contact
C	Treatment planning
D	Training course attendance/meetings
E	Administration/travel
F	Other communications aids related function

	Date	1	2	3	4	5	6	7	8	9	10	11	12	13	14	15	16	17	18	19	Total time
		Funtion (letter) and time involved																			
1	12.3.88	A ½ hour	A 10 mins	C 15 mins																	
2	13.3.88	C 1 hr	A 10 mins																		
3																					
4																					
5																					

Do you undertake work as a link Therapist (please ring) Y/N
Total hours worked over the period: 35
Comments:

Source: Department of Health (1991)
Note: * This form was originally used in an assessment of the time use of specialities providing a communication aids service for speech impaired patients

is equivalent to more than one working day per week. For less regular or small inputs the diary method may represent an unwieldy method for identifying time use. In such cases a monitoring form is likely to be more appropriate.

Evaluator observation

A simple and low-cost approach to resource use data collection is to use estimates derived from researcher observation. The evaluator in the North Brownstead practice (e.g. a GP in the practice) might be able to use his or her experience and judgement to estimate the time input of the counsellor, clinical psychologist, GPs and other health professionals involved in each option. Similar estimates of the materials and facilities used could be attempted. This approach is easily administered (using, for example, a personal interview or self-completion questionnaire) but has low precision. A range of estimates would need to be provided to allow for imprecision in the 'best estimate' of the chosen 'expert' (see Chapter 10).

Secondary data sources

Routine records and documentation can provide further information. The Smithland Trust Hospital might use a hospital activity system to record the staffing and material inputs used in the provision of a staff support group. If such planning records are kept, this can provide information for the costing exercise.

The evaluator might also examine the possibility of using routine databases. The North Brownstead Practice may be one of the many practices which maintains a computer database with details of all patient consultations, drugs prescribed, other activity and outcomes. This could be used over the evaluation period to provide resource use data for the counselling service. The evaluator might also modify an existing database for the trial period to track more accurately consultations with patients with psychosocial problems, the time involved per patient, drug prescriptions, other activity and materials used.

Using strictly defined options

A requirement of a rigorous controlled trial (especially one measuring efficacy) is that the active options have strictly defined boundaries. This requirement makes it possible to estimate the physical resource input and cost for each option without the need for data collection. For example, the options included in the North Brownstead Practice could be defined in detail prior to the trial. The counselling option might be specified as the provision, for each patient, of 25 minutes of counselling in a room at the surgery, a self-help leaflet and a 15-minute follow-up session 2 weeks later. Five minutes administration by a receptionist would be involved for each patient seen. The clinical psychologist would provide the same service on a buy-in basis and the GP would provide a standard six-minute consultation and prescribe drug therapy if it was felt to be appropriate. In the Smithland

Trust evaluation the staff support group option might be defined as meeting weekly for one hour, led by a counsellor (who is also a member of the medical staff), with participation from ten nurses each taking an hour off work. The alternative option might be defined as the provision of individual counselling sessions lasting a maximum of thirty minutes. A monitoring exercise could be undertaken to check that options were being provided as specified.

ESTIMATING THE UNIT COST OF RESOURCES

The final part in producing a cost estimate for each option is to derive an accurate valuation of the unit costs of the resource inputs used (e.g. the cost of one hour of counsellor time, the cost of a self-help leaflet, the hourly/daily/weekly/annual cost of overheads). The appropriate unit costs of each resource input needs to be defined (some examples are provided in Column 3 of Table 8.3). This unit cost or price is then multiplied by the resources (Column 2, Table 8.3) to produce a total cost estimate for each type of resource input, cost component and option.

The estimation of unit costs within an economic evaluation should be based on the principle of the opportunity cost of resource inputs. As opportunity cost is the value of the resource in its next best use, the question to be posed is whether a resource (such as an hour of the counsellor's time) has an alternative use value, and if so, how to identify the best proxy measure of opportunity cost. Unpriced resources, such as volunteer time, unpaid overtime by a counsellor and materials financed by charitable donations, should also be examined to see if they have an alternative use value. A cost should be attached to these inputs if they could have been beneficially used in some other way. For example, there are usually a variety of other services which could benefit from the time of volunteers such as home support for elderly people; unpaid overtime is provided at the cost of giving up leisure time, which has a value; and charitable donations to a counselling service are then not available for other 'worthy' causes. In addition, personal time use should be assessed to identify whether the service users' time spent travelling for counselling was diverted from an alternative beneficial use such as shopping or working.

In a cost-effectiveness analysis, especially one conducted from a societal perspective, the principle of opportunity costing is important. In economic theory, the opportunity cost of each unit of resource used in a counselling programme would be represented by their market price in a perfectly free market (i.e. one with no public sector with all health care provided privately, no taxes on goods, subsidies or government intervention in the health sector). In practice, perfectly free markets do not exist. Even in 'free market' economies such as the UK there is state intervention (taxation, public sector services).

The health service is a mixture of private and public provision. In the UK counselling services in the primary and secondary care sectors may be provided within the National Health Service. For services provided privately, market prices will exist. However, even within public provision it is possible to identify market prices for resources used in the provision of counselling services. Market prices can be identified for resources such as counsellor time, health professionals' time, equipment and materials. Counsellor time is valued using the salary paid for such professionals which is determined within the market for health professionals' skills. In general, such prices provide the most readily available and convenient estimate of the opportunity cost of resources.

In some cases, a resource has a price that is substantially different from that which would occur in a perfectly free market. For example, the prices paid by a hospital pharmacy department for drugs may not reflect their true cost, but instead reflect a negotiated discounted deal between the hospital and pharmaceutical companies. In this case the price reflects the financial cost to the hospital but may be a poor estimate of the opportunity cost of the drug. The evaluator would have to judge whether an adjustment needs to be made to the prices to derive a more accurate 'proxy' estimate.

The evaluator could define a proxy price to reflect the opportunity cost of unpriced resources used in a counselling programme, such as counsellor overtime or self-help leaflets distributed at the counselling session. For example, the cost of the production of each leaflet could be estimated or the price charged to customers of similar leaflets or booklets might provide a proxy estimate.

The evaluator must decide whether to attempt to place a value on the unit cost of each resource input or whether to include only resources for which market price information is readily available. If the latter, only a limited perspective may be adopted for the evaluation, such as that of the main providing agency. The appropriate market prices to use for estimating unit costs and the principles underlying the selection of a proxy price for each type of resource are considered in detail below.

Labour resources

This covers the time of staff involved directly or indirectly in the provision of services. In the North Brownstead Practice, this would include the counsellor, clinical psychologist, GPs and receptionists. The market price of their time is represented by their gross salary. Gross salary is payment before tax, superannuation and national insurance contributions have been deducted. The unit cost per hour (or per day/week) can be calculated by dividing the gross annual/monthly or weekly salary by the number of hours (days/weeks) worked over this period. If a counsellor or health professional is paid on a fee or hourly/daily basis, this payment rate can be used as long as it represents gross cost (or hourly/daily payment rate).

Non-labour resources

The costs of materials such as leaflets and postage, relaxation tapes and so on can be estimated using the market price or a proxy price for these items. In the UK standard prices for medications can be derived from publications such as the *British*

National Formulary (BNF) published twice a year by the British Medical Association and the Royal Pharmaceutical Society of Great Britain or the *Monthly Index of Medical Specialities* (MIMS). However, as we noted earlier, the price actually paid by hospitals usually reflect arrangements between individual pharmacists and drug companies resulting in price variations across sites. Low and high price estimates could be used to allow for uncertainty regarding the most appropriate price (the concept of uncertainty is discussed further in Chapter 10).

Travel costs can be estimated from various sources. The price of petrol for private transport or the fare paid for public transport can be used to estimate travel costs incurred by counsellors and others. If data on petrol use is not available, the cost can be estimated using Automobile Association mileage cost estimates. These have the advantage of incorporating cost for car wear and tear in addition to petrol costs. Another alternative is to use NHS mileage allowances which are available for calculating the travel reimbursement of NHS staff using private cars for NHS business.

Capital resources

Capital resources (e.g. buildings and equipment) are a form of non-labour input and are reusable. If capital resources have a useful life longer than one year then an adjustment to the total cost is required to estimate the cost per year (and derive from this a cost per month/week/day). This is known as the production of an equivalent annual cost (EAC). The Smithland Trust Hospital might want to build new premises in which to provide a staff support service. The total cost of the capital resource needs to be estimated. If the new premises have a market price this can be used to estimate total cost. However, as the new premises are part of the NHS they are unlikely to have an available market value, such as that of a new private building. Instead an estimate of the replacement or construction cost can be used. Once an estimate of the total cost and lifespan has been made, a formula exists that can be applied to calculate the EAC for the capital resource (see Table 8.3):

$$EAC = MV \text{ or } RC \times [1 - (\frac{1}{1+r})^n]$$

$MV =$ Market value of capital resource
$RC =$ Replacement cost of capital resource

The formula includes a discount factor (r) which accounts for the loss due to the depreciation of the capital resource over time and for the opportunity cost of investing in capital resources, rather than an interest-bearing investment or other resources such as staff time, for which all the benefits are realised in the short-term. Non-economists need not worry over the application of the formula as Annex 8.1 provides the calculated values (known as annuity values) for each lifespan and discount rate combination. The non-economist needs simply to multiply the relevant figure in the table by the estimated RC or MV of the capital resource to derive an EAC.

For example, the replacement cost of the new premises for the staff support group at the Smithland Trust Hospital might be estimated at £30,000 and the potential lifespan of the premises might be estimated by hospital managers as a maximum of 25 years. The annuity value for a 6 per cent discount rate and 25-year lifespan is 12.7834 (Annex 8.1). The EAC is calculated by dividing the replacement cost estimate by the annuity value.

$$EAC = £30,000/12.7834 = £2,347$$

The EAC for the premises are £2,347. If all other costs have been expressed in units of less than one year the EAC can be adjusted accordingly. So an equivalent monthly or weekly cost is derived by dividing the EAC for the premises by 12 and 52 respectively (the monthly cost of capital is £2,347/12 = £195).

Overheads

The use of overheads such as office space, utilities, administration of a counselling service may be difficult to identify, especially if counselling is one of many services being provided. Table 8.3 outlined types of overheads that might be used in the provision of a counselling service.

The first task is to identify the overheads used in the interventions. This information could be derived by one or more of the data collection methods considered earlier, such as the questionnaire or monitoring form. The facilities (e.g. office space, computing facilities) used by the counselling service at the North Brownstead Practice could be identified by means of a questionnaire completed by the counsellor.

If overhead resources can be attributed to a counselling service then a direct estimate of quantity and cost can be made. If detailed service accounts do not exist or do not cover all overhead items (such as the opportunity cost of office space used by the counsellor), separate cost estimates are required. Whatever method is used the process is likely to produce a minimum cost estimate as there will remain identified overhead resources for which it is not possible to estimate the amount used or their costs. These should be listed alongside the costed overheads.

It may be difficult to identify the amount of overhead resources used in counselling services that are shared with other services and activities. Estimation of the overhead costs will require an assessment of the proportion of the total overheads used by the counselling service. None of the methods used to apportion overhead costs are ideal but they provide a means of including costs which may represent a significant part of the total cost of a counselling service.

First, if there is evidence that the counselling service uses overhead resources that would have been incurred without the service and have not been diverted from any other use then an opportunity cost of zero can be assumed. For instance, if a spare office in the GP surgery that was inappropriate for any other use was utilised for the counselling service, then a zero opportunity cost can be assumed. Similarly, no overhead cost for heating exists if the counsellor used the main surgery which would have been heated without the existence of the counselling service.

Second, if it is not practicable to estimate the amount of overhead resources used in the counselling service, then judgement should be used to estimate the 'add-on' cost for overhead resources. A rule of thumb is that this should be 5–40 per cent on top of all other costs, depending on the range and type of overheads identified. While this is a simple method of including overhead costs there is, of course, the problem of uncertainty means that a range of high and low estimates for add-on overhead costs should be included in the evaluation (see Chapter 10). This approach can be used for overheads that are fully attributable to the counselling options and those which are shared with other services (for the latter a lower 'add-on' will be estimated).

An alternative approach is to estimate a proportion of overhead costs attributable to the counselling services from the general accounts for the GP surgery or hospital department. The less disaggregated the accounts (for example if they are produced only for the whole hospital), the more difficult it is to estimate accurately a proportion of overheads attributable to the counselling service.

Personal and intangible costs

An opportunity cost exists for personal inputs into a counselling service if the service user and any companions have incurred a monetary or time outlay they would not have otherwise made. The expenses incurred through travel can be based on the price paid for petrol and car wear and tear, or the public transport fare. A patient questionnaire would request information about the mode of transport, public transport or taxi fare paid, or distance travelled by car. Given information on car distances travelled (and assuming a certain size of car engine and annual mileage), annual schedules of estimated vehicle running costs produced by motoring organisations such as the Royal Automobile Club (RAC) or the Automobile Association (AA) can be used to estimate the per mile cost of petrol and wear and tear. In addition to travel there may be other out-of-pocket expenses incurred by the service user, such as charges for the counselling service.

The unit cost of time incurred by the service users and companions in travelling to and attending the counselling service can be estimated by a variety of means, depending on whether work or leisure time is given up in order to receive counselling. If work time has been given up, the personal cost is calculated as the loss of earnings (which may be zero if the individual is still paid). For example, if a patient attending the North Brownstead Practice for counselling takes one day off work without pay in order to do so (and assuming no other activities are undertaken), the cost is the net wage lost for that time period (i.e. what they would have earned after tax and other contributions have been deducted). It is important to use the net wage rather than the gross wage to estimate the personal cost. The latter figure is assumed to represent the loss of productivity to society and is therefore used to estimate indirect costs of the counselling service.

For many individuals who do not work in a paid job, or who attend for counselling in their leisure time, an alternative method of valuing the unit cost of this time is needed. One approach is to use the values calculated for non-work travel time from research conducted by the Department of Transport in the 1980s (Department of Transport 1987), which produced a standard value for non-work time of £2.08 per hour (1988 prices). Updated to reflect current prices, this figure can be used as an estimate of the unit cost of personal time when leisure time is foregone. The non-work values produced by the Department of Transport are about 25 per cent of their assessment of working time values of £8.42 per hour (1988 prices). The non-work valuations will, of course, vary so that the opportunity cost of time might be lower for an unemployed person than for a person who is not seeking work but carries out voluntary work. Hence, an upward adjustment on the standard figure could be made to allow for the higher opportunity cost of a voluntary worker. However, a volunteer providing a service within a counselling programme may still have a zero or low opportunity cost for their time if they would not have undertaken any other form of voluntary work, and did not value alternative uses of their leisure time.

Finally, it is difficult to estimate a unit cost for intangible costs such as stress and anxiety associated with using a counselling service (or caused to the providers – for example, staff burnout). One approach would be to construct a service user questionnaire asking consumers what they would be willing to pay to receive a counselling service if this would increase the probability of raising the quality of service provided (and hence reduce the intangible costs to the user). Consumers' hypothetical 'willingness to pay' would reflect the intangible cost associated with the current service provision. The main criticism of this approach is that it is difficult for individuals to attribute a value for a better quality service which they would not receive. It may also be difficult for users to understand the notion of increases in the 'probability' of a better quality service. Finally, because it is a hypothetical question and they do not have to pay, their response might not be a realistic estimate of their true willingness to pay.

An alternative approach is to identify a proxy intangible cost. This could be as simple as a 'guestimate' by the evaluator. It might be possible to identify an expenditure which is designed to reduce anxiety. For example, during 1992 and 1993 a number of cases of healthcare workers who were HIV positive but still seeing patients were reported and brought to public attention. The resulting anxiety among patients and the public was countered by health authorities who set up information helplines for people worried about the risks they faced. The expenditure on these phonelines could represent a crude proxy of the intangible cost from public anxiety due to the existence of HIV infection among healthcare workers.

SHORT CUTS TO ESTIMATING COSTS

Some health economists have argued that detailed costing does not necessarily produce a level of accuracy sufficient to warrant the extra time and resources required (Whynes and Walker 1995). We suggest several short cuts to costing for evaluators or service providers with limited time, money or resource use data.

Evaluator estimates

The evaluator might take a short cut by providing his or her own rough estimate of the costs of each option. However, it is still important that the evaluator carries out the first part of the costing process and identifies the cost components and types of resources used in each option according to the perspective adopted for evaluation.

Instead of collecting data to examine the physical quantities of resources used in each option, the evaluator may use his or her own judgement (and any readily available supporting evidence) to estimate the quantities. The evaluator might estimate that each weekly session on the staff support group in the Smithland Trust Hospital uses one hour of the time of a nurse to lead the session, and one hour of the time of each participant, uses a room within new staff premises, and at each session at least one self-help booklet is distributed. Unit costs can be attached to each estimated resource input to produce a total cost for this option.

If this is too complex, for example if the number of resources used is large, then it is easier to estimate the total cost of each option. So long as the relative cost differences for each option are broadly correct then the cost-effectiveness results produced should not differ greatly from those produced with more accurate total cost estimates. For example, the evaluator might estimate the cost of the staff support group as £20,000 per year and the use of a specialist counsellor as £25,000. The effectiveness of each option can be compared and the relative cost-effectiveness of each examined (although once again allowance for uncertainty should be made by including high and low cost estimates – see Chapter 10).

Financial accounts

Information from financial accounts of the providing agency represents the easiest approach to cost estimation from an agency perspective. Data collection is simplified if those resources used in the counselling option can be identified from the headings used in the accounts. If the resources are used wholly on the counselling option (e.g. such as a full-time counsellor) then the expenditures on the disaggregated accounts can be used to represent the annual cost of the resource. Other resources such as counselling information sheets may be identifiable from the accounts.

There are drawbacks to the use of accounts in cost estimation. First, as they are usually only produced annually, cost estimation is retrospective. Second, many resources used in a counselling programme do not appear as a defined cost in the accounts. The accounts are less useful the less they are disaggregated. If the accounts include details of the costs of a practice nurse, for example who also provides counselling, it is necessary to identify the proportion of the cost to be apportioned to counselling (e.g. use expert judgement, time use diaries). Third, accounts are less useful for a multi-agency perspective where several accounts would be required. Fourth, they cannot be used to estimate the costs of capital resources. Finally, they only cover resources for which a financial price exists. Resources such as volunteer time and patient/client time do not have a financial price but have an opportunity cost requiring a proxy valuation.

BOTTOM-UP COSTING OR DIRECT TOTAL COST ESTIMATION?

The methods introduced in this chapter illustrate the two approaches to costing:

1   Bottom-up costing. This is appropriate when there are clearly defined service users, and is particulary important for assessing personal costs incurred by each service user. In the North Brownstead Practice direct resource use and personal costs could be recorded for each patient using the counselling service. The data could be derived from a survey of staff and patients. For example, the resource use for a patient might consist of 25 minutes of the time of the counsellor and the provision of 1 self-help tape. In addition, an apportionment for overheads could be included. Personal costs might be recorded as 20 minutes spent in travelling to the surgery and the 25 minutes spent receiving counselling. The patient might have travelled five miles by car for which AA schedules can be used to estimate a travel cost. The process is then followed to record resource use of all other patients using the service. The cost estimate for each patient is summed to produce a total cost estimate for the counselling service.

2   Direct total cost estimation. This approach is used when individual service users are not easily identifiable or it is not possible to collect resource use data relating to each individual service user (due to expense or time constraints). Moreover, some options do not have direct service users – for instance, a campaign run by a pressure group to promote the provision of counselling facilities in a local hospital would not have any direct service users. In this case direct total cost estimation is required. This approach is suitable for an evaluation conducted from an agency perspective, but less applicable if personal costs are also included. So, in order to produce a total annual cost estimate for the counsellor option in the Smithland Trust evaluation the evaluator could estimate the annual cost of the counsellor (salary divided by proportion of time employed in providing a service) and the total non-labour costs and overheads incurred in the provision of the service. A similar process could be adopted to estimate the costs of the staff support group.

If the evaluator has data on the number of service users, the cost per service user can be derived by dividing the total cost of each option by this figure. This is known as top-down costing and is a simpler and less costly method (in terms of data collection) for producing average cost estimates. It has lower accuracy and less scope than bottom-up costing as it is difficult to estimate personal costs using this approach. However, an evaluation could use a combination of both approaches to estimate a total cost for options in an economic evaluation.

TIMING OF COSTS

In both approaches some costs may be delayed to a later date. For example, counselling provided for a patient may result in the need for further counselling sessions in one or more years time. Economic theory suggests that costs which are deferred have a lower value than costs occurring in the current time period. This is discussed in Chapter 10 (see Discounting).

TOTAL COSTS OF IMPLEMENTING AN OPTION

In a cost-effectiveness analysis, not all costs need to be included to assess relative cost-effectiveness as long as the cost is the same for each option of the excluded components. However, if there are resource constraints it is important to assess the total cost of the option and the scale of start-up costs to examine the feasibility of its implementation. Therefore, two counselling options in an evaluation may both use a practice nurse to identify patients eligible for counselling. If the time input and use of other resources is the same then their inclusion would not change the relative cost-effectiveness of the options. However, when implementing a preferred option it is important to know the total cost to ensure sufficient resources are available – at this stage the costs of the practice nurse would need to be included.

In addition, when implementing an option the service provider would need to ensure sufficient resources were available to cover start-up costs such as the provision of premises and training costs. In this case it is important to identify all the relevant start-up costs.

FIXED, VARIABLE AND MARGINAL COSTS

The discussion of cost measurement so far has described it as a static process – a single cost is calculated for a particular counselling option. However, cost calculation can be dynamic. An evaluation of the costs of altering the size of a counselling service (or the amount of any resource inputs within a service) is known as the assessment of marginal costs. This cost concept can be examined by breaking down its evaluation into two components: fixed and variable costs.

Fixed costs represent resource inputs that, within a range, do not vary with the number of service users or size of programme. This would include capital resources, overheads and the sunk costs of employing a counsellor (for example, the total salary of a counsellor on a one year contract). As the service expands the fixed cost per service user (if appropriate) will decline. Beyond a certain level of demand or size of programme, additional fixed costs will be incurred. For example, an additional part-time counsellor might be employed and larger premises might be required. Thus, in the long run the total fixed costs will increase resulting in an increase in the average cost per service user. The average fixed costs will then decline with further small changes in the number of service users or size of the programme.

Variable costs are the costs of resource inputs that vary with small changes in the size of a programme in the short run. Supposing each additional patient attending the North Brownstead counsellor is given a self-help tape. Each patient who receives a tape will be increasing the total variable cost of the service. Other variable costs include items such as stationery and telephone calls. If a counsellor is not employed to provide a fixed time input but instead is used as and when required then changes in this resource input represents a variable cost.

Figure 8.1(a) presents the probable shape of the total fixed and variable cost curves with changes in the numbers of users, or size of a counselling service. The marginal cost of a change in size (i.e. amount of resource inputs) of a counselling service could differ substantially depending on the existing position of the service on the fixed and variable cost curves in Figure 8.1(b). For example, if the current size of the programme is A1, then an expansion in the size of the service to A2 would result in a large increase in fixed costs (from FC2 to FC3), and an increase in variable costs (VCa1 to VCa2). This high fixed cost might be the need to employ a new counsellor on a one-year contract to provide a service for a greater number of people. In contrast, if the current size of the service was B1, an expansion to B2 would not increase fixed cost from FC2, only increasing variable costs (from VCb1 to VCb2). For example, the existing counsellor may be able to cope with an increased number using the service. Therefore, the marginal cost would be much lower in the latter situation due to the existence of 'spare capacity' in the use of fixed resources. This means that the expansion of a service is likely to be more cost-effective if such spare capacity exists (e.g. this could be an unused office or underused staff). Chapter 10 examines marginal costs in the analysis of cost-effectiveness.

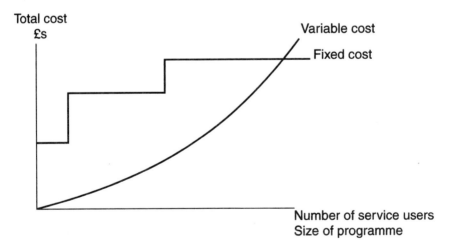

Figure 8.1 (a) Fixed and variable costs

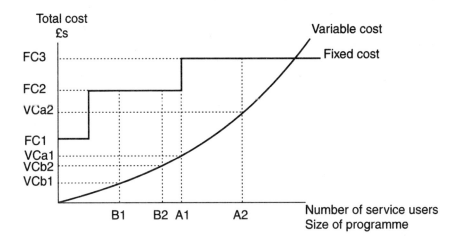

Figure 8.1 (b)   Changes in marginal fixed and variable costs

INDIRECT COSTS

The value of economic and social productivity lost due to a person attending counselling is known as the indirect cost of the intervention. Indirect costs cover work time lost and other socially productive activities given up such as voluntary work, housework and informal care. Indirect costs are usually calculated by estimating the time taken off work (or other socially productive activity) to receive a service and multiplying this by the estimated value of the lost productivity associated with this foregone time use. Because the estimation of indirect costs is neither simple nor fully accepted by health economists as relevant in a cost-effectiveness analysis of health service interventions we will not examine indirect costs in detail. The interested reader is referred to other texts which discuss the methods and pitfalls of indirect cost estimation in cost-effectiveness analysis (e.g. Drummond *et al.* 1987).

Cost-of-illness studies

Although we focus on the use of cost-effectiveness analysis, there is a further, arguably more acceptable, application of indirect costs by health economists and epidemiologists. This includes indirect costs as part of a cost-of-illness study of particular diseases or health conditions, in order to provide information on the economic burden associated with premature mortality and ill-health. For example, the indirect cost of psychosocial disorders in a community could be estimated. If these costs are combined with an estimate for the direct cost of treatment and other services provided for patients with psychosocial problems then a total cost-of-illness estimate could be produced. Such data might be useful for drawing the attention of health service managers and purchasers to the health burden associated with psychosocial problems, and for the need to identify cost-effective methods of reducing the burden. In practice, cost-of-illness studies have been conducted for several diseases and health harming behaviours including the economic cost of alcohol related illness, AIDS and Alzheimer's disease (Hay and Ernst 1987; Scitovsky and Rice 1987; Gorsky *et al.* 1988).

SUMMARY

A summary of the complete data collection phase of an economic evaluation presented in Chapters 7, 8 and 9 is presented at the end of Chapter 9.

Annex 8.1 Annuity values for calculating equivalent annual costs (EAC) (see Table 8.3, p. 103, and section on capital resources, p. 113—14)

N	1%	2%	3%	4%	5%	6%	7%	8%	9%	10%	11%	12%	13%	14%	15%
1	0.9901	0.9804	0.9709	0.9615	0.9524	0.9434	0.9346	0.9259	0.9174	0.9091	0.9009	0.8929	0.8850	0.8772	0.8696
2	1.9704	1.9416	1.9135	1.8861	1.8594	1.8334	1.8080	1.7833	1.7591	1.7355	1.7125	1.6901	1.6681	1.6467	1.6257
3	2.9410	2.8839	2.8286	2.7751	2.7232	2.6730	2.6243	2.5771	2.5313	2.4869	2.4437	2.4018	2.3612	2.3216	2.2832
4	3.9020	3.8077	3.7171	3.6299	3.5460	3.4651	3.3872	3.3121	3.2397	3.1699	3.1024	3.0373	2.9745	2.9137	2.8550
5	4.8534	4.7135	4.5797	4.4518	4.3295	4.2124	4.1002	3.9927	3.8897	3.7908	3.6959	3.6048	3.5172	3.4331	3.3522
6	5.7955	5.6014	5.4172	5.2421	5.0757	4.9173	4.7665	4.6229	4.4859	4.3553	4.2305	4.1114	3.9975	3.8887	3.7845
7	6.7282	6.4720	6.2303	6.0021	5.7864	5.5824	5.3893	5.2064	5.0330	4.8684	4.7122	4.5638	4.4226	4.2883	4.1604
8	7.6517	7.3255	7.0197	6.7327	6.4632	6.2098	5.9713	5.7466	5.5348	5.3349	5.1461	4.9676	4.7988	4.6389	4.4873
9	8.5660	8.1622	7.7861	7.4353	7.1078	6.8017	6.5152	6.2469	5.9952	5.7590	5.5370	5.3282	5.1317	4.9464	4.7716
10	9.4713	8.9826	8.5302	8.1109	7.7217	7.3601	7.0236	6.7101	6.4177	6.1446	5.8892	5.6502	5.4262	5.2161	5.0188
11	10.3676	9.7868	9.2526	8.7605	8.3064	7.8869	7.4987	7.1390	6.8052	6.4951	6.2065	5.9377	5.6869	5.4527	5.2337
12	11.2551	10.5753	9.9540	9.3851	8.8633	8.3838	7.9427	7.5361	7.1607	6.8137	6.4924	6.1944	5.9176	5.6603	5.4206
13	12.1337	11.3484	10.6350	9.9856	9.3936	8.8527	8.3577	7.9038	7.4869	7.1034	6.7499	6.4235	6.1218	5.8424	5.5831
14	13.0037	12.1062	11.2961	10.5631	9.8986	9.2950	8.7455	8.2442	7.7862	7.3667	6.9819	6.6282	6.3025	6.0021	5.7245
15	13.8651	12.8493	11.9379	11.1184	10.3797	9.7122	9.1079	8.5595	8.0607	7.6061	7.1909	6.8109	6.4624	6.1422	5.8474
16	14.7179	13.5777	12.5611	11.6523	10.8378	10.1059	9.4446	8.8514	8.3126	7.8237	7.3792	6.9740	6.6039	6.2651	5.9542
17	15.5623	14.2919	13.1661	12.1657	11.2741	10.4773	9.7632	9.1216	8.5436	8.0216	7.5488	7.1196	6.7291	6.3729	6.0472
18	16.3983	14.9920	13.7535	12.6593	11.6896	10.8276	10.0591	9.3719	8.7556	8.2014	7.7016	7.2497	6.8399	6.4674	6.1280
19	17.2260	15.6785	14.3238	13.1339	12.0853	11.1581	10.3356	9.6036	8.9501	8.3649	7.8393	7.3658	6.9380	6.5504	6.1982
20	18.0456	16.3514	14.8775	13.5903	12.4622	11.4699	10.5940	9.8181	9.1285	8.5136	7.9633	7.4694	7.0248	6.6231	6.2593
21	18.8570	17.0112	15.4150	14.0292	12.8212	11.7641	10.8355	10.0168	9.2922	8.6487	8.0751	7.5620	7.1016	6.6870	6.3125
22	19.6604	17.6580	15.9369	14.4511	13.1630	12.0416	11.0612	10.2007	9.4424	8.7715	8.1757	7.6446	7.1695	6.7429	6.3587
23	20.4558	18.2922	16.4436	14.8568	13.4886	12.3034	11.2722	10.3711	9.5802	8.8832	8.2664	7.7184	7.2297	6.7921	6.3988
24	21.2434	18.9139	16.9355	15.2470	13.7986	12.5504	11.4693	10.5288	9.7066	8.9847	8.3481	7.7843	7.2829	6.8351	6.4338
25	22.0232	19.5235	17.4131	15.6221	14.0939	12.7834	11.6536	10.6748	9.8226	9.0770	8.4217	7.8431	7.3300	6.8729	6.4641
26	22.7952	20.1210	17.8768	15.9828	14.3752	13.0032	11.8258	10.8100	9.9290	9.1609	8.4881	7.8957	7.3717	6.9061	6.4906
27	23.5596	20.7069	18.3270	16.3296	14.6430	13.2105	11.9867	10.9352	10.0266	9.2372	8.5478	7.9426	7.4086	6.9352	6.5135
28	24.3164	21.2813	18.7641	16.6631	14.8981	13.4062	12.1371	11.0511	10.1161	9.3066	8.6016	7.9844	7.4412	6.9607	6.5335
29	25.0658	21.8444	19.1885	16.9837	15.1411	13.5907	12.2777	11.1584	10.1983	9.3696	8.6501	8.0218	7.4701	6.9830	6.5509
30	25.8077	22.3965	19.6004	17.2920	15.3725	13.7648	12.4090	11.2578	10.2737	9.4269	8.6938	8.0552	7.4957	7.0027	6.5660
35	29.4086	24.9986	21.4872	18.6646	16.3742	14.4982	12.9477	11.6546	10.5668	9.6442	8.8552	8.1755	7.5856	7.0700	6.6166
40	32.8347	27.3555	23.1148	19.7928	17.1591	15.0463	13.3317	11.9246	10.7574	9.7791	8.9511	8.2438	7.6344	7.1050	6.6418
45	36.0945	29.4902	24.5187	20.7200	17.7741	15.4558	13.6055	12.1084	10.8812	9.8628	9.0079	8.2825	7.6690	7.1232	6.6453
50	39.1961	31.4236	25.7298	21.4822	18.2559	15.7619	13.8007	12.2335	10.9617	9.9148	9.0417	8.3045	7.6752	7.1327	6.6605

N = Lifespan
Note: To find the appropriate discount factor identifying the cell corresponding to expected lifespan of the capital/premises and chosen discount rate.

Chapter 9

Data collection III

Outcome measurement

Introduction
Types of outcome measure
Types of final outcome measure
Methods for collecting outcome data
The relationship between outcome measures
Short cuts to outcome measurement
External benefits

INTRODUCTION

Different types of outcome measure can be used in a cost-effectiveness analysis depending on the objective of the evaluation. Process indicators are used when the objective is to evaluate two or more approaches to the delivery of a service. Intermediate outcomes measure attitudes and behavioural response of service users and can be used to compare different types of counselling service. Final outcomes, such as change in well-being or quality of life, enable comparisons between counselling options and other healthcare or preventive services.

A controversial form of final outcome measure used in cost-utility analysis (defined here as a special form of cost-effectiveness) is the quality adjusted life year (QALY). This combines estimates of life years gained and the quality of those years to enable comparisons of a wide range of health interventions, including counselling services.

A number of methods exist for collecting outcome data in a cost-effectiveness analysis, for example, monitoring forms and questionnaire surveys. Ideally, QALY data require a special questionnaire survey. However, the evaluator may not have the time or resources to use these approaches. Instead, a short-cut method to estimating QALYs or other outcomes from counselling interventions is to use 'expert judgement' (i.e. the best estimates of, for instance, the service provider, the evaluator, counsellor, other health professionals or a 'panel' of experts).

TYPES OF OUTCOME MEASURE

To compare the cost-effectiveness of alternative counselling options, an appropriate outcome measure is required. Just as the same cost components should be assessed for each option so the same outcome measure should be used to compare relative effectiveness.

Three types of outcome measure appropriate for measuring the relative effectiveness of counselling interventions in the healthcare setting are considered here. These are: process indicators, intermediate outcomes and final outcomes. These were briefly introduced in Chapter 4. Which one is used, and when, depends on the perspective adopted, the objectives of the evaluation and the options included.

The use of process indicators

Process indicators are suitable for evaluations of alternative counselling options within the same healthcare setting (Method 1 CEA– see Chapter 6). The objectives and options have to be narrow in scope in order to use process indicators to compare effectiveness in the delivery or uptake of a counselling service. Examples of relevant process indicators for alternative counselling interventions are the numbers using each counselling intervention over a defined time period, the number of information sheets distributed and the numbers presenting for counselling.

The use of intermediate outcomes

Intermediate outcomes are suitable for evaluations within the same healthcare setting or for comparisons across healthcare settings (Method 2 CEA – see Chapter 6) but the objectives are different than in evaluations using process indicators. While the latter are generally used to examine the best approach to providing a counselling service, intermediate outcomes are used to measure the effectiveness of alternative counselling options on the attitudes, intentions or behaviour of the service users. As these are more general indicators of effectiveness a wider set of options can be compared.

Intermediate outcomes are related to a specific objective, such as to measure the relative cost-effectiveness of each counselling option in reducing nurse absenteeism in the Smithland Hospital. The counselling options might have other impacts, such as improving staff morale. However, the evaluator might decide that the important outcome measure to include in the cost-effectiveness analysis is 'nurse absenteeism rates' as it is of major concern to hospital management. Changes in staff morale can still provide supporting evidence in comparing counselling options.

Across settings, a common outcome measure could be used to compare the cost-effectiveness of employing a counsellor in a GP surgery or using a Community Psychiatric Nurse to provide a similar service in the community. A reduction in number of patients presenting at the GP surgery with psychosocial problems or reduction in expenditure on psychotropic drug prescriptions over a defined period could be used as the common outcome measure to compare these interventions. Differences in outcomes could be analysed for statistical significance (see Chapter 6).

In contrast, it would not be possible to compare directly the effectiveness of a counselling option in the Smithland Hospital, where the main objectives might be to reduce staff absenteeism and raise staff morale, with general practice counselling that has primary objectives of reducing the number of consultations by patients with psychosocial problems, a reduction in drug prescriptions and improvements in patient well-being. To compare the effectiveness of such diverse counselling services a common final outcome measure is needed.

The use of final outcomes

Final outcomes measure the mortality, morbidity, well-being or quality of life benefits of healthcare interventions. Final outcome measures often used in economic evaluations are life years gained/saved, gains in health status or quality of life rating and quality adjusted life years (QALYs). Because life years gained only reflect mortality benefits, this measure would appear to be the least appropriate for an evaluation of counselling services whose main objective is to assess the impact on the psychosocial well-being, quality of life, health status or health utility of the service user.

Because final outcomes represent general measures of effectiveness, it is possible to compare different counselling and non-counselling options both within and across care settings. A final outcome measure could be used to compare the effectiveness of the staff support group in the Smithland Trust Hospital with the counsellor service in the North Brownstead Practice. For example, the quality of life gains of patients receiving counselling at the GP surgery and of patients treated at the Smithland Trust Hospital could be compared. In the latter case the link between the staff support service for nurses and patient quality of life is indirect. The benefit is achieved by higher morale, less staff absenteeism and turnover resulting in greater quality of care, higher patient satisfaction and quality of life.

Life years saved and QALYs gained are frequently used in order to assess the cost-effectiveness of the use of healthcare resources for a wide range of interventions. Similarly, within a cost-effectiveness analysis across health programmes (Method 3 CEA – see Chapter 6), a measure such as the QALY could be used to compare one or more counselling interventions with other uses of health service resources (e.g. treatment for hypertension, 'quit smoking' health education and surgery for angina).

TYPES OF FINAL OUTCOME MEASURE

Quality of life measures

Alternative counselling options could be compared using a specific measure of patient/client psychosocial well-being or quality of life. The measure could be designed for the purpose of comparing the options in the evaluation or use could be made of one of many of the existing measures of well-being. Use of a tailor-made measure has the advantage of adaptability to the evaluation objectives, but has several practical disadvantages. These include the high effort and cost involved in designing a new measure of psychosocial well-being that is valid and reliable. For many service providers the limited usefulness of a specific well-being measure, the high degree of technical know-how and time and money resources required to overcome the inherent design problems mean the adoption of such an approach is impractical. For this reason we will not cover the methods for designing a well-being/quality of life measurement instrument, which is complex and beyond the scope of this book. Instead we focus on existing measures that have (to some extent at least) been validated and tested in previous studies. A large number of instruments can be used to assess the general well-being or quality of life of patients prior to and after receiving counselling. These can be classified into two types:

1   Specific measures which incorporate only psychological or psychosocial aspects of well-being. Examples are the General Health Questionnaire, the Delighted-Terrible Faces scale, the (psychological) General Well-Being Schedule (GWBS), the Affect-Balance Scale and the Life Satisfaction Index.
2   General measures of well-being or quality of life. These usually incorporate psychosocial dimensions but combine this with indicators of physical pain and ailments, mobility/disability and social functioning. Examples are the SF 36, the Nottingham Health Profile, the Sickness Impact Profile, Spitzer's Quality of Life index and the Karnofsky Performance Scale.

Many other measures exist within these categories, measuring specific health or quality of life dimensions. These include measures of functional ability/disability (e.g. the Arthritis Impact Measurement scale and Townsend's Disability Scale); measures of depression (e.g. Beck Depression Inventory) and social support measures (e.g. The Family Relationships Index). A short paper by Donovan *et al.* (1993) provides a summary of the different instruments and assesses their validity, reliability and applicability. Alternatively, a specialist text by Bowling (1991) provides further information on these instruments.

Almost all quantitative quality of life measures allocate a number on a scale or index to represent the level of well-being of the individual (pre and post intervention). Psychological well-being measures might be particularly appropriate for assessing the outcomes expected from a counselling intervention, and so are useful when comparing two or more different counselling interventions (within or between settings; Method 1 or 2 CEA – see Chapter 6).

In contrast, the main purpose of a general measure is to enable comparisons between different health interventions in terms of their overall effect on quality of life. Some of these measures, such as the Karnofsky Performance Scale, were originally developed for a specific patient group (patients with cancer) but have since been used as a general measure to derive quality of life gains for other patient groups. Health profiles differ from the other general quality of life scales in that they provide a separate numerical scale for each dimension included in the measure, rather than one scale combining all dimensions. For example, the Nottingham Health Profile includes a scale of 0–100 for each of six dimensions of well-being – pain, social isolation, physical mobility, energy, emotional reactions and sleep (Hunt *et al.* 1980). Respondents' scores are generated by means of a questionnaire interview – a low score reflects a low level of health problems.

Counselling interventions might be expected to produce a relatively greater gain in terms of the psychosocial and social disability dimensions of a general quality of life instrument, while other interventions, such as the provision of improved mobility aids for people with cerebral palsy, would be expected to have a greater impact on the physical disability dimensions. However, such diverse interventions could be compared using a general quality of life gain measure.

QALYs

General well-being measures do not take account of the impact of a healthcare intervention on mortality. It may be appropriate, especially for cost-effectiveness analyses that involve comparisons with health care interventions which are expected to produce life year gains, to use a composite indicator of health status. The QALY is a measure of quality of life which combines length of survival with an attempt to measure the quality or utility[1] of that survival time (Williams 1985). Quality of life in a QALY is measured by a numerical utility scale with values ranging from 0 (zero quality of life equivalent to being dead) to 1 (maximum quality of life equivalent to perfect health). The essence of a QALY is that one year of healthy life expectancy represents a value of one, but a year of less than perfect health is worth less than one. The precise value is lower the worse the quality of life of the unhealthy person (which is what the quality adjusted bits are all about). If being dead is worth zero, it is, in principle, possible to be QALY negative (i.e. for someone's quality of life to be judged worse than being dead). For example, there is ongoing medical debate about turning off life support machines. The main thrust of the argument is that the patient's current and potential quality of life on a life support machine is so poor as to be QALY negative (i.e. the patient would be better off dead).

There are many instruments available for calculating QALYs. The standard features are a questionnaire for classifying individuals according to their physical, psychosocial and social well-being and a numerical utility scale providing a corresponding value for each category of well-being or quality of life. In each case the numerical scale has been derived from initial surveys designed to elicit society's preferences for different health states (Kind *et al*. 1982).

Health economists and health researchers have invested a great deal of time and effort into producing reliable and valid utility scales for valuing quality of life. However, to date no single scale has been accepted as the best measure. One British utility scale that has been used in a number of cost-utility analyses over the last ten years is the Rosser matrix. This combines measures of physical and social functioning (disability rating) with an assessment of the psychosocial state of the individual (distress rating). A utility value between 0 and 1 is associated with each of 29 disability/distress combinations (Kind *et al*. 1982). The Rosser matrix has been criticised as unreliable due to the small and unrepresentative sample used to elicit public values for health states (Carr-Hill and Morris 1991). The original utility values were derived from a survey of only 70 respondents consisting of 6 groups – doctors, health volunteers, medical patients, psychiatric patients, medical nurses and psychiatric nurses (Gudex 1986).

As a result of these criticisms the Rosser matrix has largely been discredited as a reliable utility scale. Hence, recent research has been directed to producing and testing more detailed utility-based measures of quality of life using larger, more respresentative survey samples. One such measure is the EuroQol index produced from collaborative survey work by a team of European health researchers (EuroQol Group 1990). The most recent version of the EuroQol instrument used by researchers at York University contains five dimensions of quality of life, each with three rating levels. These are mobility, self-care, ability to perform usual activities, pain/discomfort and anxiety/depression level (Dolan *et al*. 1994).

The EuroQol team have generated values between 0 and 1 for 243 quality of life categories, (which is much greater than the 29 values in the Rosser matrix). Preliminary results from a representative UK sample of 3,395 adults have been presented by the York University team (Dolan *et al*. 1994).

In parallel with the development of the EuroQol scale, a health profile measure, the SF-36, has been advocated for use in economic evaluations (Brazier 1993). The SF-36 has been validated as a good general measure of health status, and is considered easy to administer and complete (Brazier *et al*. 1992). It has been tested alongside the EuroQol classification and found to be as reliable but a more sensitive instrument for health status measurement (Brazier 1993). Although the production of a single utility scale from the eight dimensions of quality of life in the most recent SF-36 measure is still in the developmental stage, it is likely that much debate will be generated on the relative merits of this measure and the EuroQol (and any other scales that might be promoted) for use in economic evaluations in the UK.

Other utility indices have been developed in North America, but have not yet been used in a UK economic evaluation. For example, a measure developed in the USA is Kaplan's quality of well-being scale (QWB). This integrates three subscales representing mobility, physical activity and social activity and relates this to a utility scale with values from 0 to 1. In this measure fine distinctions between utility values are possible due to a negative weighting given to 22 specific symptoms of ill-health such as headaches, lisps and wearing glasses (Kaplan and Anderson 1988).

A Canadian instrument based on mathematical modelling is Torrance's multi-attribute utility scale, which has been used in the study of the cost-effectiveness of neonatal intensive care for low birth weight infants (Boyle *et al.* 1983). This version contained 960 health categories each with a corresponding utility score between 0–1, but has been continually updated since this study (Torrance *et al.* 1992).

Calculating QALYs

The quality of life score of patients after they have received counselling is compared with their pre-counselling score and then combined with their life expectancy pre and post counselling to calculate QALYs gained. Life expectancy at any age can be estimated using life tables produced by the World Health Organisation (Campbell 1977). Within a before/after evaluation, a questionnaire survey of the patients attending the North Brownstead Practice counselling service might find that the average pre-counselling QoL score of patients was 0.6 and they had an average age of 46. From this information, a normal average life expectancy might be predicted at, say, 30 years. Post-counselling follow-up (at 6 months) might produce an average QoL score of 0.8 (no change in life expectancy). The average gain in QALYs per service user are therefore:

$$
\begin{array}{llll}
\text{Without} & \text{With} & & \\
\text{counselling} & \text{counselling} & & \\
[30 \times 0.8] & - \quad [30 \times 0.6] & = & 6 \text{ QALYs gained} \\
& & & \text{per service user}
\end{array}
$$

In the example above, if 300 people use the service per year the total estimated annual QALY gain is 1800. If the cost per service user for the counselling programme is £3,000 the cost per QALY gained is £500 (£3,000/6 QALYs). This calculation assumes the gain in quality of life lasts for the whole 30-year period. Different scenarios of quality of life gain could be examined. For example, it might be estimated that the gain will last for a shorter time period, say 10 years after the counselling programme, and then quality of life is assumed to return to the pre-counselling level of 0.6. The average QALY gain per service user is then:

$$
\begin{array}{lllll}
\text{Without} & \text{With} & & & \\
\text{counselling} & \text{counselling} & & & \\
[30 \times 0.8] & - \quad [10 \times 0.6] & - \quad [20 \times 0.8] & = & 2 \text{ QALYs gained} \\
& & & & \text{per service user}
\end{array}
$$

Total QALY gain is 600 and the cost per QALY gained is now £1,500 (£3,000 per service user/2 QALYs).

The examples used above have been kept simple to illustrate the methods of calculating QALYs. More complex combinations of gains and life expectancies could be incorporated in an evaluation. As future QALY gains are being estimated this is often an area of high uncertainty in the evaluation. The impact on the relative cost-effectiveness results of different assumptions concerning QALY gain could be tested by undertaking a sensitivity analysis (discussed in Chapter 10).

Cost per QALY gained estimates for counselling services could be compared with other healthcare and prevention interventions drawn from several studies within a cost per QALY league table (see Chapter 10). In theory, a beneficial healthcare activity is one that generates a positive amount of QALYs and an efficient healthcare activity is one where the cost per QALY is as low as possible. A high priority healthcare activity is one where the cost per QALY is low and a low priority activity is one where the cost per QALY is high (Drummond et al. 1993).

QALYs might be used to determine which of rival therapies to give to a particular patient or which procedure to use to treat a particular condition. For a given cost, the one generating the most QALYs will represent the best use of society's scarce resources. However, QALYs might also be used to determine which conditions and treatments to give priority to in the allocation of health service resources. QALYs could then be used in priority setting in the healthcare system in general (Ham 1993).

Problems with QALYs

The most vehement objections to QALYs have focused on the ethical issues surrounding their use (this was discussed in depth in Chapter 2). However, even if the principle of using a utility-based measure was accepted on ethical grounds the problem remains that the currently available quality of life measures are technically flawed (Carr-Hill and Morris 1991). For example, each of the instruments available employ a different method of utility calculation which makes comparison between results from studies difficult. Moreover, the utility valuations are meant to reflect society's preferences for different health states. This would be the case if a survey was conducted to generate utility values which covered a representative cross-section of the population. However, in most utility indices the sample sizes are small and unrepresentative (e.g. top-heavy in doctors, health service personnel and patients, while being under-represented by non-medical members of the population). Attempts have been made to produce a 'gold standard' quality of life scale for use in producing QALYs, such as EuroQol, but progress has been slow.

METHODS FOR COLLECTING OUTCOME DATA

The method of collecting outcome data depends on the type of study design chosen.

If an RCT or other controlled study design is used, then the evaluation will involve prospective data collection for one or more intervention groups and a control group, who represent the baseline or 'do-nothing' option. If there is limited time and funds to conduct an evaluation, a before/after intervention analysis is best.

There are three main methods for collecting data on outcomes. First, monitoring forms can be used to record process indicators such as the number of patients with psychosexual problems seen by a counsellor in a GP surgery, the number of information sheets distributed to patients or the number of days of nurse absenteeism that may be related to job stress (for an example, see Table 9.1). In addition, records could be kept of the basic characteristics of service users such as age, sex, medical history. This data may already be routinely collected by the service providers or it may be possible to incorporate the collection of such information within existing record-keeping mechanisms. It may even be possible to collect data for assessing intermediate outcomes using this approach. If so, this will reduce the cost of data collection.

Second, service users in each group (including the do-nothing) could be surveyed. This approach is usually required for the accurate measurement of intermediate and final outcomes. This could involve the use of a standard questionnaire covering all individuals (with filters to avoid asking inappropriate questions) or several questionnaires for different groups of service user. Indeed, a questionnaire could be designed to collect information assessing both personal costs and the effectiveness of each option. The use of several questionnaires might improve the accuracy of data collection but increase evaluation costs. As with the collection of cost data these could be self-completion or interview-based questionnaires. If a before/after design is adopted the format of the questionnaire could provide information on such items as the characteristics of the service users and changes in intermediate or final outcome after receiving the intervention.

Third, classifications of well-being or quality of life outcomes are generated from survey work. The responses are used to produce utility scores for different patient groups. Modifications can be made to such questionnaires to make them more appropriate for measuring outcomes associated with counselling. However, if the objective of the evaluation is to compare the cost-effectiveness of counselling with other healthcare interventions, care must be taken that the modifications do not substantially reduce the generalisability of the instrument selected (i.e. so that it becomes a counselling specific measure making it less reliable for comparing outcomes with other health care interventions).

THE RELATIONSHIP BETWEEN OUTCOME MEASURES

Process indicators, intermediate outcomes and final outcomes represent a linked set of outcome measures. The collection of data to measure final outcome maybe difficult to undertake in service settings. An alternative strategy is to measure

Table 9.1 Recording nurse absenteeism in a hospital setting – an example of a monitoring form

SMITHLAND HOSPITAL

Staff name		Day of Month 1	2	3	4	5	6	7	8	9	10	11	12	13	14	15	16	17	18	19	20	21	22	23	24	25	26	27	28	29	30	31
Jane Roach	Code	A	A	…	…																											
	Time off	FD	HD	…	…																											
Alison Smith	Code																															
	Time off																															
Rosie Legget	Code		B	B	B	B	…	…																								
	Time off	FD	FD	FD		…	…																									
Amy Town	Code																															
	Time off																															
John Curtis	Code			A																												
	Time off			2																												
Sarah Joppy	Code																															
	Time off																															

Record absenteeism according to following codes:
A: Sick   B: Holiday/annual leave   C: Other, e.g. maternity leave

Time off:
FD = Full day   HD = Half day
If less than HD record hours

intermediate outcomes and project the impact on final outcomes. However, the reliability of this approach depends on the extent to which reasonable estimates can be made of the association between intermediate and final outcomes.

SHORT CUTS TO OUTCOME MEASUREMENT

As a substitute for the use of questionnaires or other survey techniques, a short-cut approach useful for assessing final outcomes is to use expert judgement of the likely effectiveness of different counselling options. It is a crude approach to quality of life estimation but has the merit of simplicity and can produce quick and useable data (if used with caution). Using expert judgement requires the identification of an appropriate expert or set of experts. These might be the evaluator, the counselling service providers, counsellor, or other health professionals such as GPs. In a more sophisticated analysis a 'panel of experts' consisting of a number of specialists can be set up to provide estimates of outcomes. Expert judgement could be used to estimate QALY gains, whereby the designated experts could provide a best guess of the patient gain in quality of life (using a utility scale) and life years from an intervention. For example, in the study by Williams (1985) of the cost per QALY gained due to coronary artery bypass grafting (CABG), he asked three cardiologists to provide their expert judgement as to the expected utility gain for a typical patient with different degrees of angina. This represented a relatively sophisticated use of the expert judgement approach and may not be feasible in a counselling evaluation. The evaluator may feel that his or her own judgement of quality of life or utility gain is sufficient or is the best that can be attempted given limited time and resources for the study. For example, the evaluator of the counselling service in the North Brownstead Practice may estimate that the average quality of life or utility score of patients with psychosocial problems prior to receiving counselling from a counsellor or clinical psychologists is 0.7, but judges that this would increase to 0.8 at 6 months after receiving counselling. The assumption might be that no change in quality of life is expected for patients who receive the do-nothing option – GP care and support. The evaluator may check his or her estimates by asking the opinion of a number of GPs or other health professionals not involved in the evaluation.

Expert judgement can be used for other types of outcome measure, in particular intermediate outcomes. For instance, best estimates could be made of the expected change in staff absenteeism from staff counselling programmes introduced into a Trust hospital, such as the Smithland Hospital. Similarly, process indicator effectiveness could be estimated such as the number of people expected to take an information sheet publicising the availability of a counselling service.

As an alternative or a complement to the use of expert judgement, the evaluator may be able to use evidence from previous evaluations of the cost-effectiveness or effectiveness of counselling interventions. However, given the paucity of such evaluations it may be difficult to find appropriate and reliable empirical evidence of outcomes.

In using a short-cut approach to outcome measurement, caution must be exercised not to assume high reliability in the estimates produced. Because of the uncertainty over reliability a range of high and low estimates should be tested using sensitivity analysis to examine the effect on the cost-effectiveness results (see Chapter 10 for details of sensitivity analysis).

EXTERNAL BENEFITS

In measuring intermediate and final outcomes a distinction can be made between the direct and a secondary (or 'external') impact of a counselling intervention. A direct impact of the counselling service provided in the GP surgery might be that patients presenting with a psychosocial problem alter their lifestyle in some way to improve their personal well-being. An external benefit may be achieved if, as a result of the patients' behaviour change, other people that they interact with, such as family and friends, also change their lifestyle as an attempt to improve their well-being. However, a complex study design is needed to measure accurately secondary benefits, so that, for reasons of time and expense, most economic evaluations of counselling programmes are likely to focus on direct benefits.

SUMMARY OF THE DATA COLLECTION PHASE (I, II AND III)

Chapters 7, 8 and 9 have outlined the steps in the data collection phase of a cost-effectiveness analysis. A range of methods has been presented for choosing a study design, measuring costs and evaluating outcomes. In Chapter 7 two types of study design for collecting cost and outcome data are presented as randomised controlled trials and before/after studies; the former is the more rigorous but also the more time consuming, costly and complex approach for evaluating counselling interventions in service settings. A large part of Chapter 8 focused on the detailed measurement of costs – what cost components to include, how to collect resource use data for calculating costs and the problem of attaching a unit cost to different resource inputs. Some short-cut approaches to costing were presented for those evaluations with limited time and money resources available. In a cost-effectiveness analysis a common outcome measure is required to compare the effectiveness of the options. In Chapter 9 three types of outcome measure were considered – process indicators, intermediate outcomes and final outcomes. Final outcomes such as quality of life scales and QALYs enable counselling options to be compared with a wide range of healthcare interventions. However, given the large number of QoL or health status instruments available caution should be exercised in the choice of measure for a cost-effectiveness analysis of counselling programmes. Finally, a number of short-cut approaches to the evaluation of outcomes were presented.

NOTE

1   Economists use the term utility to represent satisfaction. Health economists use the term in cost-utility analysis to represent a value for quality of life.

Chapter 10

Analysing cost-effectiveness data

Introduction
Cost-effectiveness measures
Discounting costs and benefits
Dealing with uncertainty
Using sensitivity analysis

INTRODUCTION

In the analysis of data the first and most important problem is how to combine cost and outcome data to determine the relative cost-effectiveness of the options in the evaluation. Two types of cost-effectiveness measure can be presented using average or marginal costs. These correspond to the different economic objectives set in the evaluation planning stage (see Chapter 5).

Economic theory suggests that institutions and individuals in society, in choosing how to use resources, prefer to delay incurring costs but wish to obtain immediate benefits. The adjustment of the cost-effectiveness ratios to allow for the differential timing of costs and outcomes in counselling evaluations is known as 'discounting'. The discount rate represents the rate at which the value of future costs and benefits declines over time. This means that a counselling programme that has immediate benefits in terms of the reduction in stress levels among the service users will be preferred to a programme which only produces the same benefits after two years for the same cost. If discounting is included in an evaluation of such options, the counselling programme with immediate benefits will represent the more cost-effective option.

The level of uncertainty in an evaluation needs to be assessed. The principle of uncertainty implies that the estimates of costs, outcomes and the discount rates used in the evaluation may be incorrect. There is bound to be some level of error and imprecision in the data collection and analysis and in the assumptions used to produce cost and outcome estimates. Whether the level of error threatens to invalidate the cost-effectiveness results depends on the level of uncertainty about the accuracy of the data.

Uncertainty should be incorporated into the cost-effectiveness analysis by the use of a range of high and low estimates for the key variables, costs, outcomes and the discount rate used. The technique used to examine the sensitivity of the cost-effectiveness results with different estimates for these key variables is known as sensitivity analysis. If a counselling option was found to be the most cost-effective using the initial cost, outcome and discount rate estimates but was less cost-effective once uncertainty was assessed then measures should be taken to improve the accuracy of the original data.

There are a number of issues regarding the presentation and interpretation of the cost-effectiveness results. One topical issue is the use of 'league tables' for examining the relative cost-effectiveness of a wide range of alternative healthcare and prevention options. There is much debate about the usefulness of cost-effectiveness league tables for assisting purchasing decisions in the NHS (Drummond *et al.* 1993).

Finally, cost-effectiveness analysis is typically used to examine value for money and efficiency in the use of provider agency, health service and society's resources. However, equity objectives may be at least as important as efficiency objectives in the use of resources. Equity considerations question whether a certain use of resources, such as the provision of a counselling service for people with psychosexual problems rather than expanding health education services for smokers, is fair and just.

In this chapter the North Brownstead evaluation is primarily used to illustrate the analysis of cost-effectiveness data. However, the same principles apply for the Smithland Trust evaluation and interested readers could follow the same process with this case study.

COST-EFFECTIVENESS MEASURES

The analysis of the costs and outcomes data and presentation of the cost-effectiveness results depend on the economic objectives that were defined for the evaluation (see Chapter 5). Three cost-effectiveness measures are used to address different economic objectives: average, incremental and marginal cost-effectiveness. Average cost-effectiveness corresponds to the set of economic objectives concerned with achieving the greatest outcome for lowest cost. Incremental cost-effectiveness corresponds to the set of objectives concerned with assessing the value of achieving a higher outcome through the use of a more costly option. Marginal cost-effectiveness relates to objectives defined as achieving a greater outcome from an expansion of an option.

Average cost-effectiveness

With average cost-effectiveness (ACE) the option which has the lowest cost per unit of outcome or greatest outcome per £1 of cost represents the most cost-effective option. For example, alternative screening techniques may be considered in a breast cancer screening programme. The technique that produces the greatest number of true positives for each £1 spent will be the most cost-effective option. In practice, analysis is likely to involve more detailed examination of the costs and outcomes data. In the North Brownstead evaluation total costs over a one-year trial might be estimated at £25,000 and £20,000 respectively for the counsellor and clinical psychologist options and £5,000 for the do-nothing option. Table 10.1 presents figures for two types of outcome measure (i.e. the number of patients seen and the reduction in patients attending with psychosocial problems at the end of the trial period). The former measure is a process indicator and the latter is an intermediate outcome measure. This data could be used to examine cost-effectiveness relating to a number of economic objectives. One objective might be to identify the option with the lowest cost per patient seen. In total, 250 patients saw the counsellor, 100 saw the clinical psychologist and 50 saw a general practitioner (the numbers are deliberately high in order to simplify the calculations). The lowest cost option at £100 per patient seen would be the counsellor (ACE = £25,000/250) or the do-nothing option (ACE = £5,000/50).

Table 10.1   Total costs and average cost-effectiveness of interventions in the North Brownstead evaluation (six-month trial)

Intervention	Patients seen	Total cost £s	Cost per patient seen £s	Reduction in psycho-social problems %	Cost per 1 % reduction in psychosocial problems £s
Counsellor	250	25,000	100	30	833
Clinical psychologist	100	20,000	200	10	2,000
Do-nothing (GP care)	50	5,000	100	4	1,250

However, number of patients seen is a poor indicator of relative effectiveness, especially if a controlled study design is used. A more meaningful outcome measure would be to use the percentage reduction in patients consulting the GP up to three months after the intervention. Using this outcome measure the most effective option is the counsellor with a 30 per cent reduction in patients returning with psychosocial problems ($n=75$). Ten of the 100 patients attending the clinical psychologist did not return to the GP with similar problems (a 10 per cent reduction). Table 10.1 shows that the most cost-effective option using this outcome measure is the counsellor at £833 per one per cent reduction (ACE = £25,000/30) compared to £2,000 (ACE = £20,000/10) for the clinical psychologist.

It is important to include a 'do-nothing' option. If 2 of the 50 patients (4 per cent) with psychosocial problems who consulted the GP did not return after 3 months the average cost-effectiveness for the do-nothing option would be £1,250 (ACE = £5,000/4). These results suggest that the clinical psychologist option would not be a cost-effective option relative to existing practice.

It may be necessary to examine cost-effectiveness within certain constraints such as the requirement to meet a defined outcome target and/or the need to operate within a cost limit. If a target was set of a 10 per cent reduction in the percentage of patients with psychosocial problems returning after 3 months to the North Brownstead Practice, then only the 2 active counselling interventions could be considered in the cost-effectiveness analysis. If the target was 20 per cent, only the counsellor would meet this criteria. In this example, setting targets would not alter the selection of the 'best' option. However, if a cost limit of £20,000 was applied the most cost-effective option, the counsellor, would not be affordable as the total cost of this option was £25,000. In this case, maintaining current practice (i.e. the GPs caring for patients) would be the most cost-effective choice of the two options that are within the cost limit.

Incremental and marginal cost-effectiveness

Incremental cost-effectiveness refers to a situation in which an intervention that is more effective than the next best alternative is also more costly. In contrast, marginal cost-effectiveness includes an investigation of the marginal cost or marginal saving from expanding or contracting a particular counselling service.

The use of incremental cost-effectiveness can be illustrated using the example of a breast cancer screening programme, comparing alternative techniques for the detection of abnormalities. In this programme technique A, used for the screening of 1,000 women with breast cancer, might detect 800 true positives at a cost of £5,000, while technique B used with the same women might detect 900 true positives but at a higher total cost of £6,000. The cost per true positive case for technique A is £6.25 (£5,000/800) compared to £6.66 (£6,000/900) for technique B. Therefore, on the basis of average cost-effectiveness technique A will be chosen. However, the evaluator is in a dilemma in that a greater effectiveness (i.e. 100 additional true positives, can be obtained by using technique B although average cost-effectiveness is poorer for this option). This is where incremental cost-effectiveness is a useful aid to decision-making. The important evidence may not be the average costs but consideration of the question of what additional outcome can be achieved at what additional cost? For example, the incremental cost per additional true positive case for technique B compared to technique A is £10 (£1,000/100). Whether the identification of an additional 100 true positives is deemed worth the extra cost per case then rests with the decision-maker and depends on the original economic objectives.

An assessment of marginal cost-effectiveness involves judgements about the value of extra benefits from the expansion of a health programme. A classic example of this approach is provided in a study of the cost-effectiveness of the use of the guaiac stool test for detecting asymptomatic colonic cancer (Neuhauser and Lewicki 1975). The clinical literature at the time argued that up to six sequential sets of stool tests were required in order to determine the presence of colonic cancer. Neuhauser and Lewicki examined the average and marginal costs of conducting each additional test on a population of 10,000 people (of whom 72 were subsequently found to be true positives for cancer), with marginal effectiveness measured by the additional percentage of true positives detected. Table 10.2 presents their findings.

Table 10.2 The average and marginal costs of screening for colonic cancer by sequential guaiac tests

Number of test sets	Total cases*	Total costs $s	Average costs $s	Marginal costs $s
1	65.9469	77,511	1,175	1,175
2	71.4424	107,690	1,507	5,492
3	71.9003	130,199	1,811	49,150
4	71.9385	148,116	2,059	469,534
5	71.9417	163,141	2,268	4,724,695
6	71.9420	176,331	2,451	47,107,214

Source: Neuhauser and Lewicki (1975)
Note: * True positives

The first stool test identified 91.6 per cent of true positives and each further test was found to identify a further 91.67 per cent of the remaining undetected cases so that by the sixth test virtually all the cases were identified. While the average cost per case detected appeared reasonable at $2,451, analysis of the marginal cost-effectiveness of conducting the sixth test was extremely high at $47 million, demonstrating the minute benefit to be had from carrying out six rather than fewer tests. The marginal cost evidence suggests that carrying out more than two tests would not be a worthwhile use of resources in terms of the very small number of extra true positives that could be identified. It is probable that diverting the resources that would otherwise be committed to conducting the six tests to another health intervention would yield greater benefits.

While this example is a good illustration of the potential importance of assessing marginal as well as average costs, the analysis of Neuhauser and Lewicki has been criticised by Brown and Burrows (1990). They argue that the calculations of the guaiac test's sensitivity (how accurately it records a true positive) and specificity (how accurately it records a false negative) are incorrect, as a result of which the false positive rate is underestimated. If corrected, the marginal cost estimates are drastically reduced and are much closer to the estimates of average cost.

Despite the potential error in the Neuhauser and Lewicki analysis the main point we want to make is that in evaluations of the expansion or contraction of a counselling service it is important to assess marginal cost-effectiveness in addition to average cost-effectiveness, as different results with different policy implications could be produced.

In both incremental and marginal analysis one option represents the do-nothing or baseline. In the case of the breast cancer screening programme the baseline would be the use of technique A. In the six guaiac stool test study the sixth test is the baseline as this represents the scientific recommendation that would otherwise be adopted if no cost data was presented. In this case the aim of marginal cost-effectiveness analysis was to demonstrate the benefits of contracting the programme (i.e. conducting fewer tests).

In the North Brownstead evaluation the do-nothing option (i.e. GP usual care) achieved a 4 per cent reduction in patients returning with psychosocial problems (Table 10.1). In terms of average cost-effectiveness this option was more cost-effective than the use of a clinical psychologist or counsellor. While both the clinical psychologist and counsellor options are more effective they also have a higher cost. If the evaluator wanted to obtain a greater outcome than a 4 per cent reduction, further analysis is needed. The difference in costs between the do-nothing option and the clinical psychologist is £15,000, with the latter achieving a further 6 per cent reduction in patients with psychosocial problems. Therefore, the incremental cost of using the clinical psychologist compared to the do-nothing option is £2,500 per additional one per cent reduction in patients returning with psychosocial problems (ICE = £15,000/6). Using the same approach the incremental cost of the counsellor option compared to the do-nothing option is £769 per additional one per cent reduction in patients returning with psychosocial problems (ICE = £20,000/26). Table 10.3 summarises the incremental cost-effectiveness results.

Table 10.3 Incremental cost-effectiveness of the clinical psychologist and specialist counsellor options in the North Brownstead evaluation

Intervention	Total cost £	Additional % reduction in psychosocial problems* %	Incremental cost per extra 1 % reduction in psychosocial problems* £'s
Counsellor	25,000	26	769
Clinical psychologist	20,000	6	2,500
'Do-nothing' (GP care)	5,000	–	–

Note: * Relative to baseline 'do-nothing' option

As a second stage of the North Brownstead evaluation, the evaluator might want to assess the marginal costs of expanding the clinical psychologist option. For example, the possibility of employing a full-time clinical psychologist in the GP surgery working alongside a counsellor might be examined. If this were found to result in an additional 4 per cent reduction in patients returning with psychosocial problems after a one-year trial period at an extra cost of £10,000 the marginal cost-effectiveness would be £2,500. The evaluator would need to consider the evidence alongside service objectives and other criteria to determine whether the expansion of the counselling programme (as provided by the clinical psychologist) was a worthwhile use of resources.

DISCOUNTING COSTS AND BENEFITS

As we discussed in Chapter 3, cost-benefit analysis is a technique in which all the costs and benefits are valued in monetary units. A general principle of cost-benefit analysis is that people and agencies prefer to delay costs but desire immediate benefits. Hence future benefits and costs should have a lower valuation compared to current benefits and costs. This is known as time preference, and explains why, for example, consumers may prefer to pay for a washing machine on hire purchase or interest-free credit, or will not deposit money in a restricted access savings account unless a high rate of interest is paid on the sum. Similarly, an individual's decision to smoke tobacco and consume alcohol may reflect his or her preference to enjoy these activities now at the potential cost of an increased risk of ill-health in the future.

In health economics there is general agreement concerning the rationale and logic for discounting costs and monetary savings (Keeler and Cretin 1983). The degree of time preference for costs is represented by a discount rate. The use of a 10 per cent discount rate means that individuals value future costs less than if the discount rate was 5 per cent. For example, if the credit period on a £500 washing machine was 50 weeks the application of a social discount rate of 10 per cent would make this deal appear more attractive than if preferences for delaying costs were lower, for example if a 5 per cent discount rate was applied.

In the UK the evaluation of a counselling programme provided with public funds within the NHS would apply social discount rates that reflect society's time preferences. In contrast, investment in counselling services in the private sector, for example a staff support service in a private hospital, should reflect the time preference of the owners of the hospital. Their time preference is different from members of society, and will more closely reflect the returns that could be obtained by investing funds in other assets (e.g. returns depend on prevailing rates of interest set in the UK money market for different types of investment or borrowing arrangement). Hence for private sector initiatives, costs and financial returns should be discounted at a private discount rate.

Having identified future costs that require discounting, the main problem is to select an appropriate discount rate. The prevailing interest rates in the UK money market (where funds might instead be invested) could be utilised to determine the appropriate private discount rate to use in an evaluation of a private sector counselling service. In general, the baseline rate adopted in most UK evaluations of healthcare interventions provided within the NHS is the rate used by the UK Treasury for appraising their investment in public sector schemes (known as the test discount rate, currently at 6 per cent – 1993 figures). Because there is no agreement that this is the best rate to use, previous economic evaluations in healthcare settings have used a baseline social discount rate between 0 per cent and 10 per cent.

It is less straightforward to determine an appropriate social discount rate for use in evaluations such as the North Brownstead Practice and Smithland Trust Hospital. There is a formula for discounting costs (see Table 10.4), but it is more practical to use a discounting table (reproduced in Annex 10.1). Let us assume that the counsellor options in the North Brownstead evaluation result in a need for follow-up counselling of patients at one-and-a-half and two years after the initial intervention. These future costs should be discounted. The method to calculate the discounted costs involves three main steps:

1 Select a baseline discount rate, for example 6 per cent.
2 Produce an estimate of the expected time period for future costs, for example two years.
3 Choose a discount rate and the expected time period for future costs to identify the appropriate discount factor using the discounting table (Annex 10.1). Annex 10.1 shows that the discount factor for a 6 per cent discount rate and 2–year time period is 0.890. Multiplying 0.890 by the expected second year costs produces an estimate of the present value of these future costs.

Table 10.4 Formula for discounting costs

Total cost =	Year 0	Year 1	Year 2	Year 3	Year 4
	C_0 +	C_1 +	C_2 +	C_3	— C_n
		$1+r$	$(1=r)^2$	$(1=r)^3$	$(1=r)^n$

$$(\text{Present discounted value}) = \sum \frac{C_j}{(1+r)^j}$$

Where C = annual cost, n=discount rate and years, $j=0 - - - n$

Source: Pearce and Nash (1981)
Note: It may be more practical to use the table in Annex 10.1 and assume that any costs incurred within a year are discounted at a zero rate

There is no minimum time period for discounting. However, economic evaluations of health programmes generally do not apply discounting to costs occurring less than one year after the initial intervention. This is partly due to the argument that society does not have a time preference for incurring costs within the time period, and partly because the tables of discount factors operate on an annual basis. Therefore, any costs incurred within a year do not need to be discounted.

In the Smithland Trust evaluation the costs of follow-up counselling of nurses 3 years after the initial intervention might be estimated at £15,550. From the discount table in Annex 10.1 the appropriate discount factor is 0.890 relating to a 6 per cent discount rate and costs expected 2 years after the first year of the intervention (for reasons outlined in the previous paragraph any costs incurred in the first year are not subject to discounting). The discounted cost estimate produced is £13,894. It is this figure that should be used in the cost analysis. Any costs expected in subsequent years should also be discounted in the same way. In addition, if future savings to the health sevice were predicted, for example due to reduced sick leave payments to staff, the discounted value should also be included in the evaluation.

It is important to note that if the evaluation lasts for more than one year, this does not necessarily mean that the costs occurring in the second and subsequent years should be discounted. Discounting should be applied if costs occurring in the second year are related to the intervention in the first year or resources for use in the second year are diverted from other uses in the first year. Employing a counsellor in the second year is a current cost that results from inputs incurred in that same year.

The discounting of costs and monetary benefits should be adopted in all types of economic evaluation, except financial appraisals. The principle of discounting does not apply to process indicators (which measure effectiveness of the delivery of a service and occur only in the current time period) or intermediate outcome measures such as behaviour change (the value of which cannot be quantified by a single common unit). The validity of discounting final outcomes such as QALYs is debatable. Because outcomes are not usually expressed in monetary terms in a cost-effectiveness study there is no consensus on whether QALYs or other measures of health benefit should be discounted. The debate concerning the discounting of QALYs has centred around the question of whether individuals have a time preference for health gain now rather than in the future in the same way they might have a preference for gaining monetary benefits now rather than later in life (Cairns 1991; Coyle and Tolley 1992; Parsonage and Neuberger 1992). However, it will only be an important issue in analysis of the cost-effectiveness of counselling programmes if these interventions produce benefits lasting longer than one year. If the evaluator considering the use of QALYs decides to discount them, it is advisable to use sensitivity analysis to allow for uncertainty regarding the appropriate rate.

DEALING WITH UNCERTAINTY

Uncertainty exists in the accuracy of estimates and assumptions used in a cost-effectiveness analysis. Uncertainty relates to three sets of data:

1   Cost estimates.
2   Outcome measurement.
3   Appropriate discount rate for costs (and outcomes).

It is important that the evaluator identifies areas of uncertainty in the evaluation, decides the level of uncertainty that exists and then tests the impact this has on the reliability of the cost-effectiveness results. Where uncertainty exists a range of cost-effectiveness results should be produced using the high and low estimates for costs, outcomes and discount rates. The techniques used to examine the importance of uncertainty in these variables in terms of reducing the reliability of the relative cost-effectiveness results is known as sensitivity analysis, which is examined in the next section.

Uncertain costs

Uncertainty in cost estimates could be a consequence of imprecision in one or more parts of the costing process. The cost estimates produced for the Smithland Trust Hospital evaluation might be examined for uncertainty in three areas of the cost measurement process.

First, the evaluator may be uncertain about the accuracy of the estimates of resource inputs for each option. The level of evaluator uncertainty is likely to be higher the less rigorous the method of data collection used. Hence, for the counsellor option if the estimation of the hours of counsellor time spent in direct contact with nurses was based on the observation of a third person (e.g. a manager) this would be expected to be less reliable than a recording procedure completed by the counsellor immediately after seeing a client.

A second area of uncertainty concerns the unit cost valuation for each resource input. For example, the best estimate for the unit cost of the counsellor in the Smithland Trust Hospital might be £10.41 per hour based on a gross salary of £417 per week (£20,000 per annum divided by 48 working weeks after subtracting holiday and assuming that the counsellor works a 40-hour week). However, the evaluator might be uncertain about whether the unit cost should be derived assuming a 40-hour week or a 48-week year given that the counsellor in a typical week undertakes unpaid overtime, but would also be expected to take time off work for sickness and to spend time on administration, record keeping and supervision.

Third, if intangible and personal costs were included in the evaluation the precision of the estimates produced for these might be uncertain. For example, it might be estimated that the nurses attending the staff support group in the Smithland Trust study spend an average one and a half hours per week preparing for, getting to and attending each session. If an average of 10 people attended the group each week the estimated total weekly time input would be 15 hours. However, the evaluator might not trust the accuracy of the time estimate as the data were derived from the use of a very simple self-completion questionnaire completed by each participant retrospectively. In addition, if the session was conducted in out-of-work hours the opportunity cost for the nurses' time might be estimated at £3.00 per hour, on the assumption that this represents the value of leisure (or at least non-work) time given up to attend. However, this value might represent the 'best guess' of the evaluator and so would be unreliable.

In each of the examples above the level of evaluator uncertainty could be accounted for by the production of high and/or low estimates for the quantity of tangible and intangible inputs and the unit costs (prices and values). The less certainty regarding the precision of the original estimate the greater should be the difference between this and the high/low estimates. For example, the best estimate of the Smithland Trust Hospital manager of counsellor time spent seeing nurse employees is 15 hours per week. The evaluator might consider this to be an imprecise estimate. Therefore, if a prospective monitoring exercise to assess the time use of the counsellor over one week was carried out which produced an estimate of 20 hours the evaluator might decide this was a more reliable estimate. However, it might be that this represented a week in which the counsellor saw more clients than usual. Hence in the final evaluation 20 hours could represent the high estimate, 15 the low and 17.5 (the mid-point) as a 'best estimate'. The unit cost of £10.41 could be adjusted to allow for a 45-week working year (i.e. subtracting maximum expected sick days), producing a high unit cost estimate of £11.11, and a 50-hour working week (i.e. 10 hours unpaid) producing a low unit cost estimate of £8.33. Indeed, if the principle of opportunity costing is to be applied the 10 hours unpaid work should be costed at a rate reflecting the value of foregone leisure (non-work) time.

In addition, low and high estimates could be produced for the personal costs of the time incurred by nurses attending the staff support group. For example, the low estimate may involve an assumption of one hour attendance time, the high estimate might involve one and a half hours attendance time. The cost estimates could then be adjusted accordingly. If it is assumed that nurses attend the staff support group in their own time, the opportunity cost would be the value of their foregone leisure time.

Dealing with uncertainty involves examining each part of the costing process. In practice, the costing may not include as many cost components as have been used in this example. The cost assessment from the perspective of the Smithland Hospital might only include the direct costs of counsellor time, overheads and materials for each option, making dealing with uncertainty much simpler. Even in a more thorough costing the evaluator may simply produce high and low estimates for the total cost of each option, based on an estimate of the overall level of uncertainty in the cost estimation process. Thus, original estimates for the total cost of the counsellor and staff support group options in the Smithland Trust evaluation of £30,000 and £25,000 respectively might be produced. The cost of the former option might then be adjusted by 10 per cent upwards and downwards and the latter by 5 per cent to allow for evaluator uncertainty in the various parts of the cost estimation process so that the cost range for the counsellor is £27,000 to £33,000 and for the staff support group is £23,750 to £26,250. If the outcome measure used was the reduction in staff absenteeism with the counsellor producing an estimated saving of five working days and the staff support group three days, the relative cost-effectiveness results for the high, low and original cost estimates can be calculated. These are presented in Table 10.5.

Table 10.5 Average cost-effectiveness results for the Smithland Trust Hospital evaluation: allowing for uncertainty in the cost estimates

Intervention	Total cost range £	Working days saved	Average cost-effectiveness. Cost per working day saved using:		
			High cost estimate £	Low cost estimate £	Original cost estimate £
Counsellor	27,000– 33,000	5	6,600	5,400	6,000
Staff support group	23,750– 26,250	3	8,750	7,917	8,333

Although allowing for uncertainty is a relatively simple process, it is important that the evaluator identifies as accurately as possible the areas of uncertainty so that the high and low total cost adjustments made are justifiable.

Uncertain outcomes

Imprecision in the measurement of process indicators, intermediate outcomes or final outcomes occurs in two main areas. First, the approach to data collection influences the reliability of the outcome estimates. A prospective questionnaire survey which follows patients with psychosocial problems who have seen a counsellor over a one-year period can be expected to produce more reliable outcome estimates, for example, reduction in numbers of these patients presenting to the practice, than a similar questionnaire with only one-month follow-up. Second, the problem of attributing specific outcomes to an intervention causes uncertainty in the results. However sophisticated the method of data collection, it is difficult to be certain that the reason for the reduction in consultations of patients with psychosocial problems can be attributed to the counsellor or clinical psychologist options. It is even more difficult to attribute outcomes, such as well-being gains among patients seeing a counsellor in the GP surgery, which may only be identified well after the intervention (for example, six months to a year).

The level of imprecision varies with the type of outcome measure used. Process indicators, such as the numbers of relaxation tapes handed out at the staff support group sessions in the Smithland Hospital, are relatively easy to measure accurately.

In contrast, final outcomes from counselling programmes are difficult to measure accurately. One factor is that the instruments, such as those available to measure quality-of-life or well-being outcomes, have differing degrees of reliability and validity (Bowling 1991). Utility measures used in the estimation of QALYs have been criticised on theoretical, practical and ethical grounds (see Chapter 2).

As we demonstrated in Chapter 9, QALY-gained estimates are highly uncertain as they are usually based on a relatively short post-intervention follow-up and simplistic assumptions of the future quality-of-life benefits. These problems are likely to exist in an evaluation of counselling interventions. The only way to reduce significantly this uncertainty would be to conduct a large-scale evaluation with quality-of-life outcomes measured for several years after the intervention. However, the cost and complexity of such an evaluation means this is unlikely to be a feasible strategy.

Uncertainties are likely to be greatest for final outcomes, less so for intermediate outcomes and lowest for process indicators. Given these differences in uncertainty of outcomes it would be expected that a wider range of estimates would be used for final outcomes than intermediate outcomes, and that some process indicators may not need any application of high and/or low estimates. In the North Brownstead evaluation a range of estimates can be produced for the reduction in patients presenting with psychosocial problems after three-month follow-up. The best estimate for the counsellor was a 20 per cent reduction, but the evaluator may consider that the uncertainty of this outcome warrants high and low estimates of 25 per cent and 12 per cent respectively. These would then be included in the analysis of cost-effectiveness. If quality-of-life was measured using a specially constructed instrument designed for use with patients with psychosocial problems the uncertainty over the reliability of the questionnaire and the responses of individuals completing the questionnaire could be included by the production of high and low estimates for quality-of-life scores.

Uncertain discount rates

The biggest problem in discounting future costs is the appropriate discount rate to use. Uncertainty over the timing of future costs and the choice of social discount rate is best dealt with using a range of estimates (high and low), rather than attempting to identify the 'correct' rate (for which there is currently no consensus amongst policy-makers or economists). The approach used in most cost-effectiveness analyses of healthcare programmes is to take a discount rate equal to the standard UK Treasury level of 6 per cent as the best estimate, an upper limit of a 10 per cent discount rate and a lower limit of 3 per cent. The evidence that individuals or agencies have a preference for delaying costs is theoretically and empirically appealing so that there seems no justification for including a zero discount rate for future costs as a low estimate.

In the previous section it was demonstrated that an undiscounted cost of £15,550 for follow-up counselling occurring two years after the initial intervention in the

Smithland Trust evaluation would be £13,894 if discounted using a 'best estimate' of a 6 per cent discount rate. If a 10 and 3 per cent discount rate was applied to allow for uncertainty, the discounted cost range for follow-up counselling would be £12,850 to £14,657. (Using Table 10.4 or Annex 10.1 the discount factor for a 10 per cent discount rate and a 2-year time period is 0.8264 and for 3 per cent is 0.9426.) Unless a prospective randomised controlled trial (RCT) is undertaken there may be uncertainty regarding the timing of the expected costs. Hence the future costs of follow-up may be predicted to occur anything up to five years after the intervention. In this case the 5-year timing could be used to produce a low-cost estimate combined with a 10 per cent discount rate. From the discount factor (Table 10.4) the new low-cost estimate would be £9,655. This is substantially below the estimate for a 10 per cent discount rate and 2-year follow-up costs, demonstrating the sensitivity of the cost estimates according to when they are expected to occur.

As was discussed earlier the evaluator also faces the problem of whether to discount final outcomes that occur in the future, for example, life years or QALYs gained from counselling. There is no standard practice and health economists disagree not only over whether discounting of health-related benefits should be undertaken but also, if discounting is undertaken, whether the rate used should be the same or differ from that used for costs (Coyle and Tolley 1992). The best advice seems to be that provided by the Department of Health stating that all new cost-utility analyses should include an assessment of undiscounted costs (Parsonage and Neuberger 1992). We suggest that this should also represent the best estimate for the evaluation of counselling programmes in which life years gained or QALYs are the outcome measures used. As with costs, discount rates of 6 per cent and/or 10 per cent could then be used as high estimates for final outcomes (benefits).

USING SENSITIVITY ANALYSIS

Sensitivity analysis provides information to assess whether the relative cost-effectiveness of various options alters due to the inclusion of high and low estimates for one or more of the key variables of costs, outcomes and discount rates. The range of estimates are produced to allow for uncertainty in the assumptions used and in the precision of the original estimates. Low reliability due to high uncertainty in the original cost-effectiveness estimates for each option is implied if relative cost-effectiveness is changed when high or low estimates are applied. In this case, the evaluator may need to increase the level of precision, (for example, through better data collection or more careful analysis) to achieve meaningful results in those key variables with the highest level of uncertainty (i.e. to reduce the range between the high and low estimate).

Table 10.6 outlines the use of sensitivity analysis for the counsellor and clinical psychologist options in the North Brownstead evaluation. The effect of including high and low estimates for the costs and outcomes of these two options on the average and marginal cost-effectiveness results are presented in the table.

The lowest estimated average cost-effectiveness result for the clinical psychologist option is £1,000 per one per cent reduction in patients returning with psychosocial problems. This is based on a low total cost of £15,000 and a high estimate of a 15 per cent reduction in patients presenting with psychosocial problems. This is lower than the average cost estimate for the 'do-nothing' option of £1,250 but above the original estimate for the counsellor option (£833). Hence, the counsellor remains the most cost-effective option even after allowing for uncertainty in the cost and outcome estimates of the clinical psychologist intervention.

However, the evaluator might believe that the cost estimate for the counsellor is underestimated. A high cost estimate of, for example, £36,500 might be applied to examine the impact on the cost-effectiveness results. Combining this cost figure with an original outcome of a 30 per cent reduction in patients returning with psychosocial problems the average cost is £1,217 per one per cent reduction. This is below the original estimates for the other two options but is less cost effective relative to the most favourable estimate for the clinical psychologist (£1,000). In this case the problem of uncertainty has led to ambiguous cost-effectiveness results, depending on which cost and outcome estimates are applied. The reliability of selecting any one option using this data is questionable and other non-economic information would be useful for making a decision. Alternatively, the evaluator could attempt to collect more reliable cost and outcome data.

A sensitivity analysis could be conducted to assess the impact of uncertainty on the incremental cost-effectiveness results. Relative to the do-nothing option the incremental cost per additional one per cent reduction in patients returning with psychosocial problems based on a high cost estimate for the counsellor option is £1,211 ([£36,500–£5,000]/[30–4]), and £909 for the clinical psychologist based on the high outcome and original cost estimate ([£15,000 – 5,000]/[15–4]). The interpretation of these results depends on the value judgements of the decision-makers. If decision-makers are willing to accept the risk of, at worst, an incremental cost-effectiveness of £1,211 for the counsellor then this option should be selected. This choice would also depend on whether the high cost of the counsellor, £36,500, exceeded a cost limit determined by the decision-makers.

Sensitivity analysis could be used to examine the impact on the marginal cost-effectiveness of small changes in the composition of one or more options. For example, the staff support group option in the Smithland Trust evaluation might be modified if there was uncertainty concerning its format. Minor changes might be a longer length of session or more frequent meetings. Adjustments may be made to the counselling option by comparing the effect on the costs and outcomes of extending the counselling service availability on an 'on-call' basis compared to the original situation of fixed hours during the week.

Net costs approach

A further approach to analysis of relative cost-effectiveness is to subtract from the

Table 10.6   The impact of uncertainty on the average cost-effectiveness of interventions in the North Brownstead evaluation

Intervention	Total cost estimates £	Outcome estimates % reduction in patients returning with psychosocial problems:	Average cost-effectiveness cost per 1% reduction in patients returning with psychosocial problems using a:		
			High cost per unit outcome estimate £	Low cost per unit outcome estimate £	Original cost per unit outcome estimate £
Clinical psychologist	15,000– 20,000	10–15	–	1,000	2,000
Counsellor	25,000– 36,500	30	1,217	–	833
Do-nothing (GP care)	5,000	4	–	–	1,250

total costs of each option any monetary benefits or savings occurring as a consequence of the counselling options. Combined with the outcomes data this produces estimates of net cost-effectiveness. The range of savings included in the evaluation depends on the perspective adopted. If the perspective was the North Brownstead Practice, for example, it would be relevant to include reductions in psychotropic drug expenditures.

If the net costs approach was not adpted, the post-counselling expenditure on items such as psychotropic drugs could be assessed and included as part of the total costs of each option. For example, drug prescribing costs for the counsellor, clinical psychologist and GP options in the North Brownstead Practice of £700, £880 and £1,000 respectively might be estimated at post-counselling follow-up. Relative cost-effectiveness would be compared by including these costs as part of the total cost for each option. If we assume the original total cost estimates for the options in Table 10.1 did not include drug costs, a new set of total cost estimates can be produced including these figures. These are presented in the second column of Table 10.7.

The net costs approach does not include these drug costs in the evaluation. Instead the original cost estimates for the three options are used (third column of Table 10.7) and the savings in drug prescribing are estimated. If the pre-counselling drug costs were estimated at £1,000 then the saving for the 'do-nothing' can be estimated at zero, £300 (£1,000-£700) for the counsellor option and £120 (£1,000-£880) for the clinical psychologist option (assuming these figures are based on adjustments to allow for differences in time period covered and to numbers of patients seen before and after the counselling intervention).

Using these data a new set of cost-effectiveness results can be produced using the outcome results from Table 10.1. These are presented in Table 10.7. The estimated net costs per one per cent reduction in patients reconsulting with psychosocial problems becomes £823 for the counsellor option (£24,700/30) and £1,988 for the clinical psychologist (£19,880/10) with the do-nothing option remaining at £1,250. Including savings has improved the relative cost-effectiveness of the two 'active options'.

Net incremental cost-effectiveness can also be calculated using data from Table 10.3 (although this is not attempted here) and interpreted in the same way as the results based on gross costs (Table 10.1). The ranking of cost-effectiveness will be the same whether adopting the net costs approach or the usual approach of including drug expenditure within total costs (as in column 2 of Table 10.7). However, the cost effectiveness statistics will be different (i.e. they will be lower if the net costs approach is used), which may have an impact on decision-makers' perceptions of the cost-effectiveness of a counselling option.

If the perspective were wider, for example the health service or society, then other monetary savings are likely to be included in a net costs approach. This might include an assessment of the future hospital treatment cost savings from early intervention to reduce levels of psychosocial problems among patients attending the North Brownstead surgery. An assessment of personal cost savings might be included in this evaluation, with the results presented as net costs per QALY gained. This type of evaluation is complex in that it involves estimation of future uncertain

Table 10.7 Net cost-effectiveness for interventions in the North Brownstead evaluation[*][+]

Intervention	Total costs (including drug costs) £	Original total costs (excluding drug costs) £	Drug saving estimate £	Net cost (original total cost minus savings) £	Average cost effective- ness (per 1% reduction in psychosocial problems) £	Net cost effective- ness (per 1% reduction in psychosocial problems) £
Specialist counsellor	25,700	25,000	300	24,700	833	823
Clinical psychologist	25,880	20,000	120	19,880	2,000	1,988
Do-nothing (GP counselling)	6,000	5,000	–	5,000	1,250	1,250

Notes: [*] Reproduced from Table 9.1
[+] Outcome data derived from Table 9.1

benefits and the extensive use of sensitivity analysis. In each case expected future monetary savings should be discounted using the same rate as for future costs.

The main advantage of the net costs approach is that it allows some of the benefits of interventions that are usually only considered in a full cost-benefit analysis to be included in a cost-effectiveness analysis. We have argued earlier (Chapter 3) how cost-benefit analysis represents the economic evaluation technique with the greatest foundations in economic theory, but how difficulties in its application preclude its use for most evaluations of healthcare or counselling interventions. The net costs approach explicitly incorporates savings into the analysis of the cost-effectiveness or cost-utility (i.e. costs per QALY gained) of counselling programmes. This is very important for providing health service decision-makers and purchasers with more appropriate and realistic information of the 'real' cost-effectiveness of each option in the evaluation. One possible disadvantage with this approach is that it is currently rarely used in economic evaluations. Hence, if net cost-effectiveness results were produced for counselling options it would be difficult to compare these results with those for other healthcare interventions (for example, within a cost per QALY league table) as the latter are generally not based on the use of net costs.

Cost-effectiveness league tables

An important issue is how best to present the cost-effectiveness results of the counselling evaluation in order to have most influence on health service decision-making.

Prior to an evaluation managers may have agreed to fund a programme to reduce absenteeism due to burnout among nursing staff at the Smithland Trust Hospital. The purpose of a cost-effectiveness analysis might then be to identify the most cost-effective means of meeting this objective. The relative effectiveness of the two options in the Smithland Trust evaluation may have been assessed in terms of a percentage reduction in staff absenteeism, which represents an intermediate outcome measure. On this basis if the staff support group is the most cost-effective in terms of average cost data the decision will be to implement that option. The assumption is that the decision-makers in the health service responsible for adopting the programme are convinced that the implementation of a counselling programme is a worthwhile use of health service resources.

However, the hospital management or health authority may want to assess the results in a wider health service context and assess the relative cost-effectiveness of staff support or counselling options with other health programmes. This is only possible if a final outcome measure, such as a gain in quality of life or QALYs gained has been used to assess the relative effectiveness of the counselling options in the evaluation. This enables comparisons to be made with a variety of healthcare and preventive interventions for which cost-effectiveness results using final outcome measures have been derived (usually from other published studies). The counselling options can then be ranked in a cost-effectiveness league table to determine their relative cost-effectiveness in the use of health services resources.

Table 10.8 reproduces a cost-effectiveness league table for cost per QALY gained results which have been drawn from a number of studies undertaken between 1985 and 1991 (Maynard 1991). Any final outcome measure can be used; league tables also exist for cost-per-life-years-saved estimates with regard to interventions which have a major impact on survival probabilities rather than quality of life (e.g. HIV prevention initiatives). In principle, the nearer to the top of the table the counselling programme is placed the greater its relative cost-effectiveness and the higher priority such services will receive in the allocation of health service resources. The use of such tables began in the UK when the health economist Alan Williams produced a number of cost per QALY gained estimates for interventions aimed at the reduction of the risk of heart disease, including hypertension management drug therapy, coronary artery bypass grafting and GP advice to quit smoking (Williams 1987a). The updated average cost results for each of the interventions in this study have been included in Table 10.8.

Cost-effectiveness league tables (i.e. cost for life year gained or cost per QALY) provide a short cut to comparing the cost-effectiveness of counselling with other healthcare programmes. They are meant to combine the results from a diverse set of studies that have used similar methods of economic evaluation and so reduce the need to collect original data on alternative health service interventions. To conduct a separate assessment of the cost-effectiveness of a sufficiently wide range of alternative health programmes would be a large and costly exercise.

If we assume that a health authority purchases services from both the Smithland Trust and the North Brownstead practice and so would potentially fund the counselling programmes in each setting. If cost per QALY estimates of £500 and £833 respectively were produced for the two 'best' options in the North Brownstead and Smithland Trust evaluations (for example, the specialist counsellor and staff support group respectively) these could be ranked in Table 10.8 allowing the health authority to assess their relative priority in making purchasing decisions. In effect, a higher priority should be given to funding the counselling service in the North Brownstead Practice, but if sufficient funds were available the Smithland Trust intervention appears to represent good value for money relative to other interventions.

Problems with league tables

Cost-effectiveness league tables offer some scope for presenting the results from a counselling evaluation in a wider decision-making context. However, there are a number of difficulties in interpreting relative cost-effectiveness from a league table, in particular cost per QALY league tables.

First, although each study in Table 10.8 has produced cost per QALY gained estimates the studies have not used a standard method for calculating costs or producing the QALY gained estimates. Differences in methods used reduces the

Table 10.8   Cost per quality adjusted life year (QALY) gained of alternative
therapies

	Cost/QALY gained (£ Aug 1990)
Cholesterol testing and diet therapy only (all adults, aged 40–69)	220
Neurosurgical intervention for head injury	240
GP advice to stop smoking	270
Neurosurgical intervention for subarachnoid haemorrhage	490
Anti-hypertensive therapy to prevent stroke (ages 45–64)	940
Pacemaker insertion	1,100
Hip replacement	1,180
Valve replacement for aortic stenosis (narrowing)	1,140
Cholesterol testing and treatment	1.480
Coronary artery by-pass graft (CABG), left main vessel disease, severe angina	2,090
Kidney transplant	4,710
Breast cancer screening	5,780
Heart transplantation	7,840
Cholesterol testing and treatment (incrementally) of all adults aged 25–39 years	14,150
Home haemodialysis	17,260
CABG, 1 vessel disease, moderate angina	18,830
Continuous ambulatory peritoneal dialysis	19,870
Hospital haemodialysis	21,970
Erythropoietic treatment for anaemia in dialysis patients (assuming a 10% reduction in mortality)	54,380
Neurosurgical intervention for malignant brain tumour	107,780
Erythropoietic treatment for anaemia in dialysis patients (assuming no increase in survival)	126,290

Source: Maynard (1991)

comparability of the estimates and agreement has yet to be reached as to the most appropriate core concepts to use within a cost-utility analysis (Gerard 1992).

Second, there are only a limited set of interventions included in current cost-effectiveness league tables. The league table is deficient in health education interventions, nursing and community care and counselling programmes. The main use of the league tables to date has been to compare the relative cost-effectiveness of surgical interventions such as heart transplants with mass screening programmes (e.g. breast cancer screening).

Third, the league tables are a relatively new approach to making comparisons so they are relatively crude including only estimates of average costs (not marginal costs) produced at a national level. It has been argued that they are of little use for local decision-making (in such settings as the North Brownstead Practice or the Smithland Trust Hospital) but that league tables produced for specific and smaller geographical areas could be useful for setting priorities in local healthcare settings.

While outlining a range of objections to cost-effectiveness league tables in health service decision-making, Drummond *et al.* (1993) argue that in the absence of better alternative processes for decision-making (the alternative being informal and subjective value-for-money comparisons) the league table approach at least offers a formal and objective instrument. Controversial though they are, tables such as Table 10.8 are beginning to have an impact on decision-making in the NHS (Gerard 1992).

Although counsellors should exercise caution the best approach may be to incorporate counselling interventions within current cost-effectiveness league tables rather than waiting for improvements in the methodology of cost-utility analysis. Given the potential power of these tables it may be better to have counsellor interventions in the table (however crude the estimate) than not, and so avoid leaving the fate of counselling programmes open to subjective decision-making alone.

What about equity?

Incorporating the issue of equity information in a cost-effectiveness analysis is problematic. The traditional role of cost-benefit analysis is to examine efficiency in the use of resources, whereas equity has been considered a separate and subjective concept outside the remit of economists (Pearce and Nash 1981). However, in the financing and delivery of health care equity has become a core issue for consideration by health economists (Donaldson and Gerard 1993).

Equity is a multi-faceted concept relating to the fairness of a programme, concerning issues of who benefits and who pays. It has many definitions but two main types appear most relevant for incorporating equity objectives for different population groups into the economic analysis of the delivery of counselling services such as those included in the North Brownstead and Smithland Trust evaluations. These are:

- equity of access;
- equity of outcome.

The pursuit of absolute equality is only one interpretation of equity. Strict equality is an egalitarian concept implying that each individual who receives counselling gets and achieves the same amount. This is an untenable objective. A more realistic objective is to define equity of access as equal access for equal need or equity of outcomes as equal amount of treatment gain for equal capacity to benefit. Using these concepts equity of access means that each patient with psychosocial problems registered with the North Brownstead Practice has an equal opportunity to see the counsellor according to their level of need. Equity of outcome means that they will obtain the same level of service and benefit as others with the same capacity to benefit (e.g. the same time input from the counsellor and a minimum expected improvement in quality of life).

There are other notions of equity that could be applied to assessing the fairness of patients' access to the service, level of service received and quality-of-life outcomes. For example, an equity objective for a health programme might be based on the principle of 'just deserts' (i.e. the principle that if you smoke and have heart disease you do not deserve equal access to health care compared to a person with the same disease but related to family history). The value judgements of the service providers will determine which notion of equity to use.

Using alternative equity concepts the service provider could redefine economic objectives to incorporate a set of equity objectives, such as to ensure that people under 50 years have access to the service, or people from a disadvantaged background receive counselling support. For the purposes of a cost-effectiveness analysis the evaluator can define desirable equity objectives, even if this results in a less cost-effective option being selected. An appropriate joint efficiency/equity objective might be to determine the most cost-effective counselling option in the North Brownstead Practice for achieving a reduction in patients returning with psychosocial problems subject to a target reduction of 10 per cent being achieved amongst known patients from deprived housing estates within the practice boundaries. Subject to the equity target being reached the most cost-effective option would be selected.

There is a question mark over whether purchasers and providers for counselling programmes will or should be concerned with equity objectives. Certainly, the current incentive in the NHS is to achieve efficiency objectives with less attention paid to ensuring universal and equitable access to services (and virtually no attention given to assessing whether the benefits from the health service are being distributed equitably). In a financial appraisal of how to allocate the practice or hospital budget, equity is of little importance. However, if a societal perspective is adopted in an evaluation equity objectives should be incorporated. Evaluations from single agency or multi-agency perspectives may vary in the extent to which equity is considered; it is the decision of the service providers or those funding the evaluation. We suggest that even if equity objectives are not set, the evaluator should include broad equity principles that have to be met for an otherwise cost-effective option to be considered suitable for implementation.

SUMMARY

This chapter has outlined the issues involved in the analysis of the cost and outcome data after the study trial has been completed. We have demonstrated that a full evaluation of cost-effectiveness can involve much more than just the simple comparison of the average cost-effectiveness of each option, with the option with the lowest cost per unit of outcome selected as the most cost-effective. Other important aspects to consider in the analysis phase are the examination of the incremental and marginal cost-effectiveness of more costly options, the use of discounting to allow for the differential timing of costs and outcomes, the problem of uncertainty over the precision of the cost, outcome and discount rate estimates used and the use of sensitivity analysis to examine the impact of this uncertainty on the results. In addition, the inclusion of monetary savings into cost-effectiveness analysis and the use of cost-effectiveness league tables could be considered. Finally, equity objectives might be considered alongside the selection of the most cost-effective option.

The preceding four chapters have explained how to conduct a comprehensive analysis of the cost-effectiveness of counselling programmes. A detailed checklist of the steps in the planning and implementation of a cost-effectiveness analysis is provided in the context of the case studies in Chapter 11.

While most evaluations will only use some of the techniques discussed, these chapters should enable the evaluator to identify the most appropriate approach for assessing the cost-effectiveness of a counselling service within the constraints of service practice, time available and the research budget. With this information, it should be possible for the evaluator to clearly understand and justify the limitations of the analysis.

Annex 10.1 Discount factors for calculating the present value of future costs

| Years | Discount rates | | | | | | | | | | | | | | |
	1%	2%	3%	4%	5%	6%	7%	8%	9%	10%	11%	12%	13%	14%	15%
1	0.9901	0.9804	0.9709	0.9615	0.9524	0.9434	0.9346	0.9259	0.9174	0.9091	0.9009	0.8929	0.8850	0.8772	0.8696
2	0.9803	0.9612	0.9426	0.9246	0.9070	0.8900	0.8734	0.8573	0.8417	0.8264	0.8116	0.7972	0.7831	0.7695	0.7561
3	0.9706	0.9423	0.9151	0.8890	0.8638	0.8396	0.8163	0.7938	0.7722	0.7513	0.7312	0.7118	0.6931	0.6750	0.6575
4	0.9610	0.9238	0.8885	0.8548	0.8227	0.7921	0.7629	0.7350	0.7084	0.6830	0.6587	0.6355	0.6133	0.5921	0.5718
5	0.9515	0.9057	0.8626	0.8219	0.7835	0.7473	0.7130	0.6806	0.6499	0.6209	0.5935	0.5674	0.5428	0.5194	0.4972
6	0.9420	0.8880	0.8375	0.7903	0.7462	0.7050	0.6663	0.6302	0.5963	0.5645	0.5346	0.5066	0.4803	0.4556	0.4323
7	0.9327	0.8706	0.8131	0.7599	0.7107	0.6651	0.6227	0.5835	0.5470	0.5132	0.4817	0.4523	0.4251	0.3996	0.3759
8	0.9235	0.8535	0.7894	0.7307	0.6768	0.6274	0.5820	0.5403	0.5019	0.4665	0.4339	0.4039	0.3762	0.3506	0.3269
9	0.9143	0.8368	0.7664	0.7026	0.6446	0.5919	0.5439	0.5002	0.4604	0.4241	0.3909	0.3606	0.3329	0.3075	0.2843
10	0.9053	0.8203	0.7441	0.6756	0.6139	0.5584	0.5083	0.4632	0.4224	0.3855	0.3522	0.3220	0.2946	0.2697	0.2472
11	0.8963	0.8043	0.7224	0.6496	0.5847	0.5268	0.4751	0.4289	0.3875	0.3505	0.3173	0.2875	0.2607	0.2366	0.2149
12	0.8874	0.7885	0.7014	0.6246	0.5568	0.4970	0.4440	0.3971	0.3555	0.3186	0.2858	0.2567	0.2307	0.2076	0.1869
13	0.8787	0.7730	0.6810	0.6006	0.5303	0.4688	0.4150	0.3677	0.3262	0.2897	0.2575	0.2292	0.2042	0.1821	0.1625
14	0.8700	0.7579	0.6611	0.5775	0.5051	0.4423	0.3878	0.3405	0.2992	0.2633	0.2320	0.2046	0.1807	0.1597	0.1413
15	0.8613	0.7430	0.6419	0.5553	0.4810	0.4173	0.3624	0.3152	0.2745	0.2394	0.2090	0.1827	0.1599	0.1401	0.1229
16	0.8528	0.7284	0.6232	0.5339	0.4581	0.3936	0.3387	0.2919	0.2519	0.2176	0.1883	0.1631	0.1415	0.1229	0.1069
17	0.8444	0.7142	0.6050	0.5134	0.4363	0.3714	0.3166	0.2703	0.2311	0.1978	0.1696	0.1456	0.1252	0.1078	0.0929
18	0.8360	0.7002	0.5874	0.4936	0.4155	0.3503	0.2959	0.2502	0.2120	0.1799	0.1528	0.1300	0.1108	0.0946	0.0808
19	0.8277	0.6864	0.5703	0.4746	0.3957	0.3305	0.2765	0.2317	0.1945	0.1635	0.1377	0.1161	0.0981	0.0829	0.0703
20	0.8195	0.6730	0.5537	0.4564	0.3769	0.3118	0.2584	0.2145	0.1784	0.1486	0.1240	0.1037	0.0868	0.0728	0.0611
21	0.8114	0.6598	0.5375	0.4388	0.3589	0.2942	0.2415	0.1987	0.1637	0.1351	0.1117	0.0926	0.0768	0.0638	0.0531
22	0.8034	0.6468	0.5219	0.4220	0.3418	0.2775	0.2257	0.1839	0.1502	0.1228	0.1007	0.0826	0.0680	0.0560	0.0462
23	0.7954	0.6342	0.5067	0.4057	0.3256	0.2618	0.2109	0.1703	0.1378	0.1117	0.0907	0.0738	0.0601	0.0491	0.0402
24	0.7876	0.6217	0.4919	0.3901	0.3101	0.2470	0.1971	0.1577	0.1264	0.1015	0.0817	0.0659	0.0532	0.0431	0.0349
25	0.7798	0.6095	0.4776	0.3751	0.2953	0.2330	0.1842	0.1460	0.1160	0.0923	0.0736	0.0588	0.0471	0.0378	0.0304
26	0.7720	0.5976	0.4637	0.3607	0.2812	0.2198	0.1722	0.1352	0.1064	0.0839	0.0663	0.0525	0.0417	0.0331	0.0264
27	0.7644	0.5859	0.4502	0.3468	0.2678	0.2074	0.1609	0.1252	0.0976	0.0763	0.0597	0.0469	0.0369	0.0291	0.0230
28	0.7568	0.5744	0.4371	0.3335	0.2551	0.1956	0.1504	0.1159	0.0895	0.0693	0.0538	0.0419	0.0326	0.0255	0.0200
29	0.7493	0.5631	0.4243	0.3207	0.2429	0.1846	0.1406	0.1073	0.0822	0.0630	0.0485	0.0374	0.0289	0.0224	0.0174
30	0.7419	0.5521	0.4120	0.3083	0.2314	0.1741	0.1314	0.0994	0.0754	0.0573	0.0437	0.0334	0.0256	0.0196	0.0151
35	0.7059	0.5000	0.3554	0.2534	0.1813	0.1301	0.0937	0.0676	0.0490	0.0356	0.0259	0.0189	0.0139	0.0102	0.0075
40	0.6717	0.4529	0.3066	0.2083	0.1420	0.0972	0.0668	0.0460	0.0318	0.0221	0.0154	0.0107	0.0075	0.0053	0.0037
45	0.6391	0.4102	0.2644	0.1712	0.1113	0.0727	0.0476	0.0313	0.0207	0.0137	0.0091	0.0061	0.0041	0.0027	0.0019
50	0.6080	0.3715	0.2281	0.1407	0.0872	0.0543	0.0339	0.0213	0.0134	0.0085	0.0054	0.0035	0.0022	0.0014	0.0009

Chapter 11

Counselling case studies

Introduction
Case study one: Is it cost-effective to employ a counsellor in general
practice?
Case study two: The cost-effectiveness of counselling nurses in a hospital
setting

INTRODUCTION

In this chapter we present two case studies to describe and work through the use of
cost-effectiveness analysis in evaluating counselling programmes in medical settings. The case studies demonstrate the problems to be considered in carrying out
an evaluation. In each study we consider the planning of the evaluation, its
implementation and the analysis of results, bearing in mind the perspective of the
evaluation and the resources available to carry out the evaluation.

Table 11.1 is a checklist covering four stages in the planning and implementation
of a cost-effectiveness analysis. It provides practical guidance to counsellors,
service purchasers and providers attempting to evaluate the cost-effectiveness of
counselling interventions. The checklist is employed in the two case studies in this
chapter.

The first case study represents an evaluation within a primary care setting – the
North Brownstead Practice. This study illustrates three main issues in conducting
a cost-effectiveness analysis:

1 An illustration of the evaluation planning process. The example demonstrates
   how the doctors in the North Brownstead Practice might use stages 1–2 of the
   checklist to guide their general discussion in planning a cost-effectiveness
   analysis of counselling in their practice. We assume that the project is discussed
   mainly at the monthly practice meetings. This phase is time-consuming; the
   doctors spend a year discussing and planning the project.
2 Implementing a cost-effectiveness analysis. The next problem facing the North
   Brownstead doctors is how to ensure the cost-effectiveness analysis will go

ahead. This includes questions concerning who will conduct the research and what financial arrangements are possible to fund the study (stage 3 in the checklist). They need to assess the cost of the evaluation and possible sources of funding (e.g. the evaluator's costs, support costs and the provision of counselling services).

3   The evaluation. We assume that the FHSA decides to fund a six-month trial of a counselling service in several practices, including the North Brownstead Practice (total funding for a researcher for one year). A health economist, Ms Penn, is employed to review the decisions taken by the doctors, coordinate data collection, conduct the analysis and present the results (stage 4 of the checklist).

The same procedure is adopted for the second case study. This demonstrates the planning of a cost-effectiveness analysis of staff support mechanisms within a hospital setting – the Smithland Trust Hospital. However, less emphasis is given to the initial discussions and development of a protocol for funding in the second study. In both case studies a health economist is employed to refine and carry out the evaluation. We have tried to demonstrate, especially in the first case study, how service providers and purchasers could and should (if they are to obtain the funds for the project) play an active part in planning and designing an evaluation. Although we conveniently assume a professional health economist was recruited in these studies, not all evaluations will be blessed with the funds to enable this. We hope that the case studies provide readers with the confidence and some of the skills to be able to substitute for Ms Penn and carry out a cost-effectiveness analysis themselves. We would suggest, however, that counsellors who undertake audit or evaluation studies seek advice and supervisory support from academics experienced in research. Information is given at the end of the book on how to obtain help from research departments.

Table 11.1

Cost-effectivness analysis: a checklist for evaluation
planning and analysis

Stage 1 – Setting up the cost-effectiveness evaluation

1.1   Defining the study problem

- Identify the issue for evaluation.

- Choose an appropriate method of cost-effectiveness
analysis

Table 11.1   (continued)

[(i) same type of intervention within a setting; (ii) same type of

intervention across settings; (iii) different types of intervention across

settings].

- Determine a perspective for the evaluation.

[single agency, multi-agency, societal].

1.2   Defining evaluation objectives

- Define general objectives.

- Define specific economic objectives.

1.3   Selecting options for analysis

- Identify an initial list of possible options.

- Select final options for analysis ('active' options)

[reject those from initial list that are not politically, ethically, financially or otherwise feasible/acceptable].

- Identify the 'do-nothing' option (if appropriate)

[this represents the current situation].

1.4   List the expected costs and benefits of the active options.

Stage 2 – Planning data collection

2.1   Identify an appropriate and feasible study design and time scale

[possibilities are the controlled trial and the before/after study].

CASE STUDY ONE

Is it cost-effective to employ a counsellor in general practice?

The evaluation planning process

In this section we demonstrate the discussion among service providers and the timetable involved in planning an evaluation to examine the cost-effectiveness of employing a counsellor in general practice. The planning process is followed from the first time the idea of such an evaluation was raised by a doctor at the North Brownstead Practice at a practice meeting on 1 April.

As the case study shows, an essential part of the process of evaluation is the qualitative debate which precedes the formal collection of data, because it enables interested parties to discuss ideas, aims, values and available information.

The setting: the North Brownstead Practice

1 April   North Brownstead represented a fund-holding practice and consisted of six doctors (Doctors Pill, Bottle, Kind, Golf, Senior and Junior), eight part-time receptionists, a practice manager, two practice nurses, and the shared services of a health visitor, a chiropodist and an audiologist. At their weekly practice meetings the only female general practitioner, Dr Junior, mentioned that more and more of her consultation times were taken up with extended appointments for patients with psychosomatic or psychological problems and she wondered if the other doctors shared her experience. Dr Senior said that he thought patients always found their way to the doctor who would give them what they wanted, and that since Dr Junior had joined the practice he had far fewer depressed women in his surgery, but he still had his depressed elderly patients, whom he had known for a number of years. Dr Kind commented that he was continuing to see quite a few patients with social problems. It was noted that while Doctors Kind and Junior tried talking cures with these patients, Drs Golf and Pill had the highest prescription rates for tranquillisers and repeat prescriptions of anti-depressants and that a small number of women were approaching Dr Golf asking to be taken off tranquillisers and sleeping pills, often with deleterious consequences, including increased anxiety and concomitant symptoms. All the partners agreed that it would be useful to decrease the costs of psychotropic medicines and all agreed that they should be prescribed carefully, in keeping with current concepts of good clinical practice and cost consciousness. Doctors Junior and Kind raised the possibility of employing a counsellor part time to deal with the more difficult psychosocial problems and perhaps to raise skills in the practice team in general. Dr Bottle thought this was an unnecessary expense and Dr Senior thought the practice ought to be able to look after all its patients' physical and psychological needs. Dr Junior and Dr Kind persuaded Drs Bottle and

Pill that counselling might be a valid alternative to the prescription of psychotropic drugs. After heated discussion it was agreed that the general practitioners would investigate options, including the possibility of employing a counsellor.

Stage 1 – Setting up the Cost-Effectiveness Evaluation

Defining the study problem

2 May   At the next practice meeting the issue of a counsellor attachment to the practice was raised again. With the aid of the practice manager, the doctors discussed how they might set up a counsellor attachment and how it might be evaluated. Dr Kind brought a checklist which he had come across in a medical journal, outlining the steps of economic evaluation (Table 11.1). He thought it might be useful in helping his colleagues think through the project. The checklist contained four main stages and several sub-stages. The first stage was how to set up the cost-effectiveness analysis. As far as he could tell, he thought they were currently in Stage 1.1, that is defining the study problem. The three aspects to be considered were (see Chapter 6):

1   Identification of the issue for evaluation.
2   Identification of the appropriate method of cost-effectiveness analysis.
3   Identification of the perspective for evaluation.

Dr Kind pointed out that they had already discussed the issue for evaluation. He believed this was to identify the most cost-effective way of dealing with patients with psychosocial problems, to improve their well-being and reduce the burden on the practice. This included attempting to reduce prescription of psychotropic and related drugs.

According to the checklist the next task in defining the study problem was to decide which method of cost-effectiveness analysis was appropriate. They decided that of the methods listed, they were most interested in method 1– identifying the most cost-effective approach to the study problem within a setting – in this case the practice. The analysis should therefore be conducted from the perspective of the North Brownstead Practice – a single agency perspective.

Economic Objectives

Stage 1.2 of the checklist was to define the general and economic objectives of the evaluation. Dr Junior and Dr Kind felt that doctors in the practice lacked the time and expertise to deal with the psychosocial and psychosomatic problems presented by their patients and that the partners needed to consider alternative ways of dealing with them. In particular they wanted to assess the costs and benefits of employing a counsellor in the practice. The doctors defined several general objectives for a counselling service, in a loose order of priority:

1   Improve patients' psychological well-being.
2   Reduce the costs to the practice of prescribing psychotropic medication.
3   Reduce GP consultation time spent on patients with psychological problems.
4   Improve patient satisfaction and quality of care.
5   Improve doctor workload satisfaction.
6   Improve reputation of practice.

In terms of economic objectives they thought that the priority should be to identify whether a counselling service could, at an acceptable cost, improve patient well-being, reduce drug expenditures and reduce GP consultation time spent with patients with psychosocial problems. The doctors felt they were not yet in a position to set targets for effectiveness or specify a cost limit. They decided to return to this issue at a later stage.

What are the alternative options?

1 June   Stage 1.3 on the checklist was to define specific options to include in the cost-effectiveness analysis. At the next practice meeting (1 June) Dr Junior pointed out that it would be useful to identify a range of options that would address the study problem before deciding which to try. Such discussion would also enable them to think carefully about the options and the possible reasons for rejecting some of them. Some options might be rejected if some of the doctors found them to be ethically unacceptable, or impossible to implement due to high set-up costs. All sorts of reasons might be put forward for rejecting options. However, it is important to consider as wide a range of options as is possible and agree on the reasons for the rejection of particular options from the final evaluation. Although some providers may have a firm idea of the type of service they want to evaluate and eventually implement it is better to consider a range of alternatives at the outset.

Thus, the doctors discussed in detail a range of options that might address the needs of patients with psychosocial problems (and might help reduce their drug expenditures). Dr Senior suggested that Dr Junior go on a counselling training course and specialise in this area of work. Dr Junior thought that while she would benefit from a short weekend counselling skills course it would cost too much time to train as a counsellor; besides she enjoyed the general medical work and her major interest was in fact dermatology. She felt that most of the female patients came to talk to her about their problems because she was the only woman doctor in the practice. Dr Golf suggested that things were fine as they stood and that it was better to carry on as before (the 'do-nothing' alternative). Dr Pill suggested that patients with intractable psychosocial problems should be referred to the Community Mental Health Team but Dr Kind and Dr Senior felt that the doctors in the practice had a responsibility to look after their patients and that while the Community Psychiatric Nurses and psychiatrists in the mental health team were skilled in dealing with more acute psychological problems, the Director of Community Mental Health Services had recently indicated that it would be inappropriate to refer patients who were experiencing marital or occupational problems as the services were under intense pressure. Dr Kind thought that a counsellor in their practice might help patients and might also help the team members improve their counselling skills. Dr Bottle agreed and added that a practice counsellor might add to the reputation of the practice, thus attracting more patients, although Dr Golf was not sure he wanted the practice to be seen as the 'problem practice' with neurotic patients joining because a counsellor was employed. Having agreed that the majority of problems presented by patients were 'life problems' that might be dealt with by a counsellor rather than needing help from a psychiatrist or the Community Mental Health Team, the doctors finally agreed that employing a counsellor for a trial period of six months was their preferred choice. They thought that this 'active' option could be compared with the current practice of patients with 'life problems' receiving routine care (a 'do-nothing' option).

To help guide future discussions Dr Junior was asked to make a list of potential costs and benefits of employing a practice counsellor. Dr Junior and the practice manager listed all the important costs and outcomes they could think of, but did not apply figures to the items included.

Expected costs of counsellor option:

- Cost of counsellor's salary.
- Extra administration costs – GP time, receptionist time.
- Prescription costs for patients with psychosocial problems.
- Cost of facilities for the counsellor.
- Cost of referrals to psychiatric services in hospitals.
- Cost of referrals to Community Mental Health Team and other agencies.
- Cost of the evaluation.
- Cost of distress to patient and family.
- Cost of patients' travel expenses to receive counselling at the practice.

Expected costs of 'do-nothing' option:

- Cost of GP consultation time.
- Administration costs.
- Cost of referrals to psychiatric service, CMHT, other services.
- Cost of distress to patient and family.
- Cost of patients' travel expenses for GP consultation.
- Prescription costs for patients' with psychosocial problems.

Dr Junior listed the additional benefits they expected from the counselling option compared to the 'do-nothing':

Expected benefits (counsellor v. 'do-nothing'):

- Improved health and well-being of patients with psychosocial problems.
- Savings in prescription costs.
- Fewer GP consultations.
- Saving in other staff time, e.g. receptionists having to spend less time with distressed patients on the phone and at the desk, the practice nurse getting more appropriate referrals.
- Fewer referrals to outside agencies such as Community Mental Health Teams and psychiatrists.
- Improved image of practice in having a counsellor.

1 July   At the next practice meeting there was only time for Dr Junior to present her list of costs and benefits. She explained that the list was extensive and reflected costs and benefits to the practice, patients and other health service providers (i.e. societal perspectives). Although they were planning to restrict their analysis to the perspective of the practice, she argued it was useful to list other costs and benefits to provide supporting qualitative information on the relative value of the introduction of a counselling service.

Stage 2 – Planning Data Collection

The study design

1 August   At the next practice meeting the doctors wanted to discuss the next stage of the evaluation process. This was to plan the collection of costs and outcome data. In order to do this the doctors realised that they first had to identify an appropriate study design. Drs Senior, Golf and Pill felt this was difficult as they had no experience of designing evaluations. The checklist identified two types of design – the controlled trial and a before/after study design. Dr Kind pointed out that the latter appeared to be a more pragmatic approach as they could continue their normal service and at the same time monitor the costs and effectiveness of a counsellor attachment. Dr Bottle interjected that a randomised controlled trial (RCT) would provide a more rigorous study design and give more credibility to their findings. The other doctors argued that the set-up costs of a controlled trial and their lack of experience in designing RCTs meant that they should not take this approach. Dr Senior also pointed out that as they were mainly interested in deciding whether to employ a counsellor in their own practice they need be less concerned about the wider credibility of their findings. However, Dr Junior pointed out that the FHSA might need to be convinced of the cost-effectiveness of the service if they were expected to contribute to the cost of employing a counsellor. She mentioned that the checklist (Table 11.1) referred to a book on the evaluation of the cost-effectiveness of counselling in which study design was discussed in more depth. Dr Junior argued that they should not immediately discard the use of a controlled trial but should find out more about it. Dr Kind suggested that they defer making a decision on study design at this stage but continue to work through the checklist.

Cost measurement

The next step was to consider the measurement of the costs of the options in the cost-effectiveness analysis (Stage 2.2 in Table 11.1). The checklist identified three components to cost measurement (see Chapter 7):

1   Identifying the cost components appropriate for the perspective adopted.
2   Measuring the quantity of resource inputs.
3   Identifying appropriate unit costs (if relevant) and estimating the total cost of each option.

The doctors decided that the best approach would be to try to clarify the specific cost components appropriate for the perspective of the North Brownstead Practice. Their list consisted of the following cost components.

For the counsellor option:

- Time input of the counsellor.
- Time input of receptionist handling referrals to the counsellor and booking appointments.
- Running expenses (e.g. stationery, telephone, postage).
- Additional overheads, compared to the 'do-nothing' (i.e. office space, electricity).
- Drug prescription costs.

For the 'do-nothing' option:

- Time input of the GP providing counselling in consultations.
- Running expenses (e.g. stationery, telephone, postage).
- Drug prescription costs.

Overheads were not included in the list for the do-nothing option because they would have been incurred even if there were no patients with psychosocial problems presenting at the surgery.

Measuring the quantity of resource inputs and estimating the total costs of each option (parts (2) and (3) above) relates to the method of data collection to be used and the approach to estimating unit costs for resource inputs. As the doctors had not yet decided what type of study design to adopt, they felt it was not possible to decide on detailed methods of data collection. Dr Bottle pointed out that it should not be difficult to identify the time input of a counsellor. However, the other cost components might necessitate the use of monitoring forms and other methods of data collection in order to estimate the physical quantities of the resource used. The doctors were concerned about how the costs of employing a counsellor would be met. Under current arrangements the FHSA would possibly fund 70 per cent of the counsellor costs and the practice would meet the other 30 per cent of the costs. Dr Senior stated this was something they would have to consider further before they could implement the trial.

Outcome measurement

1 September   At their next practice meeting the doctors tackled the issue of outcome measurement (Stage 2.3 and 2.4 of the checklist). To help start the discussion, Dr Junior read aloud a section from the book she had recently purchased on the economic evaluation of counselling. The text was as follows:

> What is the appropriate effectiveness measure? Having identified the problem, the objective of the evaluation and considered the cost components to include, the next step in the planning process is to identify appropriate outcome measures. In a cost-effectiveness analysis there is a need to choose a quantifiable measure of the effectiveness of counselling and other options. One common measure of effectiveness must be selected to compare options, although if possible, several different effectiveness measures should be tested. Choice of measure depends on the perspective adopted (i.e. the perspective of a specific agency, individual participants, society-wide perspective and so on), as well as the resources available to the evaluator.

Dr Junior summarised the different types of outcome measures they could use. The effectiveness of service delivery is measured using process indicators. There-fore, if the doctors wanted to examine the cost-effectiveness of the delivery of a counselling programme in the practice a process indicator such as number of patients per week identified as having psychosocial problems and seen by the counsellor might be used. This could be compared with the number seen by the GPs. In contrast, a final outcome measure should be used in evaluations with patient welfare oriented objectives. Thus, at a later stage the cost-effectiveness of employing a counsellor could be compared with alternative counselling options or other healthcare interventions using a common final outcome measure such as QALYs, or a well-being index (see Chapter 7). Finally, Dr Junior stated that intermediate outcomes represented an alternative to measuring process indicators or final outcomes, if the objective was to compare different counselling interven-tions. Reductions in consultation rates and psychotropic drug prescriptions due to counselling are examples of such measures.

The doctors were faced with the task of identifying appropriate outcome measures and selecting one (or more) with which to compare the options' effec-tiveness. After further debate, the outcome measures and methods of data collection were defined as:

1   Assess patient psychological well-being using an available scale.

2   Monitor prescription rates before and after the counsellor attachment to see if there is any reduction in the prescription of psychotropic medication.

3   Monitor consultation rates to see if there is any reduction in consultation rates of patient (and patients' family) before and after the counsellor attachment.

4   Monitor referral patterns to external agencies and the psychiatric services.

5   Assess patient and doctor satisfaction through brief questionnaires.

They decided not to choose outcome measures to use in the cost-effectiveness analysis, but to wait until the evaluation was funded before deciding this.

Stage 3 – Implementing a Cost-Effectiveness Analysis

1 October   The process so far had taken up a great deal of time at the doctors' monthly practice meetings, but they felt as if they were beginning to be clear about what they were trying to do. Dr Kind offered to contact the British Association for Counselling (BAC) for advice on how to employ a counsellor in general practice and information about hours, insurance, pay, accountability and so on. At the next meeting he brandished the *Counselling in Medical Settings (CMS) Guidelines on the employment of counsellors* and suggested that the practice contact the FHSA regarding financing a practice counsellor. The counsellor could share the practice nurse's room and arrangements would be made so that the room was used at different times by nurse and counsellor. Finally, Dr Senior offered to furnish the practice nurse's room with two old armchairs from his attic, to ensure the comfortable setting which appeared to be essential to the process of counselling.

Implementing the cost-effectiveness analysis

Having thought about the practical details of employing a counsellor in the surgery (Stage 3.1, Table 11.1), the doctors held a further meeting to discuss who could undertake data collection and analysis of results. After setting up the procedure by which to employ a counsellor, decisions needed to be made about the method of evaluation, who would do the evaluation, how much it would cost and who would provide funding. The doctors thought it would be best to put a proposal to the FHSA to obtain funding for the evaluation. Dr Golf thought the counsellor ought to carry out the evaluation, but Dr Kind thought that while counsellors were often experienced in small scale service audit and evaluation, the likelihood of getting a counsellor who could undertake an economic evaluation seemed remote. Dr Golf argued that as doctors they were hardly experienced economists themselves and perhaps they were biting off more than they could chew and the whole thing should be called off. Dr Junior felt that having got so far it would be a shame to abandon the project, although like the other doctors she did not feel she had the time or experience to do research. Dr Senior insisted, however, that some sort of costing should take place, if a counsellor were employed, given that there were budgetary considerations and practice funds at stake. He suggested that when he contacted the

FHSA to ask about reimbursement of the counsellor's salary, he should also ask for suggestions about who might carry out some sort of economic audit for the practice and whether this was an area that the FHSA saw as a priority. The general practitioners called the meeting to an end and left it to Dr Senior to try to sort something out.

Funding the project (stages 3.2 to 3.3 of Table 11.1)

1 December   The Director of the FHSA, Mr Money, was invited to come to the practice to discuss the project. At the meeting, Mr Money expressed interest in what the GPs were trying to do and said that he had been approached by several practices who wanted to employ counsellors and that this inevitably raised funding issues and resource implications for the FHSA. He was particularly concerned about the distribution of resources across the locality and worried that counsellors would duplicate the work of local Community Mental Health Teams, and that there would be an increasing demand for surgery-based counsellors without anyone really knowing whether this was an efficient and effective use of resources. Mr Money said that the FHSA had been wrestling with this problem for some time and that it might be possible to coordinate a small working group with staff from interested practices, perhaps with a view to funding a small research project into the deployment of counsellors in general practices in the area. It might then be possible to employ a researcher with expertise in economic analysis to manage the project, refine the study design, implement the evaluation and analyse the results (Stage 3.2 in Table 11.1). Dr Junior agreed to represent the practice at the meeting convened by the Director of the FHSA, who began work to set up a small steering group which would meet in the new year.

12 January   Four practices were represented at the general meeting, all of which had previously requested funding from the FHSA to employ a counsellor. In the discussion which ensued it emerged that the general practitioners and FHSA Director were interested in a wide range of questions, including fundamental ones such as: How does counselling work? Can GPs do it? What is the most effective method of counselling? Which patients does it work best for? All the doctors agreed that they wanted to employ a counsellor in their practice for a trial period, and to assess the costs and benefits of the attachment before making a decision as to whether to continue to provide a counselling service. Mr Money was equally keen to look at costs and benefits to the FHSA in terms of funds and staff resources. He asked that a budget be drawn up outlining the funds required for an evaluation. A number of the GPs argued that it was difficult for them to produce an accurate budget until the research design was clarified. However, Dr Junior had already made some calculations. The cost of the evaluation was likely to be about £20,000 covering the one year part-time salary of a health economist-researcher, and travel expenses, stationery, photocopying and overheads. It was agreed that the costs of employing counsellors and associated expenses for a trial period would be presented to the FHSA for agreement as soon as the researcher had more clearly defined the options and study design. Mr Money said he would recommend that the FHSA agree to pay for the researcher post for one year, and would contribute 70 per cent towards the costs of counsellors and supervisors from non-recurring funds.

A contract was drawn up with the local university's Centre for Health Economics, to provide the services of a health economist (Ms Penn) part time for one year.

Stage 4 – Conducting the Research

Reviewing the study problem, evaluation objectives and options

1 April On taking up her post on 1 April Ms Penn's first task was to review the evaluation planning originally undertaken by the North Brownstead doctors (Stage 4.1 in Table 11.1). In doing this she worked closely with Drs Junior and Kind at the North Brownstead Practice. They provided Ms Penn with a written summary of the steps and decisions they had made in the original planning of the evaluation using the checklist.[1] In reviewing the doctors' original intentions (Stage 4.1 in Table 11.1) it became clear that the defined study problem was to reduce, in a cost-effective manner, the burden on general practice from patients attending with psychosocial problems. Ms Penn agreed that the appropriate method of analysis was the comparison of options within a single setting – the general practice. However, as the FHSA was funding the evaluation she suggested the perspective should be extended to include the FHSA and other practices that were participating in the study.

The next step was to review the general and economic objectives of the evaluation. Ms Penn defined three general objectives as:

1 The reduction in the level of psychosocial problems and depression in patients attending the GP surgery.
2 Reduction in the prescribing of psychotropic, anti-depressant and anxiolytic drugs.
3 Reduction in consultation rates for psychosocial problems.

After discussion with Drs Kind and Junior, Ms Penn set specific economic objectives related to the general objectives. The aim was not to provide fixed targets but to give the GPs guidance so that they could assess the success of the counselling intervention and whether it had met their expectations.

Ms Penn thought that two sets of economic objectives would provide useful guidance. First, the selection of the least cost option per unit given in patient well-being (objective 1); per unit reduction in drug prescriptions (objective 2); or per unit reduction in GP consultation rates (objective 3). Second, the selection of the option with the minimum 'acceptable' cost per additional unit gain in patient well-being (objective 4); unit reduction in drug prescriptions (objective 5); or unit reduction in GP consultation rates (objective 6). She set targets for each of the six objectives:

Objective 1: a 10 per cent improvement in patient well-being.

Objective 2: a 5 per cent reduction in drug prescriptions/costs.

Objective 3: a 10 per cent reduction in consultation rates.

Objective 4: an additional 10 per cent reduction in patient well-being due to specialist counselling.

Objective 5: an additional 5 per cent reduction in drug prescriptions due to specialist counselling.

Objective 6: an additional 10 per cent reduction in GP consultation rates due to specialist counselling.

Ms Penn's next task was to respecify the original options for evaluation to reflect the wider FHSA perspective. Mr Money wanted the evaluation to focus on assessing the cost-effectiveness of employing BAC accredited counsellors in the GP setting compared to the existing practice of GPs providing care for patients experiencing psychosocial problems. Hence, the options were the same as those of the North Brownstead doctors; the active option was the employment of practice counsellors to provide a counselling service to patients who were experiencing psychosocial problems, compared with GPs providing usual care and support for such patients. Mr Money pointed out that the FHSA was keen to assess whether short-term counsellor placements in the GP setting represented a cost-effective use of health service resources. At a later stage they might want to consider the cost-effectiveness of longer term counselling interventions. As a result of this discussion Ms Penn clarified the active option as a short-term intervention consisting of each patient receiving one counselling session per week for a period of six weeks. Patients receiving usual care would obtain one consultation with the GP over this time period. To be eligible for entry into the trial, patients had to meet certain criteria: aged over 16 years and suffering from recent stress, crisis, relationship or family problems, depression, bereavement, sexual difficulties, employment and financial difficulties. Patients with severe psychiatric problems were not eligible.

In the original planning of the evaluation the North Brownstead doctors had listed the expected costs and benefits of a counselling service. Ms Penn felt it was not necessary to repeat this exercise as its purpose had been to clarify in the doctors' minds the potential value of a counselling service and to provide supporting qualitative information.

Collecting the data

1 May   By the end of April Ms Penn had completed her review of the evaluation objectives and options. It was now time to set collection in motion. The first step was to finalise the study design. Ms Penn envisaged conducting an RCT to collect data on costs and outcomes of the two options. On 27 May a meeting was held at the FHSA consisting of a representative from each of the seven general practices participating in the study, Ms Penn and Mr Money. The main item on the agenda was to obtain agreement on the use of an RCT study design. This agreement was obtained. After the meeting Ms Penn started the detailed planning of data collection. The trial (lasting six months) was to commence on 1 August.

The RCT was planned whereby all patients attending one of the participating practices over a six-month period, who met the criteria for psychosocial problems and provided verbal informed consent, would be randomly allocated between an intervention group who were offered the services of a BAC accredited counsellor and the control group, where the patient received usual GP care, support and advice. The identification of patients likely to benefit from counselling was to be made by GPs during routine consultations. This might result in patient selection bias with some people who could have benefited from counselling not being included, and others who may benefit less being included in the trial. This could be checked by measuring psychiatric disturbance using a screening instrument such as the General Health Questionnaire (GHQ). This tool was used in the evaluation to measure well-being outcomes, but it was decided not to use it to screen patients due to the extra expense and effort required, that is the use of a practice nurse or researcher to undertake this task. Following patient selection by GPs, random allocation to each option was planned to be computer generated whereby eligible patients on a routine visit would be assigned to either the intervention or control group.

Before the trial began, Ms Penn worked on the methods to be used for cost and outcome data collection and measurement. Given the study perspective she decided that cost measurement for the two options should consist of estimation of the direct costs incurred by the general practices (and the FHSA through part reimbursement). The cost components to be included were therefore the direct time input of the health professionals involved (the counsellors and GPs), the time spent on supervision of the counsellors (a requirement for the 'active' option), receptionist time involved in booking patient appointments with the GP or counsellor and the costs of psychotropic, anti-depressant and anxiolytic drug therapies prescribed and further GP consultations over the study period. Referrals to outside agencies were to be monitored but not costed.

This represents a simple costing. If a wider perspective had been adopted, for example to examine costs to the NHS generally, then inputs such as referrals to psychiatric services would have been included. The perspective adopted also meant that personal costs such as travel time and expenses incurred by patients, companions and family were not to be examined – this might be an important cost if, for instance, patients were having to make a special trip to see the counsellor (which is probable given that the 'course of treatment' is one session per week for six weeks – involving more trips to the surgery than would normally be expected).

Data collection on resource use relating to the above cost components involved two main methods:

1   Staff monitoring forms for the counsellors to check that they were completing

50-minute sessions with each patient, and for the GPs to assess the time spent providing usual care, support and advice to patients in the control group. The counsellors were also asked to specify the amount of supervision time they received. The receptionists in the practices recorded the amount of time they spent on booking appointments for patients to see the counsellor.

2   GPs were to complete three forms for each patient, the first one when the patient entered the study, another on cessation of counselling at six weeks and a follow-up at three months post counselling. This was used to collect data on the drugs prescribed to study patients and their consultation rates. The information was to be derived from patient records. In addition, the same data source could be used to monitor the number of referrals to outside agencies.

Because only the direct costs of the intervention were to be assessed Ms Penn adopted what is known as a 'bottom-up' approach to costing. This means that resource use and cost estimates were to be derived from each patient in the trial. The average cost per patient can then be derived from this data. The alternative would have been a 'top-down' approach whereby the total cost of each of the resources used is estimated and divided by the number of patients in the trial to produce a figure for the average cost per patient. This approach is useful if non-patient specific costs are to be included (e.g. overheads) in the evaluation.

For the staff time inputs hours/minutes were used to represent the measure of unit resource use covering counsellor time, counsellor supervision time, receptionist time and GP time. Resource use for drug therapy was measured by the daily dose for the three sets of drugs prescribed to patients in the trial. For drug costs, estimates of the unit cost for the daily dosage prescribed would be based on net prices published in the *British National Formulary* (BNF). Unit costs for the time inputs were to be derived from the gross salary (i.e. before tax and including superannuation and national insurance) for the counsellors and their supervisors; the average gross salary of the receptionists at the participating practices was used to estimate the unit cost of their time input. The average annual remuneration for the GPs in the study was to be used to derive a unit cost estimate for GP time.

Ms Penn then had to decide on the outcome measures to be used in the economic evaluation in order to compare the effectiveness of the options. As the evaluation issue was to identify a cost-effective approach to reducing psychosocial problems within a single setting, Ms Penn thought it would be appropriate to use a measure of psychological well-being to compare the active and do-nothing options. After considering several relevant final outcome measures for psychological well-being, including the Hamilton Depression Index and the Beck Depression Inventory, Ms Penn decided to use the General Health Questionnaire (GHQ). The GHQ was to be used to assess the extent of patients' psychological distress pre and post counselling.

Other outcome measures could be used in the cost-effectiveness evaluation if necessary. For example, the changes in drug prescriptions for the intervention and control group could be used as an alternative measure of relative effectiveness. Ms Penn also wanted to collect data on patients' own assessments of the benefits of counselling compared to support and advice from the GP. She therefore developed patient questionnaires. The first was to be completed by patients at entry to the study prior to receiving counselling or GP care. This was designed to obtain demographic information (age, sex, social class), a description of the patient's problem and it also contained GHQ questions. The second questionnaire, to be completed at the cessation of counselling at six weeks and at three months post-counselling follow-up, also contained GHQ questions and questions on the patients' assessment of the benefits of the service.

Having designed these questionnaires and piloted them on several patients in the participating general practices, the trial started on 1 August. Five trained and experienced counsellors were employed part time providing the equivalent of three full-time counsellors. Supervision was provided by a counsellor-supervisor, involving three quarters of her working time. The original estimated budget for the evaluation of £20,000 was sufficient to cover the costs of the questionnaires, data collection, analysis and dissemination. However, the total costs of 3 full-time equivalent (FTE) counsellors and supervisors employed for a 6-week period represented an additional cost of £23,500. This figure was presented to the FHSA who agreed funding of 70 per cent while the practices had to meet 30 per cent of the costs out of their own budgets. The total cost of the evaluation was estimated at £43,500 (£36,450 to be provided by the FHSA).

Data collection went smoothly, (Stage 4.2 in Table 11.1) except for a few minor modifications to the original plan. Because of poor completion of monitoring forms it was decided not to use data on the GP time spent involved in post counselling/advice consultations with the patients in the study. Hence only consultation rates were derived with no attempt made to cost these.

Analysing the data

12 January The next stage in the evaluation process is the analysis of data to produce the cost-effectiveness results (Stage 4.3 in Table 11.1). Data were coded, verified and analysed by computer using the Statistical Package for Social Sciences (SPSS). In total, 192 patients who were identified by the GP as eligible for inclusion in the study and who gave their informed consent were randomly allocated to the intervention and control groups. An additional twelve patients refused to take part in the study. Over the study period 126 patients were allocated to receive counselling and 66 were allocated to receive GP advice. The groups were found to be well matched at pre-counselling with no statistically significant differences in age, sex, social class, type of psychosocial problem, drug use or degree of psychological distress as measured by the GHQ.

Costs

Table 11.2 presents the resource use per patient, unit cost for each staff input and source of unit costs data for the counsellor and GP care groups. Table 11.3 presents

Table 11.2   Resource use and unit costs for counsellor v. GP care options
(direct staff time costs only)

	Average resource use per patient	*Unit cost*	*Source of unit costs*
Counsellor option			
Counsellor time	6 hours	£12.19 per hour	Gross salary of counsellor – FWA scale grade 6[1]
Counsellor supervision[5]	1.5 hours	£13.15 per hour	Gross salary of supervisor – FWA scale grade 7[2]
Receptionist	20 minutes	£5.07 per hour	Average gross salary of receptionists grade B[3]
GP time	5 minutes	£23.86 per hour	Average annual remuneration[4]
GP option			
GP time	9.8 minutes	£23.86 per hour	Average annual remuneration[4]

Notes: [1] £20,758 per annum gross salary
[2] £22,381 per annum gross salary
[3] £8,637 per annum gross salary
[4] £40,610 in 1993–94
[5] 75 per cent of one counsellor supervisor covering 3 full-time equivalent counsellors

cost data for drug prescriptions at three months post-counselling follow-up for the two options.[2] By multiplying the data in each row of column 2 with that in column 3 of Tables 11.2 and 11.3 an average cost per patient for each type of resource input can be determined. These costs are presented in Table 11.4. As can be seen in Table 11.4 drug costs for the two options were added on to the other costs. Ms Penn thought about using the net costs approach instead (see Chapter 10). In this case the difference in drug costs (of £0.61 per patient) could have been included as a saving from the use of a counsellor placement and subtracted from the costs of this option. The net cost for the counsellor option would be £95.94 (costs minus drug savings of £0.61) and £3.90 for the GP option (costs excluding drug costs of £1.21). This would not change relative cost-effectiveness results but would have required the assumption that average drug costs for all patients with psychosocial problems in an equivalent period prior to the intervention were the same as that for patients in the GP group at three months post-counselling follow-up (Table 11.4). Because of this Ms Penn decided to include drug costs as part of the total cost calculations for each option. The total average cost per patient for the specialist counsellor option is £97.14, and £5.11 for the GP care option.

Table 11.3   Resource use and unit costs for counselling v. GP care option –
                drugs prescribed at three months post-counselling follow-up

| Type of drug | Patient numbers[1] | | Average dose prescribed | Unit cost [2] (pence per 10 mg) |
	Counsellor option n=107	GP option n=60		
Psychotropic				
Temazepam	10	11	20mg per day (40-day course)	2.1p
Nitrazepam	4	4	10mg per day (40-day course)	0.007p
Flurazepam	3	4	30mg per day (60-day course)	3.5p
	17(16%)	19(32%)		
Anti-depressant				
Amitriptyline	7	9	100mg per day (40-day course)	0.005p
Butriptyline	3	5	75mg per day (600-day course)	0.005p
	10(9%)	14(23%)		
Anxiolytic				
Diazepam	3	2	10mg per day (40-day course)	0.25p
Bromazepam	3	3	9mg per day (150-day course)	20.7p
	6(6%)	5(8%)		
Total drugs prescribed	33 (31%)	38 (63%)		

Notes: [1] Figures in parenthesis are the percentage of patients in the group prescribed the drug
[2] Source of unit costs – BNF net prices

Cost-effectiveness results

Ms Penn's next task was to analyse the data on the cost-effectiveness of a counsellor attachment in general practice. This relates to Stage 4.3 in Table 11.1. Ms Penn conducted three sets of analysis:

1   Change in GHQ score to assess the average and incremental cost-effectiveness of the counsellor option in improving patient well-being.
2   Changes in drug prescriptions to assess whether savings are generated by the counsellor option.

Table 11.4   Costs per patient of counsellor v. GP options using GP/FHSA perspective[1] – at three months post-counselling follow-up

Cost component	Counsellor option £s	GP option £s
Health professionals direct time input: Counsellor	73.14	–
GP	1.99	3.90
Counsellor supervision time	19.72	–
Receptionist time	1.69	–
Drug prescriptions[2]	0.60	1.21
Consultations cost[3]	N/A	N/A
Referrals to other agencies[4]	N/A	N/A
Cost per patient	£97.14	£5.11

Notes: [1] Excludes costs from society perspective (i.e. patient costs and indirect costs).
[2] In the net costs approach the difference between counsellor v. GP group represents monetary benefit or savings of the counselling option (see Chapter 10).
[3] Not costed as insufficient data available. However, there were no statistically significant differences in consultation rates between counsellor groups (51 per cent) and GP group (65 per cent) at 3 months post-counselling follow-up.
[4] Not costed as relates to wider NHS perspective. However, follow-up evidence was that referrals to other NHS facilities were 4 per cent in counsellor group and 63 per cent in GP group.
N/A = not available

3   Using patient self-evaluation data analysis of average and incremental cost-effectiveness of the counsellor option in making patients 'feel happier' and improving patient perceptions that they are 'coping better'.

The first two sets of results relate to the economic objectives constructed by Ms Penn. The third set represents an additional analysis. The economic objectives for consultation rates were not examined as data were not available for this purpose. Table 11.5 presents the results for the average and marginal cost-effectiveness of the counsellor option in improving patient well-being. In both the active and do-nothing option there was a gain in the GHQ at three months post-counselling follow-up. Pre-counselling there were no statistically significant differences in GHQ scores between the intervention group (16.27) and control group (16.19). At three months post-counselling follow-up GHQ scores were reduced (representing a well-being gain) on average by 10.06 points per patient in the counsellor group (to 6.21) and 5.63 in the GP usual care (to 10.56). In terms of average costs per unit GHQ reduction, the cost-effectiveness ratio for the counsellor option was £9.66, compared to £0.91 per patient for the 'do-nothing' option. While the counsellor option was more costly than the do-nothing option (an additional £92.03 per patient), it was also more effective producing an average additional per patient

Table 11.5 Cost-effectiveness of counsellor v. GP option at three months
post-counselling follow-up (costs and outcomes per patient £s)

Cost/outcomes components	Counsellor option	GP option
Cost per patient	£97.14	£5.11
Pre-counselling GHQ score per patient	16.27	16.19
Cost-counselling GHQ score per patient	6.21	10.56
Reduction in GHQ score	−10.06	−5.63
Costs per unit reduction in GHQ score	£9.66	£0.91
Counsellor v. GP option		
Difference in costs (counsellor v. GP group)	£92.03	
Difference in GHQ score reduction	4.43	
Incremental costs per additional unit reduction in mean GHQ score	£20.77	

reduction in GHQ score of 4.43. In terms of the incremental cost-effectiveness the
extra cost per additional unit reduction in GHQ score for the counsellor option was
£20.77.

Ms Penn conducted further analysis on the drug prescriptions data related to the
two options. The 'do-nothing' option resulted in an additional drug prescription
cost at the three months post-counselling follow-up period of £0.61 per patient
(£1.21 per patient versus £0.60 per patient for the counsellor groups, Table 11.4).
Ms Penn had collected data on the prescription rates pre-counselling for the two

groups.[3] In the counsellor group 39 per cent of patients (n=3) had previously been taking psychotropic drugs, compared to 42 per cent of the do-nothing group (n=25). There was no statistically significant difference in these figures. Post-counselling, the counsellor group prescription rate was 31 per cent (n=33), while the prescription rate was higher for the GP group at 63 per cent (n=38) (see Table 11.3).

Ms Penn decided to use the patient self-evaluation data post-counselling to assess the costs per one per cent of patients stating they were 'feeling happier' and costs per one per cent stating they were 'coping better'. Table 11.6 presents the results. While 45 per cent of the GP care group reported 'feeling happier', the figure for the counsellor group was 80 per cent. The respective costs per one per cent feeling happier were £0.11 and £1.21.

Of the patients in the GP group 45 per cent stated they were 'coping better' compared to 77 per cent of the counsellor group, with cost-effectiveness ratios of £0.17 and £1.26 respectively. Ms Penn also conducted incremental analysis. For each additional one per cent of patients 'feeling happier' as a result of counselling compared to GP support the extra cost was £2.63. The incremental cost-effectiveness for those 'coping better' as a result of the counsellor intervention was slightly more favourable at £2.49.

How do these results compare with the economic objectives Ms Penn had

Table 11.6 Cost-effectiveness of counsellor v. GP option (per patient) – some self-reported benefits indicators at three months post-counselling follow-up

	Counsellor option	*GP option*
Cost per patient	£97.14	£5.11
Percentage feeling happier	80%	45%
Cost per 1 per cent feeling happier	£1.21	£0.11
Incremental cost per additional 1 per cent feeling happier due to counsellor option	£2.63	
Percentage coping better	77%	40%
Cost per 1 per cent coping better	£1.26	£0.17
Incremental cost per additional 1 per cent coping better due to counsellor option	£2.49	

Indicator: Number 'feeling happier'
Number 'coping better'

specified prior to the trial period? The first set of objectives related to average cost-effectiveness. Both options achieved Objective 1, that is, a 10 per cent improvement in patient well-being. However, the do-nothing option had achieved this at much lower average cost per patient. The outcome was different for Objective 2, the GP option resulting in an expected increase in prescribing rates, while the counsellor option achieved the target of a 5 per cent reduction (and cost saving). Objective 3, a 10 per cent reduction in GP consultation rates, could not be assessed as no pre-counselling data were available. However, there was no statistically significant difference in consultation rates between the two groups at three months post-counselling follow-up. The most important objective for incremental cost-effectiveness was Objective 4 relating to patient well-being. Despite the do-nothing option achieving the target reduction in GHQ score at a lower cost it was less effective overall than the counsellor option. Ms Penn decided she would present the average and incremental cost-effectiveness evidence to the FHSA and let them decide as to whether the additional benefits from the counsellor option were worth the additional resources that would be required.

Discounting

There was no need to perform discounting as this was an evaluation of short-term costs and benefits.

Sensitivity analysis

From the checklist in Table 11.1 the next task (under Stage 4.3) is to test the effect of uncertainty on the cost-effectiveness results. Ms Penn went through each of the cost and outcome variables in the evaluation to check for uncertainty. In most cases the level of uncertainty was so small that she did not expect the production of high and low estimates to have any impact on the relative cost-effectiveness of the options.

Her major concern was the reliability of the drug cost figures. She felt that BNF prices were an unrepresentative proxy for the true costs of the drugs prescribed in each option. In light of this uncertainty she made an arbitrary adjustment of 10 per cent higher and lower for the total cost per patient of drugs prescribed. This resulted in a range of drug costs per patient of £0.54–£0.66 for the counsellor option, and £1.09–£1.33 for the GP option. However, this had only a small impact on the cost-effectiveness ratio, changing each by only a few pence in favour of the counsellor option.

Equity

There was no analysis of equity carried out in this evaluation. Had this been desired, the economic objectives could have been modified to allow for equity criteria – for example, a target of 10 per cent overall reduction in GHQ score only if all patients counselled do not have a worse rating post-counselling. One finding from the evaluation was that six patients receiving counselling had a lower GHQ score post-counselling. This suggests that some clients may deteriorate after receiving counselling.

Presenting the results (Stage 4.4 of Table 11.1)

Towards the end of her contract Ms Penn wrote a report for the GPs and the FHSA, presenting Tables 11.2 to 11.6, discussing their implications and making recommendations. In the report she discussed a number of considerations resulting from the research. These are summarised below:

1   The counsellor option was more costly, but also more effective than the 'do-nothing' option in both improving patient well-being and reducing drug cost savings. However, the 'do-nothing' option achieved the original target for well-being gains at a low cost.
2   The fact that the 'do-nothing' option produced costs and benefits (or losses in the case of drug prescriptions) illustrates that the 'do-nothing' option is important and should be fully costed and evaluated.
3   The counsellor option produced several additional benefits, such as an improved 'image' for the practice which should be considered by decision-makers when assessing whether to implement the service.
4   The method used to calculate and compare costs of the options was a 'bottom-up' approach. In other words, only the costs incurred on providing counselling for each patient were considered. The FHSA, in deciding whether to implement a counselling service, would have to assess the total budgetary implications. For instance, it might not be possible to employ counsellors on a per patient cost basis. Instead, it might be necessary to employ a counsellor on a minimum contract (say, one year) and provide permanent facilities in the GP surgery for the counsellor. This would have important cost implications but, as Ms Penn pointed out, was beyond the scope of the current evaluation.

The FHSA Decision

The objective of the evaluation was to assess the cost-effectiveness of short-term counselling. Although the evidence appeared to be favourable for the use of a counselling service, the FHSA were keen to discover whether a longer term intervention would have an even more favourable impact. They were worried that the benefit from short-term counselling would not be maintained in the long run. On the other hand, they were concerned to discover whether the patients receiving counselling who demonstrated a poorer GHQ score would in fact demonstrate a long-term improvement.

Therefore, they decided that they would develop a limited counselling service in practices in the area, but would incorporate mechanisms for audit and evaluation from the outset. They acknowledged the need for a longer term evaluation to properly assess the cost-effectiveness of counselling but thanked Ms Penn for a well-organised project and agreed it was a useful pilot evaluation.

CASE STUDY TWO

The cost-effectiveness of counselling nurses in a hospital setting

The first case study followed the evaluation process from the initial discussion of the project at the North Brownstead Practice, planning the research and obtaining funding for it from the FHSA and the subsequent evaluation involving several general practices in the region. This process covered all four stages outlined in Table 11.1. In the second case study we assume funding is available for the recruitment of a researcher to conduct an evaluation – hence Stages 3 and 4.1 are omitted from the evaluation process. Stage 1 and 2 are worked through in order to undertake the economic evaluation conducted within Stage 4. The evaluation involves comparison of two schemes designed to address problems of stress and high levels of absenteeism amongst nursing staff.

Planning an evaluation[4]

An essential part of the evaluation process is the general debate which precedes the formulation of the study design, because it enables interested parties to discuss ideas, aims, values, available resources, information and so on.

Background discussions

In February Mr Stripe, the Unit General Manager of the Smithland Trust Hospital, called a meeting of personnel, senior nursing staff and tutors at which he discussed a paper produced by the Royal College of Nursing. The College reported that an unacceptably high percentage of student nurses leave during training and that a further percentage do not take up staff posts on completing their training. Mr Stripe wanted to know whether this was true of the Smithland Hospital and, if so, what could be done about it? Moreover, he had recently reviewed the work of the Intensive Care Unit and was concerned at the high levels of staff departure in the Unit, with consequent recruitment and training costs. The Personnel Manager, Mr Tetchwell, pointed out that personnel were concerned not only about the high turnover of staff in the Intensive Care Unit, but also in other high-stress specialties such as the Neo-Natal Unit and the Dialysis Department. He told Mr Stripe that the problem was not limited to the Smithland Trust, but that all specialist units across the country were having similar problems, despite pay increases over latter years. Mr Tetchwell said he was further concerned about the high levels of absenteeism amongst all nursing staff, including students. The nurse manager, Mrs Leftwich agreed that staff loss was high and that the nurses themselves were aware of the practical problems associated with staff shortages and low morale. Mrs Leftwich thought that the staff were demoralised and confused after a period of intense political change within the health service and that they felt unsure of the future of their jobs. Many nurses, she reported, were undertaking part-time training courses in fields such as business studies, word processing, counselling and so on, because they felt they may need to seek alternative employment in the future. Stress levels were high, said Mrs Leftwich. At this point Mr Stripe left to go to another meeting, but he asked those present to reconvene at the same time a week later, so that the problems raised could be further discussed and some solutions put forward.

At the second meeting in the middle of February, Mr Stripe asked Mr Tetchwell and Mrs Leftwich if they had any new information to add. Personnel had been doing some brief background research into the problems highlighted at the meeting the previous week, and had come up with some data and a proposed solution. Mr Tetchwell reported that approximately 8–14 million working days are lost in the UK each year, for a total cost in lost production, for 1985, of an estimated £1.5 billion (Einzig and Evans 1990). He went on to say that in the HMSO report *Mental Health at Work*, the government assumed that up to 40 per cent of absenteeism at work can be attributed to mental or emotional problems. He was not sure whether the mental or emotional problems experienced by staff in the health service were work-related. In a booklet entitled *Personal Problems at Work* the suggestion seemed to be that the majority of problems are marital, relationship and family issues (Einzig and Evans 1990). However, he was still seeking information on stress and absenteeism amongst NHS staff.

One of the ways of addressing the problem of stress and resultant poor performances at work and absenteeism was to employ a staff counsellor, or to set up some sort of Employee Assistance Programme, as many American companies were now doing, apparently to good effect (Ross 1989). Mrs Leftwich said she was interested that Mr Tetchwell had come up with the suggestion of a counselling scheme because after discussion with her colleagues and with students throughout the hospital she had thought that the best way to improve morale, decrease stress and reduce absenteeism, was to set up a staff support scheme, such as a regular staff support meeting on each ward.

Mr Stripe was very interested in the proposed solutions but suggested that if the Trust was going to attempt to solve some of the problems then the work should be done professionally (i.e. costed and evaluated). He suggested that they should seek advice as to how the Trust should go about setting up staff counselling and/or support, and how the Trust would be able to monitor whether or not the schemes were working. He offered to contact Professor Smythe at the local University's Centre for Health Economics, an academic who was currently a non-executive director of the Trust, to see what could be arranged. The three managers agreed to meet at the earliest opportunity to discuss progress.

Guidelines for planning the evaluation

Two weeks later, on Professor Smythe's recommendation, Ms Penn from the Centre for Health Economics joined the managers to discuss the proposed evaluation of a programme to address issues of stress, low morale, high turnover of staff and high levels of absenteeism, as well as the problem of student nurses' failure, to take up staff posts on completion of their course or sometimes failure to complete the course itself. Ms Penn thought the best strategy would be to help Mr Stripe and the other managers to think through the steps in planning an economic evaluation using the checklist in Table 11.1 as a guide. She began by asking the managers to identify the study problem. They defined this as 'identifying the most cost-effective counselling option to address problems of high staff absenteeism and turnover in the hospital'. The evaluation was to take place within a single setting (i.e. the hospital), from the perspective of the hospital (which was funding the evaluation). Next Ms Penn asked them to identify broad objectives (Stage 1.2 in Table 11.1). Mr Stripe said he could easily summarise the objectives, saying the main ones were to reduce absenteeism and high nurse turnover. He thought these could be achieved by improving staff morale and reducing staff stress. Ms Penn wanted to find out what would count as success for the management? What would make it worth their while to provide a counselling service or staff support system on a more permanent basis? What was the minimum to be achieved? What sorts of targets were the managers aiming at, and what percentage reduction of the target? What cost was acceptable and how much more would managers be willing to pay for a more costly but more effective option? She asked whether for a given cost they would be satisfied with a decrease in absenteeism rates alone or were they looking also for an improvement in staff morale? Ms Penn listed several possible economic objectives that a counselling intervention might be expected to achieve:

To achieve at a minimum cost a:

- reduction of 5 per cent in the amount of days lost to the hospital in staff absenteeism over 1 year.
- reduction of 5 per cent in staff turnover over 1 year.
- reduction of 2 per cent in the training budget for new nurses.

Other objectives that could not be quantified at this stage were to improve staff morale, improve take up of staff jobs by student nurses and reduce drop-out levels in nurse training. As in the first case study the objectives were set up to provide guidelines for the evaluation. The managers could alter them if that was necessary or justifiable.

What are the alternative options? (Stage 1.3 in Table 11.1)

When identifying a problem it is useful to generate a series of alternative options that might address the problem before deciding which to evaluate. Ms Penn urged the managers to think carefully about all the possible options and reasons for rejecting some of them. Perception of costs, perception of benefits, political and ethical reasons, funds available, time and interest are all important criteria for choosing options.

The alternative options discussed by Mr Stripe, Mrs Leftwich, Ms Penn and Mr Tetchwell, were either to set up a staff support scheme or to employ a staff counsellor. Mr Tetchwell thought there was a possibility of setting up an Employee Assistance Scheme, like those in the USA, but Mr Stripe felt that this would be a major undertaking involving a lot of groundwork and that he wanted something in-house and quickly accessible. Mrs Leftwich suggested that pay increases for nursing staff, now at the discretion of the Trust, might be an immediate boost to staff morale, but Mr Stripe said that it would be too expensive an option, and would not address some of the real problems of stress caused by the nature of the work of nurses. Similarly, there was no funding in the budget for increases in levels of staffing, which might be another way of alleviating some of the problems the staff were experiencing. Mr Stripe insisted that the intervention had to be low cost and should enable staff to work more happily within the existing corporate structure.

Mrs Leftwich thought that employing a staff counsellor would not work, as nurses would be too embarrassed to go to the counsellor, thus admitting they had problems. Mr Tetchwell pointed out that several of the larger London teaching hospitals employed counsellors and that problems of confidentiality were quickly ironed out. In fact, as far as he knew, the staff counsellors were always stretched for time because of the demand for their services. Mrs Leftwich thought that many of the nurses had counselling skills, however, and that it would be a waste of money to employ a counsellor to come in to counsel staff. As far as she was concerned, nurses would benefit more from sitting down together to discuss some of the problems they encountered at work, and by showing each other and nursing students that problems were common and resolvable. Mr Tetchwell said that that was all very well, but that if, as American research showed, many of the problems were family or marital, how were they going to be dealt with in a nurse support group – he for one would not be happy to discuss his personal problems (not that he had any, of course), in front of others and thought that many of the nurses would feel the same.

Mr Stripe suggested that perhaps Ms Penn ought to have some say, since she was an experienced researcher. Ms Penn suggested that the Trust set up both schemes for a trial period and monitor the effects. The do-nothing option was the current practice of no formal or informal mechanism for stress reduction. She suggested that it would be useful for the managers to try to list qualitatively all the potential costs and benefits to the hospital and staff of each option (i.e. a counsellor in the hospital and for the staff support scheme). This information could be used to support the evidence from the cost-effectiveness analysis which would focus on a smaller range of cost components and a few outcome measures.

Study design (Stage 2.1 in Table 11.1)

The managers felt that with the help of Ms Penn, they were able to clarify what they were aiming to do. Ms Penn pointed out that as well as measuring the costs, they were also trying to evaluate the effect of the competing options, and that it would be necessary to set up some sort of controlled trial, whereby half the staff had access to a counsellor and half the staff had access to a staff support group. Mr Stripe thought that the simplest way to do this would be to set up alternative schemes for the student nurses and for the staff nurses, suggesting perhaps the students had access to the counsellor and the staff had access to the support groups. Ms Penn pointed out that if this were the case, they would glean no information on whether staff support groups were more effective than counselling for students or alternatively for staff nurses and that it would be better to give both groups access to both models to enable comparison of effects. Mrs Leftwich suggested that the schemes should operate on the two sites in the hospital. The staff counsellor could perhaps be housed in the new building, which had most of the acute in-patient beds and the staff support groups be set up in the old building, which housed long-stay geriatric wards, maternity and rehabilitation. Ms Penn pointed out that although this would solve the problem of study 'contamination', there would be no across-speciality comparisons of alternative schemes. The problem seemed insurmountable until Mr Stripe suggested that the scheme be operated as a trial, and explained to nurses as such, and that a mix of wards would be encouraged to set up staff support schemes, while other wards could have access to a part-time counsellor. It was agreed that although this was not ideal, it would have to do.

In addition, it was agreed that for the purposes of the trial the services would be restricted to post-qualification staff and student nurses. Mr Tetchwell offered to set about employing a part-time counsellor, and Mrs Leftwich suggested that she met up with her nurse manager colleagues to develop the idea of the staff support groups. Ms Penn said she would address the issue of the two groups in the hospital, and they all agreed to report back to Mr Stripe in a couple of weeks time. As a result of their efforts, the alternative schemes were set up and the multi-storey new building of the hospital was split into levels, some of which had staff support groups and some of which had access to the counsellor. The levels consisted of a range of acute and non-acute specialties and there was a roughly even distribution of services when separated level by level.

Scheme 1: staff counsellor

Expected costs:

- Cost of counsellor's salary.
- Cost of staff time in attending counselling.
- Administrative costs, telephone, secretarial assistance.
- Cost of setting up a counselling room.
- Cost of anxiety caused to staff.

Scheme 2: staff support scheme

Expected costs:

- Cost of nurse time in leading the group.
- Staff time in attending groups.
- Costs of facilities (room hire).
- Administrative costs, telephone, secretarial support, etc.

Expected benefits for both schemes:

- Reduced staff absenteeism.
- Reduced staff turnover, indicating lower recruitment and training costs.
- Improved health and well-being of staff, improved morale/reduced anxiety.
- Improved status of hospital in having staff support system.
- Improved quality of patient care.

The options and data collection were planned to begin by the start of May. A counsellor was to be employed part time, on a one-year contract to be available to two levels in the hospital (covering eight wards) with extension of contract subject to review. Staff support groups were set up on two further floors of the hospital (nine wards), for an indefinite period of time. The study population was to be limited to nurses on the evaluation wards. The Trust Hospital agreed to fund the evaluation of the two options, including the appointment of Ms Penn for a year and a half full time, with administrative back up from both the Trust Hospital and the University employing Ms Penn. Data collection on costs and outcomes was to involve a mixture of retrospective analysis of data covering the period one year before the start of the scheme, and one year prospective follow-up after the start of the scheme.

Cost measurement (Stage 2.2 in Table 11.1)

Mr Stripe wanted the perspective of the evaluation to be that of the Smithland Hospital. He said that while it might be interesting to measure personal costs, these should only be assessed to the extent that nurse time incurred in attendance at a staff support group or to receive counselling represented a cost to the hospital. Hence the cost components to be included were:

- cost of counsellor time/leader of staff support group time;
- cost of providing premises (room) for the staff support group/counsellor;
- cost of nurse time attending support group/counsellor;
- cost of administration (time of secretary).

Resource use data to measure costs for these components were to be collected using a combination of monitoring forms and a standard questionnaire. The unit costs of the time of the part-time counsellor, staff support group leader and administrative support could be based on the salaries paid. An equivalent annual cost for the premises would be calculated by estimating the opportunity cost of the rooms used (including overheads, lighting, heating). The unit costs of staff time attending the support group or visiting the counsellor would be included if this was undertaken during normal work hours. Unit costs would be based on the mid-point salary estimate reflecting the skill mix of the staff attending sessions. Staff might, however, attend the support group or visit the counsellor in their own time. If this was the case, while this would reflect a personal opportunity cost (i.e. in terms of foregone 'leisure' time) it would not represent a direct cost to the hospital and so would be excluded from the analysis.

Outcome measures (Stage 2.3 in Table 11.1)

Having identified the problem, the objectives of the evaluation, the options and study design, the next step is to identify quantifiable outcome measures for the cost-effectiveness analysis. In cost-effectiveness analysis a common measure of effectiveness is needed to compare options, although if possible several different effectiveness measures should be tested. Choice of measure depends on the per-spective adopted as well as the resources available for the project.

The managers tried to decide how to gather information to achieve their objectives. After a great deal of debate, the outcome measures and methods of data collection were defined as follows:

1 Assess nurse work attendance rates for one year before and up to one year after the start of the alternative schemes to see if there is any short- and medium-term reduction in absenteeism.
2 Retrospectively assess nurse turnover in the year prior to the counselling schemes and in the year during which the schemes were in operation.
3 Test nurse stress levels, work satisfaction and morale before and after the start of the schemes by questionnaire.
4 Assess rates of nurse students who take up staff jobs one year before and one year after the start of the scheme.
5 Examine drop-out rates one year before and one year after the start of the scheme.

Conducting the Research: Data Collection and Analysis (Stages 4.2 and 4.3 of Table 11.1)

Study design and data collection   The study design selected was a controlled before/after trial involving two groups of nurses – those having access only to a counsellor on floors B and C of the hospital and those having access only to a staff support group on floors D and E of the hospital. In April the total number of qualified nurses employed in the 8 wards on floors B and C was 103, with an additional 80 student nurses. The total employment on the 9 wards on floors D and E was 115 qualified and 90 student nurses.

At the beginning of May Ms Penn arranged separate meetings with nurses from wards on floors B/C and D/E to provide details about the study and the service that was available. No other publicity was used to reduce the possibility of staff from the B/C floors attending the staff support group on D/E. Nurses eligible for the staff support group were told that this would be held weekly in a seminar room on floor E and would last for approximately one hour. This would be led by a nurse trained in counselling skills (the nurse was employed by the Smithland Hospital). No 'registration' was necessary, staff could simply turn up at the appointed time. The counsellor was given an otherwise empty office on floor B, and would work on a part-time basis for $17\frac{1}{2}$ hours per week (mainly afternoons). Appointments to see the counsellor had to be made through a designated secretary. In each ward a liaison nurse was identified to inform new staff about the existence of the appropriate scheme and to provide information about access to the scheme and answer other questions nurses might have. The liaison nurses received a training session with Ms Penn and Mrs Leftwich.

Ms Penn undertook data collection in two phases.

1 Retrospective data collection and analysis of nurse absenteeism, nurse turnover, and student nurse drop-out rates was conducted covering the year prior to the start of the schemes. This data could be derived from existing hospital records disaggregated by ward.

2 For the period one year after the start of the schemes the prospective assessment would be monitored using available records to identify changes in outcomes (at one year post-scheme). In addition, staff would be asked to complete a 'stress' questionnaire at the start of the schemes and at one year follow-up. The responses to the questionnaire would be used to derive a score for level of staff stress using a standard nurse stress index. Finally, towards the end of the study period a short self-completion questionnaire was given to each nurse to collect information on whether they had used the counselling or support group schemes, their satisfaction with the service, and whether they felt the service had helped them (e.g. less time off work, felt happier, more productive while at work).

During the evaluation period cost data were also to be collected. First, a brief general resource use proforma was used as a checklist by Ms Penn to collect information from a variety of sources on the premises used, administrative time involved and other overheads. Second, Ms Penn decided to attend and observe the staff support groups on several occasions to estimate the time input from the nurse leading the group and the average attendance. Ms Penn had access to attendance records in order to identify the numbers and skill mix of staff using the group. Records were also kept by the staff counsellor of consultations and the time involved. From these Ms Penn could calculate the time input of staff in attending the support group or the counsellor. Third, she interviewed Mr Tetchwell, the Personnel Manager, and Mr Brockbank, the Finance Officer, to identify the gross salary paid to the counsellor and any other expenses associated with the two schemes.

Analysis of the Results

After the evaluation period Ms Penn had six months to analyse the results and prepare a report. She had saved some time by analysing data during the evaluation period. The following tables represent the final results, covering the effectiveness, costs and cost-effectiveness results.

Outcomes   In total 26 nurses (13 per cent of those eligible) used the staff support group over the course of the year (with an average attendance of 10 per week). A larger proportion used the counsellor with 19 per cent of those eligible (35 nurses) booking one or more appointments during the study year.

Table 11.7 outlines the results relating to the outcomes of the two schemes. One year post-evaluation outcomes were compared with pre-evaluation outcomes for the year prior to their introduction. Nurse absenteeism was measured by days off sick (excluding certain illnesses which were almost certainly not stress-related and for which a doctor's note had been presented, and excluding maternity leave). An average of 4.4 days absenteeism per nurse over the course of the pre-evaluation year was recorded. At one year follow-up the absenteeism rate for the nurses eligible to receive the staff support group option was estimated at 3.9 days per nurse (11 per cent reduction), compared to 2.6 days for those nurses eligible for the counsellor option (59 per cent reduction).

A second measure, nurse turnover (percentage leaving the job during the year), was estimated at 5 per cent of all nurses on the study wards over the year prior to the evaluation. At one year follow-up this was recorded at 4.6 per cent for the nurses eligible for the staff support group option (8 per cent reduction) and 4 per cent of nurses eligible for the counsellor option (20 per cent reduction).

Ms Penn also analysed the pre- and post-evaluation differences in student nurse 'drop-out' rate. Pre-evaluation, the figures were 9 per cent of intake. At one year follow-up a lower drop-out rate was recorded for the staff support group option (8 per cent of intake) and counsellor option (6 per cent of student intake).

The nurse stress index used to provide a quantitative measure of staff stress and morale was administered at the start of the evaluation. An average score of 0.52 per nurse was registered for the pre-intervention level of stress. At one year follow-up when the stress questionnaire was repeated the average score recorded on the staff support group wards was 0.65 compared to 0.83 per nurse for the counselling option wards (i.e. stress was reduced in both sets of wards).

In summary, both options appeared to produce favourable outcomes for each of the measures included in Table 11.7. In each case, the counsellor option produced a larger benefit than the staff support group.

Costs

Table 11.8 outlines the costings for the two options. Column 1 of the Table illustrates the cost components relevant for the perspective of the evaluation. Column 2 represents the resource use units for each option derived from data

Table 11.7   Main outcomes : staff support group v. counsellor group

Outcome measures	Pre-evaluation outcomes (1 year)	Post-evaluation outcomes (1 year follow-up)	
		Staff support group	Counsellor group
		n=205	n=183
Nurse absenteeism	4.4 days per nurse	3.9 days per nurse (11% reduction)	2.6 days per nurse (59% reduction)
Nurse turnover (% leaving)	5% of nurses	4.6% of nurses (8% reduction)	4% of nurses (20% reduction)
Student nurse drop-out	9% of intake	8% of intake (9% reduction)	6% of intake (33% reduction)
Nurse 'stress' score[1]	0.52	0.65	0.83

Note: [1] Higher score equates to lower stress

collected by Ms Penn. Column 3 identifies the unit cost estimates applied by Ms Penn which enables calculation of the total cost of each resource input and option (column 4).

The staff support group involved 2.5 hours of the time of a nurse trained to lead the group (1 hour in the group and an average of 1.5 hours per week on preparation). Based on a unit cost for nurse time of £10.47 per hour, the total one-year cost for this resource input was estimated at £1,204 (derived by multiplying 2.5 hours by £10.47 by the 46 weeks in the year the group meets). The nurse group leader also went on a 2-day counselling skills course at a fee to the hospital of £150. The counsellor was employed part time for 17.5 hours per week at a unit cost of £11.81 per hour, producing a total cost estimate for the year of £10,050.

The value of work time lost directly due to nurses' attendance at the staff support group or for a session with the counsellor was costed. Ms Penn had collected data on the average attendance per week for each option over the course of a year (which due to holidays is 46 weeks per option). On average five qualified nurses and five student nurses attended the staff support group for one hour each week. The average weekly number receiving 50-minute sessions with the counsellor was 8 Registered General Nurses (RGNs) and 7 students. These were costed using the average gross salary for the participants producing a unit cost of £9.97 per hour for an RGN and £2.96 per student nurse. The total cost for this time input was £2,974 for the staff support group and £3,851 for the counsellor option.

Secretarial support of 2 hours was provided for the counselling option, which at

Table 11.8 Costings for the staff support group and counsellor options

Option and cost components	Resource input	Unit cost £	One year total cost £
Staff support group:			
Nurse leader	2.5 hours per week	10.47 per hour[1]	1,204
Training for nurse leader	2 days counselling course	75 per day[2]	150 (one off)
Staff attending group	Average 10 staff × 1 hour per week:		
	Av. 5 qualified nurses	9.97 per nurse[3]	2,293
	Av. 5 student nurses	2.96 per student[3]	681
Premises	Seminar room	0.78 per hour[4]	72
Administrative support – secretary time	30 minutes per week	6.83 per hour[5]	157
Administration expenses (e.g. photocopy, telephone)[7]	N/A	–	1,000[6]
			Total cost = £5,557
Counsellor option			
Counsellor	17.5 hours per week	12.48 per hour[6]	10,050
Staff time attending counsellor	15 staff × 50 mins per week:	9.97 per nurse[3]	3,057
		2.96 per student[3]	794
	Av. 8 qualified nurses		
	Av. 7 students		
Premises	Unused office	0.00[4]	0.00
Administrative support – secretary	2 hours per week	6.83 per hour[5]	628
Administration expenses (e.g. photocopy, telephone)[7]	N/A	–	500[6]
			Total cost = £15,029

Source of unit costs:

[1] Nurse leader gross salary (full time) (i.e. including tax, NI, superannuation) = £19,269 per annum.

[2] Daily fee for course.

[3] Nurses attending support group or counsellor gross salary:
   Qualified nurse (full time) = £18,352 per annum
   Student nurse = £5,443 per annum.

[4] Seminar room replacement cost = £18,000, 24-year lifespan, 6 per cent discount rate therefore EAC = £1,432. Zero opportunity cost for spare office for counsellor.

[5] Secretary gross salary (full time) = £11,630, 37-hour week.

[6] Counsellor gross salary (full time) – £20,100, part time pro-rata = £10,050, based on 35-hour week (full time).

[7] Administration expenses – derived from accounts.

Note: Unless stated above all staff work 46 weeks per year, 40 hours per week (needed to calculate hourly cost)

£6.83 per hour produced an annual cost of £628. The staff support group had no formal secretarial support, but an estimated time input for this work of 30 minutes per week was estimated, producing an annual cost estimate of £157.

A hospital seminar room on floor E was booked weekly for two hours for the staff support group (although it was only used for one hour). As the seminar room was heavily booked, this has an opportunity cost as the room could not now be used for other meetings at that time. As the seminar room was a capital item with no market prices, Ms Penn decided to calculate an equivalent annual cost for the use of this room by using an estimate of its replacement cost (i.e. construction cost) and useful lifespan (the costing of capital resources was covered in Chapter 8). From discussions with Mr Brockbank, Ms Penn produced an estimate of £18,000 for the replacement cost and 24 years useful lifespan. Using a 6 per cent discount rate she derived an annuity factor from the discounting tables of 12.5504 (see Annex 8.1). From this the EAC of the seminar room could be calculated:

$$EAC = £18,000/12.5504 = £1,432$$

The proportion allocated to the staff support group was estimated at £0.78 per hour (i.e. the EAC divided by the 46 weeks in the year and 40 hours in the week the seminar room was available) and £157 per year. The counsellor was accommodated in a previously unused office on B floor – a zero opportunity cost was recorded for this item. Finally, administrative costs were estimated from hospital accounts at £1,000 and £500 respectively for the staff support group and counsellor option respectively.

Cost-Effectiveness results

The costs per nurse counselled was £214 for the staff support group and £429 for the counselling option. However, this does not provide an indication of the relative cost-effectiveness of the services. Ms Penn used three sets of outcome data from Table 11.7 to compare their cost-effectiveness. The results are presented in Table 11.9 using both average cost and incremental cost-effectiveness analysis.

Using average costs, the staff support group was most cost-effective on two of the measures used: least cost per one per cent reduction in nurse turnover (£695 versus £751), and least cost per unit (one unit = 0.1) improvement in average nurse stress scores (£4,275 versus £4,848). However, the counsellor group had the least cost per absenteeism day reduced (possibly the most reliable of the outcome measures used) at £9,349 compared to £11,114 for the staff support group.

Ms Penn felt that as the counsellor option was more effective on all outcome measures used in Table 11.9 and the differences in average cost-effectiveness appeared quite small, an analysis of the incremental cost-effectiveness of the counsellor option would be useful (although this was not an original economic objective). This analysis demonstrated a relatively high incremental cost for achieving unit gains from the employment of a part-time counsellor. This was an additional £7,286 per extra absenteeism day reduced, £789 per additional one per

Table 11.9 Cost-effectiveness results: staff support group v. counsellor group (one-year follow-up)

Cost-effectiveness ratios (1-year follow-up)	Average cost-effectiveness		Incremental cost-effectiveness, counsellor v. staff support[1]
	Staff support group	Counsellor group	
	£	£	£
	n=205	n=183	
Cost per day of nurse absenteeism – reduced	11,114	9,349	7,286
Cost per 1% reduction in nurse turnover	695	751	789
Cost per unit (i.e. 0.1) improvement in nurse stress score	4,275	4,848	5,262

Note: [1] Calculated by dividing the difference in total cost of the two options by the difference in outcomes

cent reduction in nurse turnover and £5,262 per additional unit improvement in nurse stress score. Incremental cost analysis is revealing in quantifying the cost implications of obtaining a small additional benefit. Ms Penn decided the incremental cost-effectiveness figures should be presented to Mr Stripe and the other hospital managers to help them decide which option to choose. It was for them to identify the cost-effectiveness measure they felt was most appropriate to reflect the success of one or other option and to decide whether the cost was acceptable. Ms Penn did not include student drop-out rates in the final cost-effectiveness analysis because of high uncertainty over the reliability of the data and difficulties in interpretation.

Other Analysis

Ms Penn decided that discounting was not appropriate as there was no assessment of future costs of benefits related to the counselling and staff support group options. She thought that it might be interesting to evaluate the longer term effect of counselling on staff productivity (over a five-year period), in which case discounting would be relevant (if the outcome is measured in monetary units). However, time was limited and this would not be possible given contractual constraints.

Another requirement of an economic evaluation is to examine the effect that uncertainty concerning any of the key cost and outcome variables might have on the cost-effectiveness results. Because of the limited time left and the difficulties in identifying the extent to which the key variables were reliable estimates, but assuming that some level of uncertainty existed with each of the cost and outcome indicators, Ms Penn decided to conduct a form of sensitivity analysis. She was particularly uncertain about the outcomes for the average stress scores which appeared to show too large a gain, given that less than 20 per cent of nurses used either service. The argument in defence of the benefits achieved by non-service users was that simply having a counselling service available reduced stress and raised morale for non-users. In addition, the stress scale was a particularly sensitive instrument likely to record even small improvements. However, Ms Penn felt it was probable that some other factors not associated with the counselling interventions were responsible for a part of the reduction in stress levels demonstrated in Table 11.7. To allow for this uncertainty she decided to reduce the estimate of expected gain for the staff support group to an average per nurse of 0.05. This produced a cost per unit (0.1) reduction in nurse stress score of £11,114. She then decided to vary the estimated stress outcomes for the counsellor option until the relative cost-effectiveness of the two options was the same. The stress score required to achieve this was 0.65, an increase of 0.13 compared to the pre-evaluation year. Ms Penn felt this approach to sensitivity analysis would be useful for the hospital managers who wanted to identify the change in stress ratings required for the counsellor option to produce the same relative average cost-effectiveness as the staff support group.

Presentation of Results

A final report was produced including the tables shown here. The report contained additional analysis not contained in this case study. For example, Ms Penn produced a breakdown of the cost-effectiveness of providing a counselling or staff support group option to the two sub-groups of qualified and student nurses. In addition, she included a discussion of whether the final results had achieved the original economic objectives of the evaluation. Both the staff support group and counsellor options had met the objectives that had been set for reducing absenteeism days due to stress and reducing nurse turnover. In both cases the economic objectives in retrospect appear too pessimistic. Ms Penn also conducted further incremental analysis, not reported here.

In the report Ms Penn stressed that caution had to be exercised in the interpretation of the results as the use of a before/after study design might cause problems in reliably attributing the outcomes to the two interventions. However, as the design was as rigorous as it possibly could be for an evaluation in a service setting she felt any bias would be minimal. In a meeting with Mr Stripe, Mr Tetchwell and Mrs Leftwich at which the report was discussed the consensus was that the staff support group was currently the better option, especially as this had a low set-up cost compared to the counsellor option.

SUMMARY

This chapter provides two in-depth case studies of the processes and stages involved in planning and carrying out an evaluation of the cost-effectiveness of counselling in primary and secondary care settings. The discussions and analysis described here represent the approaches that might be expected in cost-effectiveness evaluations within different service settings. Not every service will have the funds to obtain access to a health economist such as Ms Penn, but it is hoped that at a minimum the examples will provide the basic tools for counsellors, service providers and health service managers to develop a proposal for an economic evaluation and at best design and conduct an evaluation to further our knowledge of the cost-effectiveness of counselling in health care.

NOTES

1   The following data is partly derived from an evaluation of the short-term impact of counselling in general practice involving seven general practices in Northamptonshire Health Authority (Boot *et al.* 1994). However, we have taken some liberties with the data in order to illustrate particular methods and results of cost-effectiveness analysis. We have not presented background data on the age, sex, social class breakdown of patients in the evaluation. This information is available in Boot *et al.* (1994).
2   In this case study we simplify the presentation of results by focusing on the three-month post-counselling follow-up figures only.
3   However, as the patients in the pre-counselling and post-counselling groups differ, direct comparisons cannot be made.
4   The second case study is based entirely on hypothetical data. In order to illustrate the basic techniques we have over-simplified the analysis. For example, we have not discussed the effect of nurses coming into and dropping out of the study – this problem has been avoided by (unrealistically) keeping the same numbers in each group for the entire study period. There are many other simplifying assumptions in the analysis.

Further Help

For those readers seeking further advice, there are several research centres in the UK which employ health economists. The main centres are listed below. Most will be happy to provide limited advice and assistance at no charge. However, for more substantial collaboration their service, like any other, will come at a cost. The York Health Economics Consortium specialises in short-term consultancy work, while the other institutions listed below generally focus on longer term research projects.

The Centre for Health Economics
University of York
York YO1 5DD

Tel: 01904 433718

York Health Economics Consortium
University of York
York YO1 5DD

Tel: 01904 433620

Health Economics Research Unit
University Medical Buildings
University of Aberdeen
Foresterhill
Aberdeen AB9 2ZD

Tel: 01224 681818

Keith Tolley
Department of Public Health Medicine
Queen's Medical Centre
University of Nottingham
Nottingham NG7 2UH

Health Economics Research Group
Brunel University
Uxbridge
Middlesex UB8 3PH

Tel: 01895 274000

References

Altman, D.G. (1991) *Practical statistics for medical research.* Chapman and Hall, London.

Anderson, S., Hasler, J. (1979) Counselling in general practice. *Journal of the Royal College of General Practitioners* 29: 352– 6.

Ashurst, P.M. (1979) Evaluation of counselling in a general practice setting: preliminary communication. *Journal of the Royal Society of Medicine* 72: 657–9.

Ashurst, P.M., Ward, D.F. (1983) *An evaluation of counselling in general practice.* Final report of the Leverhulme Counselling Project, unpublished, UK.

Aveline, M. (1984) What price psychiatry without psychotherapy? *The Lancet* i: 857–9.

Barr, N. (1994) *The economics of the welfare state.* 2nd edition. Oxford University Press, Oxford.

Bergner, M., Bobbit, R.A., Kressel, S. (1981) The sickness impact profile. Development and final revision of a health status measure. *Medical Care* 19: 787–805.

Blakey, R. (1986) Psychological treatment in general practice: its effect on patients and their families. *Journal of the Royal College of General Practitioners* 36: 299–311.

Bloch, S., Lambert, M.J. (1985) What price psychotherapy? A rejoinder. *British Journal of Psychiatry* 146: 96–8.

Bolger, T. (1989) Research and evaluation in counselling. In: Dryden, W., Charles-Edwards, D., Woolfe, R. (eds) *Handbook of counselling in Britain.* Tavistock/Routledge, London: 385–401.

Bond, T. (1990a) Towards defining the role of counselling skills. *Counselling* 69.

Bond, T. (1990b) Counselling supervision – ethical issues. *Counselling* 1 (2): 43–6.

Boot, D., Gillies, P., Fenelon, J., Wilkins, M. (1994) Evaluation of the short-term impact of counselling in general practice. *Patient Education and Counselling*: in press.

Borus, J.F., Olendzki, M.C., Kessler, L., Burns, B.J., Brandt, U.C., Broverman, C.A., Henderson, P.R. (1985) The 'offset effect' of mental health treatment on ambulatory medical care utilization and charges. *Archives of General Psychiatry* 42: 573–80.

Bowling, A. (1991) *Measuring health. A review of quality of life measurement scales.* Open University Press, Milton Keynes.

Boyle, M.H., Torrance, G., Sinclair, J.C., Horwood, S.P. (1983) Economic evaluation of neonatal intensive care of very low birth weight infants. *New England Journal of Medicine* 308: 1330–37.

Brazier J. (1993) The SF-36 health survey questionnaire – a tool for economists. *Health Economics* 2: 213–15.

Brazier, J., Harper, R., Jones, N.M.B., O'Caithain, A., Thomas, K.J., Usherwood, T., Westlake, L. (1992) Validating the SF-36 health survey questionnaire: new outcome measure for primary care. *British Medical Journal* 305: 160–4.

British Association for Counselling (BAC) (1987) Information sheet 8. *Supervision of counselling*. BAC, Rugby.

British Association for Counselling (BAC) (1988) Information sheet 12. *Identifying appropriate supervision*. BAC, Rugby.

British Association for Counselling (BAC) (1989a) *Code of ethics and practice for counselling skills*. BAC, Rugby.

British Association for Counselling (BAC) (1989b) B3.1. *Supervision*. BAC, Rugby: 8.

British Association for Counselling (BAC) Research Committee (1989c) Evaluating the effectiveness of counselling. Counselling 69: 27–9.

British Association for Counselling (BAC) (1993) *Code of ethics and practice for counsellors*. BAC, Rugby.

Brown, K., Burrows, C. (1990) The sixth stool guaiac test: $47 million that never was. *Journal of Health Economics* 9: 429–45.

Bryan, S., Parkin, D., Donaldson, C. (1991) Chiropody and the QALY: a case study in assigning categories of disability and distress to patients. *Health Policy* 18: 169–85.

Cairns, J.A. (1991) Health, wealth and time preference. Discussion paper 07/91. Health Economics Reasearch Unit, Aberdeen.

Campbell, H. (ed.) (1977) *Manual of mortality analysis*. World Health Organisation, Geneva.

Canter, A. (1991) A cost-effective psychotherapy. *Psychotherapy in Private Practice* 8 (4): 13–17.

Carr-Hill, R. (1989) Assumptions of the QALY procedure. *Social Science and Medicine* 28: 469–77.

Carr-Hill, R.A., Morris, J. (1991) Current practice in obtaining the 'Q' in QALYs: a cautionary note. *British Medical Journal* 303: 699 – 701.

Catalan, J., Gath, D.H., Edmonds, G., Ennis, J. (1984) The effects of non-prescribing of anxiolytics in general practice. Controlled evaluation of psychiatric and social outcome. *British Journal of Psychiatry* 144: 593–602.

Chamberlain, M.A., Rowley, C., Hennessy, S., Leese, B., Tolley, K., Wright, K. (1991) *An evaluation of communication aids centres for the speech impaired*. Report to the Department of Health, Rehabilitation and Research Unit, University of Leeds and Centre for Health Economics, University of York.

Cochrane, A.L. (1972) *Effectiveness and efficiency: random reflections on health services*. Nuffield Provincial Hospitals Trust, London.

Corney, R. (1990) Counselling in general practice – does it work? *Journal of the Royal Society of Medicine* 83: 253–7.

Corney, R. (1992) *Evaluating counselling in counselling in general practice*. Royal College of General Practitioners, Clinical Series, London.

Coyle, D., Tolley, K. (1992) The discounting of health benefits in the pharmacoeconomic analysis of drug therapies: an issue for debate? *PharmacoEconomics* 2 (2): 153–62.

Cubbon, J. (1991) The principle of QALY maximisation as the basis for allocating health care resources. *Journal of Medical Ethics* 17: 181–4.

Culyer, A.J. (1980) *The political economy of social policy*. Martin Robertson, Oxford.

Daniels, M.H., Mines, R. Gressard. C. (1981) A meta-model for evaluating counselling programmes. *Personnel and Guidance Journal* May: 578–82.

Davis, H., (1992) *The design and development of a questionnaire for the evaluation of counselling*. Presentation at the Association for Student Counselling Research Sub-Committee Conference, London.

Davis, H., Fallowfield, L. (1991) *Counselling and communication in health care*. Chichester, John Wiley and Sons.

Demuth, N.M., Yates, B.T. (1981) Improving psychotherapy: old beliefs, new research, and future directions. *Professional Psychology* 12 (5): 587–95.

Department of Health (1992) *The health of the nation*. HMSO, London.

Department of Transport (1987) *Values for travel time savings and accident prevention.* HMSO, London.

Dolan, P., Gudex, C., Kind, P., Williams, A. (1994) *The measurement and valuation of health : First report on the main survey.* The MVH Group, Centre for Health Economics, University of York.

Donaldson, C., Gerard, K. (1993) *Economics of health care financing: the visible hand.* Macmillan Press Ltd, London.

Donovan, J., Frankel, S. J., Eyles, J.D. (1993) Assessing the need for health status measures. *Journal of Epidemiology and Community Health* 47: 158–62.

Dowrick, C. (1992) Improving mental health through primary care. *British Journal of General Practice* 42: 382–6.

Drummond, M.F. (1989) Output measurement for resource allocation decisions in health care. *Oxford Review of Economic Policy* 5(1): 59–74.

Drummond, M.F., Stoddart, G.L., Toprrance, G.W. (1987) *Methods for the economic evaluation of health care programmes.* Oxford Medical Publications, Oxford.

Drummond, M.F., Torrance, G., Mason, J. (1993) Cost-effectiveness league tables: more harm than good? *Social Science and Medicine* 37 (1): 33–40.

Dryden, W., Charles-Edward, D., Woolfe, R. (1989) *Handbook of counselling in Britain.* Tavistock/Routledge, London.

Earll, L., Kincey, J. (1982) Clinical psychology in general practice: a controlled trial evaluation. *Journal of the Royal College of General Practitioners* 32: 32–7.

Einzig, H. (1993) *Counselling and psychotherapy: is it for me?* British Association for Counselling, Rugby.

Einzig, H., Evans, R. (1990) *Personal problems at work.* British Association for Counselling, Rugby.

EuroQol Group (1990) EuroQol a – new facility for the measurement of health related quality of life. *Health Policy* 16: 199–208.

Eysenck, H.J. (1952) The effects of psychotherapy: an evaluation. *International Journal of Psychiatry* 16: 319–24.

Fallowfield, L., Davis, H. (1991) Organisational and training issues. In: Davis, H., Fallowfield, L. (eds) *Counselling and communication in health care.* John Wiley & Sons Ltd, Chichester.

Freeman, G., Button, E. (1984) The clinical psychologist in general practice: a six year study of consulting patterns for psychosocial problems. *Journal of the Royal College of General Practitioners* 34: 377–80.

Gerard, K. (1992) Cost-utility in practice: a policy maker's guide to the state of the art. *Health Policy* 21: 249–79.

Ginsberg, G., Marks, I., Waters, H. (1984) Cost-benefit analysis of a controlled trial of nurse therapy for neuroses in primary care. *Psychological Medicine* 14: 683–90.

Goldberg, D.M., Jones, R. (1980) The costs and benefits of psychiatric care. In: Robins, L. N., Clayton, P.J., Wing, J.K. (eds) *The social consequences of psychiatric illness.* Brunner/Mazel, New York.

Goldberg, I.D., Krantz, G., Locke, B.Z. (1970) Effect of a short-term outpatient psychiatric therapy benefit on the utilization of medical services in a prepaid group practice medical program. *Medical Care* 8 (5): 419–28.

Goodwin, P.J., Feld, R., Warde, P., Ginsberg, J. (1990) The costs of cancer therapy. *European Journal of Cancer* 26: 223–5.

Gorsky, R.D., Scwartz, E., Dennis, D. (1988) The mortality, morbidity and economic costs of alcohol abuse in New Hampshire. *Preventive Medicine* 17: 736–45.

Gudex, C. (1986) *QALYs and their use by the health service.* Discussion Paper 20, Centre for Health Economics, University of York.

Ham, C. (1993) Priority setting in the NHS: reports from six districts. *British Medical Journal* 307: 435–8.

Harris, J. (1987) QALYfying the value of life. *Journal of Medical Ethics* 13: 117–23.

Harris, J. (1991) Un-principled QALYs: a response to Cubbon. *Journal of Medical Ethics* 17: 185–8.

Hay, J., Ernst, R.L. (1987) The economic costs of Alzheimer's disease. *American Journal of Public Health* 77: 1169–75.

Hengeveld, M.W., Ancion, F.A.J.M., Rooijmans, H.G.M. (1988) Psychiatric consultations with depressed medical inpatients: a randomized controlled cost-effectiveness study. *International Journal of Psychiatry in Medicine* 18 (1): 33–43.

HMSO (1988) Mental Health at Work. HMSO, London.

Hunt, S.M. (1986) Measuring health in clinical care and clinical trials. In: Teeling-Smith, G. (ed.) *Measuring health: a practical approach.* John Wiley, Chichester.

Hunt, S., McKenna, S., McEwan, J., Backett, E.M., Williams, J., Papp, E. (1980). A quantitative approach to perceived health status: a validation study. *Journal of Epidemiology and Community Health* 34: 281–6.

Ingelfinger, J., Mosteller, F., Thibodeau, L.A., Ware, J.H. (1994) *Biostatistics in clinical medicine.* 3rd edition. McGraw-Hill Inc, New York.

Ives, G. (1979) Psychological treatment in general practice. *Journal of the Royal College of General Practitioners* 29: 343–51.

Kaplan, R.M. (1988) New health promotion indicators: the general health policy model. *Health Promotion* 3 (1): 35–50.

Kaplan, R.M., Anderson, J.P. (1988) The quality of well-being scale: rationale for a single quality of life index. In: Walker, S.R., Rosser, R. (eds) *Quality of life: assessment and application.* MTP Press, London: 51–77.

Keeler, E.B., Cretin, J. (1983) Discounting of life saving and other non-monetary effects. *Management Science* 29: 300–6.

Kind, P., Rosser, R., Williams, A. (1982) Valuation of quality of life: some psychometric evidence. In: Jones-Lee, M.W. (ed.) *The value of life and safety.* The North-Holland Publishing Co., Netherlands: 159–70.

Koch, H.C.H. (1979) Evaluation of behaviour therapy interventions in general practice. *Journal of the Royal College of General Practitioners* 29: 337–40.

Lancet Editorial (1984) Psychotherapy: effective treatment or expensive placebo? *The Lancet* i: 83–4.

Lesser, A.L. (1979) Psychotherapy, benefits and costs. *The Psychiatric Journal of the University of Ottawa* 4 (2): 191–6.

Loewy, E. L. (1980) Cost should not be a factor in medical care. (letter) *New England Journal of Medicine* 302: 697.

McGrath, G., Lowson, K. (1986) Assessing the benefits of psychotherapy: the economic approach. *British Journal of Psychiatry* 150: 65–71.

Maguire, P., Tait, A., Brooke, M., Sellwood, R. (1980) The effects of counselling on the psychiatric morbidity associated with mastectomy. *British Medical Journal* 281: 1454–6.

Maguire, P., Pentol, A., Allen, D., Tait, A., Brooke, M., Sellwood, R. (1982) Cost of counselling women who undergo mastectomy. *British Medical Journal* 284: 1933–5.

Marks, I.M., Waters, H., Lindley, P. (1983) *Nurse therapy in primary care: a controlled clinical and epidemiological study.* Department of Health and Social Security, London.

Martin, E. (1988) Counsellors in general practice. *British Medical Journal* 297: 637.

Maynard, A. (1991) Developing the health care market. *The Economic Journal* 101: 1277–86.

Mooney, G. (1984) Medical ethics: an excuse for inefficiency. *Journal of Medical Ethics* 10: 183–5.

Mumford, E., Schlesinger, H.J. (1987) Assessing consumer benefit. Cost offset as an incidental effect of psychotherapy. *General Hospital Psychiatry* 9: 360–63.

Mumford, E., Schlesinger, H.J., Glass, G.V., Patrick, C., Cuerdon, T. (1984) A new look at evidence about reduced cost of medical utilization following mental health treatment. *The American Journal Of Psychiatry* 141 (10): 1146–57.

Neuhauser, D., Lewicki, A.M. (1975) What do we gain from the sixth stool guaiac? *New England Journal of Medicine* 293: 226–8.

Parsonage, M., Neuberger, H. (1992) Discounting and health benefits. *Health Economics* 1: 71–6.

Pearce, D.W., Nash, C.A. (1981) *The social appraisal of projects: a text in cost-benefit analysis.* Macmillan Press Ltd, London.

Personal Social Services Research Unit (1989) *The methodology for costing community and hospital services used by clients of the care in the community demonstration programme.* Discussion Paper 647. University of Kent, Canterbury, UK.

Pringle, M., Laverty, J. (1993) A counsellor in every practice? *British Medical Journal* 2: 306–7.

Prioleau, L., Murdock., M., Brody, N. (1983) An analysis of psychotherapy versus placebo studies. *Behavioural Brain Science* 2: 275–310.

Robinson, R. (1993) Economic evaluation and health care. What does it mean? *British Medical Journal* 307: 670–73.

Robson, M.H., France, R., Bland, M. (1984) Clinical psychologist in primary care: controlled clinical and economic evaluation. *British Medical Journal* 288: 1805–8.

Ross, P. (1989) Counselling and accountability. *Counselling* 69: 11–18.

Rowland, N. (1992) Counselling and counselling skills. In: M. Sheldon (ed.) *Counselling in general practice. RCGP, Clinical series, London.*

Rowland, N., Tolley, K. (1995) Economic evaluation. In: Keithley, J., Marsh, G. (eds). *Counselling in general practice: process and outcomes.* Oxford University Press.

Ruark, J.E., Raffin, T.A., Stanford University Medical Center Committee on Ethics (1988) Initiating and withdrawing life support. *New England Journal of Medicine* 318: 25–30.

Schlesinger, H.J., Mumford, E., Glass, G.V. (1983) Mental health treatment and medical care utilization in a fee-for-service system: outpatient mental health treatment following the onset of a chronic disease. *American Journal of Public Health* 73 (4): 422–9.

Scitovsky, A.A., Rice, D.P. (1987) Estimates of the direct and indirect costs of aquired immunodeficiency syndrome in the United States, 1985, 1987, 1991. *Public Health Reports* 102: 5–17.

Scott, A.I.F., Freeman, C.P.L. (1992) Edinburgh primary care depression study: treatment outcome, patient satisfaction and cost after 16 weeks. *British Medical Journal* 304: 883–8.

Shepherd, M. (1985) What price psychotherapy? *British Journal of Psychiatry* 146: 555–7.

Sibbald, B., Addington-Hall, J., Brenneman, D., Freeling, P. (1993) Counselling in English and Welsh practices: their nature and distribution. *British Medical Journal* 306: 29–33.

Smith, M.L., Glass, G.V., Miller, T.I. (1980) *The benefits of psychotherapy.* Johns Hopkins University Press, Baltimore, USA.

Sugden, R., Williams, A. (1978) *The principles of practical cost-benefit analysis.* Oxford University Press, Oxford.

Tolley, K., Gillies, P. (1994) *The cost-effectiveness of a specialist counsellor in a GP setting.* Unpublished. University of Nottingham, Nottingham.

Torrance, G. (1986) Measurement of health state utilities for economic appraisal. *Journal of Health Economics* 5: 1–30.

Torrance, G., Zhang, Y., Feeny, D., Furlong, W., Barr, R. (1992) Multi-attribute preference functions for a comprehensive health status classification system. Working paper number 92-18, Centre for Health Economics and Policy Analysis, McMaster University, Ontario, Canada.

Walker, S.R., Rosser, R.M. (1993) *Quality of life assessment: key issues in the 1990s.* Kluwer Academic Publishers, Lancaster.

Ware, J., Sherbourne, C.D. (1992) The SF36 short-form health status survey. Conceptual framework and item selection. *Medical Care* 30: 473–83.

Waydenfeld, D., Waydenfeld, S.W. (1980) Counselling in general practice. *Journal of the Royal College of General Practitioners* 30: 671–7.

Whitehead, M., Dahlgren, G. (1991). What can be done about inequalities in health, *Lancet* 338: 1059–63.

Whynes, D.K., Walker, A.R. (1995) On approximations in treatment costing. *Health Economics:* 4 (1): 31–41.

Wilkinson, G. (1984) Editorial: psychotherapy in the market-place. *Psychological Medicine* 14: 23–6.

Williams, A. (1985) Economics of coronary artery bypass grafting. *British Medical Journal* 291: 326–9.

Williams, A. (1987a) Screening for risk of CHD: is it a wise use of resources? In: Oliver, M. (ed.) *Screening for risk of coronary heart disease.* John Wiley and Sons, London.

Williams, A. (1987b) Response: QALYfying the value of life. (letter) *Journal of Medical Ethics* 13: 117–23.

Williams, A. (1992) Cost effectiveness analysis: is it ethical? *Journal of Medical Ethics* 18; 7–11.

Williams, A. (1994) *Economics, QALYs and medical ethics. A health economist's perspective.* Discussion Paper 121. Centre for Health Economics, University of York.

Wolberg, L.R. (1981) Editorial: cost effectiveness in psychotherapy. *Journal of The American Academy of Psychoanalysis* 9 (1): 1–5.

Woolfe, R., Dryden, W., Charles-Edwards, D. (1989) The nature and range of counselling practice. In: Dryden, W., Charles-Edwards, D., Woolfe, R. (eds) *Handbook of counselling in Britain.* Tavistock/Routledge, London: 3–40.

Yates, B.T., Newman, F.L. (1980a) Approaches to cost-effectiveness and cost-benefit analysis of psychotherapy. In: Vandebos, G.R. (ed.) *Psychotherapy: practice, research and policy.* Sage Publications, Beverly Hills, USA.

Yates, B.T., Newman, F.L. (1980b) Findings of cost-effectiveness and cost-benefit analysis of psychotherapy. In Vandebos, G.R. (ed.) *Psychotherapy: practice, research and policy.* Sage Publications, Beverly Hills, USA.

Index